Differentiating Instruction
for Gifted Learners

A Case Studies Approach

Differentiating Instruction
for Gifted Learners

Christine L. Weber, Ph.D.,
Wendy A. Behrens, M.A. Ed.,
and Cecelia Boswell, Ed.D.

A COPUBLICATION OF THE

NATIONAL ASSOCIATION FOR
Gifted Children

PRUFROCK PRESS INC.
WACO, TEXAS

Library of Congress Cataloging-in-Publication Data

Names: Weber, Christine L. | Behrens, Wendy A. | Boswell, Cecelia.
Title: Differentiating instruction for gifted learners : a case studies
  approach / by Christine L. Weber, Ph.D., Wendy A. Behrens, M.A. Ed., and
  Cecelia Boswell, Ed.D.
Description: Waco, Texas : Prufrock Press, Inc., [2016] | Includes
  bibliographical references.
Identifiers: LCCN 2015044132| ISBN 9781618215314 (pbk.) | ISBN 9781618215338 (epub)
Subjects: LCSH: Gifted children--Education--Case studies. | Individualized
  instruction. | Mixed ability grouping in education.
Classification: LCC LC3993 .W369 2016 | DDC 371.95--dc23
LC record available at http://lccn.loc.gov/2015044132

Edited by Katy McDowall

Cover and layout design by Raquel Trevino

ISBN-13: 978-1-61821-531-4

Printed in the United States of America.

At the time of this book's publication, all facts and figures cited are the most current available. All telephone numbers, addresses, and website URLs are accurate and active. All publications, organizations, websites, and other resources exist as described in the book, and all have been verified. The authors and Prufrock Press Inc. make no warranty or guarantee concerning the information and materials given out by organizations or content found at websites, and we are not responsible for any changes that occur after this book's publication. If you find an error, please contact Prufrock Press Inc.

Prufrock Press Inc.
P.O. Box 8813
Waco, TX 76714-8813
Phone: (800) 998-2208
Fax: (800) 240-0333
http://www.prufrock.com

Table of Contents

Acknowledgments

The authors wish to express their appreciation to all of the administrators, teachers, counselors, parents, and students whose experiences have served as a basis for case studies in this book. Additionally, the preservice and in-service teachers who willingly agreed to share lesson and unit plans as tools for learning deserve special recognition. Gratitude is also extended to Dr. Cheryll M. Adams for providing her thoughtful reflections and to Amanda Laukitis for once again extending a tireless commitment to edit and offer valuable feedback on content. We are sincerely grateful for the contributions of everyone associated with our work.

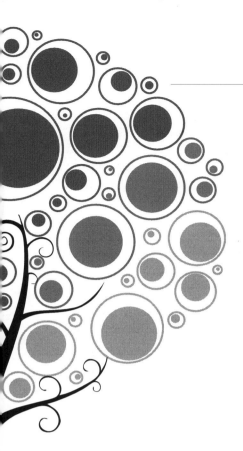

Foreword

It gives me great pleasure to introduce you, the reader, to the second book of case studies by these authors. I have worked closely in several capacities in gifted education with both Christine Weber and Cecelia Boswell, and they are wonderful contributors to the field through service on gifted boards, as national and international consultants, and as authors. All three authors have the needs of gifted learners and those who teach them at the center of their practice as professionals. They provide insight into many issues and problems facing gifted students as well as educators of the gifted and other school personnel who interact with them. They are astute in their selection of problems and issues and present each with professionalism and heightened awareness of the impact of decisions on all involved. As evidenced by the success of the first book of case studies, *Exploring Critical Issues in Gifted Education: A Case Studies Approach*, our field is in need of cases that draw on specific issues and problems that educators, administrators, consultants, parents, and other school personnel face when dealing with the various ways that giftedness may manifest itself in specific children. If there are still those who see the gifted population as homogeneous, the cases in this book will certainly dispel that myth.

One of the strengths of this book is the attention the authors have given to standards. The NAGC-CEC Teacher Preparation Standards in Gifted and

Talented Education (2013b), the NAGC-CEC Advanced Standards in Gifted Education Teacher Preparation (2013a), and the NAGC Pre-K–Grade 12 Gifted Programming Standards (NAGC, 2010) have been used as the foundation for the issues presented in the cases. There is a close alignment of each case to one or more of these standards, and a good understanding of these standards will assist with the decision making needed to find possible solutions. Moreover, the Common Core State Standards and the Next Generation Science Standards are used in cases that focus on math, science, or English language arts. This emphasis on standards ensures that the cases as well as the possible solutions are grounded in theory and research, with a focus on student outcomes.

During my career in education, I have served as a classroom math and science educator, gifted coordinator, principal of a school for gifted students, director of a university center for gifted studies, and as a member of the university graduate faculty teaching courses in gifted education. Reflecting through the lens of each of those positions as I read the cases in this book, I found myself pulled toward specific cases that would benefit me in each situation. For example, "Miss Parker" is in a situation that many educators experience on a daily basis. Thinking back to my early days as a new educator, I would have gained some important insights into how to handle a range of student learning needs if I had had an opportunity to work through this case. Having begun teaching in the era of tracking, the assumption was that the students in each track were homogeneous in learning needs.

Using my gifted coordinator lens, I found a number of cases from which to choose that would lend themselves to engaging educators in professional learning communities. One of my favorites was "Miss Wendell," a teacher who is trying to differentiate for a diverse group of learners. Throughout both of the "Miss Wendell" lessons are various opportunities for discussions on topics such as English language learners in the classroom, differentiating based on students' readiness levels, provisions for differentiated lessons that are respectful of students' time and attention, and how to develop tiered lessons that offer challenge at each level.

As a principal, I tried to challenge my faculty to broaden their knowledge about gifted learners and the models and strategies that are considered best practices in the field of gifted education. Using this lens, I was particularly drawn to those cases that seemed to challenge long-held beliefs based on myths about giftedness and gifted services. These include a teacher at the "Confucius Academy, Mandarin Language Immersion School," who wanted to use the gifted students as "teacher's helpers" for struggling students, and "Meredith," whose acceleration request is denied. I would also want to use "Differentiating and Assessing Products With Menus" and "Mr. Randall and

Natalie," a case based on using learning contracts. My school was a high school for gifted juniors and seniors, and as with most secondary teachers, the instructors were trained as content specialists. Many did not have many strategies in their toolkit, and I would have used these cases to analyze how to use the strategies effectively.

When I was the director of a center for gifted studies, I would have loved having this book because it covers myriad issues and problems in gifted education. I was often asked to provide professional development to school systems all over the nation and in Europe. Looking back, most requests were either very general, such as, "We really need our teachers to be able to differentiate," or very specific, "We are getting requests for acceleration and we aren't sure how to handle this." I believe I could find a case to cover any request for a particular focus that I ever had. The cases cover every grade level from early childhood to high school, a variety of service models such as inclusion and cluster grouping, specific strategies such as tiered lessons and menus, programs such as IB, nearly every content area, and special populations.

Finally as a university faculty member, I teach graduate-level courses in gifted education. Most often I teach an introductory course in gifted education and a curriculum course; my students are nearly all practicing professionals with occasional undergraduates who are completing a bachelor's degree and a master's degree before graduation. As I mentioned previously, the cases run the gamut of issues and problems that one would find in any classroom in any school system, charter school, private school, or other learning place. For me, I see this book as one that students would begin to use in the introduction to gifted education course and continue to work through in courses such as models and strategies, curriculum, special populations, differentiation, social and emotional needs of gifted learners, identification and evaluation, and creativity. Using the cases within coursework allows teachers to apply their knowledge to a situation, analyze the case, problem solve, and evaluate their solutions. The cases lend themselves to group and individual work. I might also choose a relevant case to use as a pre-/postassessment to demonstrate growth in specific areas based on the objectives of the course. A case might also be used as a project to determine the degree to which particular course objectives have been met. Table 2.1 (p. 19) will be helpful for assessing growth, self-reflection, goal setting, or as a rubric depending on the needs within a particular class.

This book will be a valuable addition to the library of anyone who is involved in or seeks to be involved in any aspect of gifted education. The knowledge, skills, theories, and concepts outlined in standards are evidenced to a high degree in all of the cases. The cases fall in various places along a continuum from those that could be used with novice teachers to those that require advanced knowledge and skills. The authors are to be commended for making diversity a common thread through all the cases in a sincere manner, making the cases reflective of today's educational settings. I am excited to begin planning where to use the cases in each of my courses, and I am grateful to the authors for providing a wealth of material that can be accessed by those who want to expand their knowledge and skills in meeting the needs of gifted students.

—Cheryll M. Adams, Ph.D.
Director Emerita, Center for Gifted Studies and Talent Development
Ball State University

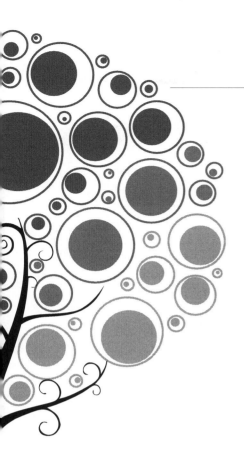

Introduction

Why Read a Book on Case Studies for Differentiating Instruction?

A teacher's role is often formal and ongoing, carried out at a school or another place for educating students. In many countries, including the United States, an aspiring teacher must first obtain specific professional qualifications or credentials from a university or college. These professional qualifications often include the study of pedagogy or the science of teaching. Teachers, like other professionals, may have to continue their education after they qualify to teach in a process known as continuing professional development. Alternatively, teachers may choose to attend a university to further their teaching credentials with a master's degree or new certification.

Thus, a teacher's professional duties may extend beyond formal teaching. Standards from various stakeholders including the National Board for Professional Teaching Standards (NBPTS), the National Association for Gifted Children (NAGC) and the Council for Exceptional Children, and The Association for the Gifted (CEC-TAG) all have clearly articulated knowledge and skill standards for teachers specifically working with the gifted. These standards guide the level of expectations in many areas for educators working with gifted children. Many educators in gifted education also continue their professional growth toward mastery of advanced professional standards to help prepare them for leadership roles in gifted education. The NAGC-CEC

Advanced Standards in Gifted Education Teacher Preparation (2013a; see Appendix A) lay out the knowledge and skills that teachers in gifted education should master as part of their preparation for advanced professional practice.

The purpose of this book is to provide case studies that (1) present opportunities for teachers and other education professionals working in various Pre-K through grade 12 instructional settings (e.g., cluster classroom, regular classroom, and full-time placement) to analyze the role and purpose of differentiation in classrooms targeting high-ability and gifted learners, (2) explore common issues related to implementing differentiation, (3) promote an application of best practice in teaching (e.g., flipped classrooms, 21st-century thinking skills, Common Core State Standards [CCSS]) for advanced and gifted learners, and (4) improve services to gifted learners by encouraging educators to reflect on their beliefs or philosophy associated with implementing differentiated instruction in their classrooms. This book details learning scenario narratives, each with a brief overview that introduces the case. Within each case, *things to consider* guide the reader's thinking without imparting an explicit action, recommendation, or solution. *Discussion questions*, *activities*, *extensions*, and suggestions for *additional readings* support the standards of excellence set forth in the revised NAGC-CEC Teacher Preparation Standards in Gifted and Talented Education and the NAGC-CEC Advanced Standards in Gifted Education Teacher Preparation. The goal is for educators to draw from these case studies, which situate learning in authentic and meaningful contexts for the purpose of improving services and programs for gifted and talented students.

Currently, there is one book developed by the authors that provides working cases on issues related to identifying and educating gifted learners including differentiation (Weber, Boswell, & Behrens, 2014), but no other resource of its kind exists. Many schools and districts espouse differentiation, supporting the need for ongoing professional development. Providing a book of cases for analyzing various strategies and their uses encourages teachers to create classrooms where every student belongs, every student is valued, and every student is nurtured. The cases facilitate conversations about children and their unique individual needs. This resource can be used in a variety of professional development settings as a vehicle to stimulate ideas and evaluate policies and procedures for improved services for gifted and advanced learners. The cases also provide an opportunity for teachers to imagine themselves in settings they might not otherwise have encountered.

What Will You Learn From Case Studies?

Students have preferred styles of learning, different interests, and different rates of learning with no two students alike. This classroom makeup requires that every preservice and in-service teacher be trained to meet the diversity of student needs. The days of teaching one traditional lesson plan and hoping that all students "get something from it" are long past. One size does not fit all (Gregory & Chapman, 2013). Teachers who vary instruction, curriculum, resources, assessments, and the classroom environment are working to provide an optimal education setting for the diversity of learners in their classrooms. Although you may have heard terms associated with differentiation such as *readiness*, *learning profile*, *interests*, *depth*, *pacing*, and *complexity*, what exactly do they mean to you and the students you teach? With research supporting the effects of differentiation (Olenchak, 2001; Smutny, 2003; Tomlinson, 2000), embracing the challenge of implementing the strategies requires a philosophy about differentiation. Consequently, providing professional development opportunities for teachers to strengthen their skills in this area is crucial to making a positive impact in the classroom. Consider the following statements by Gregory and Chapman (2013) with regard to the role of the teacher:

> In order to achieve truly differential education for students, teachers must modify standard classroom offerings in several areas. These areas include but are not limited to pacing and sophistication, depth, complexity, and personalization. The speed with which students' progress through the curriculum must be accelerated or decelerated according to student need. Students must be encouraged to delve as deeply into content as is challenging for them and then to try and delve even more deeply. Learning activities must allow for student choice at levels of complexity that are most appropriate; in other words, assignments must be tiered to take into account different ways to meet the same goal. Finally, students must be provided with reality-based opportunities to interpret and express what they are learning in ways that are personally relevant and meaningful. It is essential that we be able to distinguish between the notions of "different" and "differentiated." (p. 6)

Trying to meet the needs of individual learners in the classroom can seem overwhelming. What does a differentiated classroom look like, sound like? How does one manage a differentiated classroom? Does one need to differentiate assessments? By providing an opportunity for educators to explore issues related to differentiated curriculum and instruction for gifted and advanced learners in diverse school settings using a case studies approach, we support a philosophy in which our students are motivated and engaged in the educational process.

In order to better prepare educators and other school personnel to differentiate curriculum and instruction, this book of case studies covers various problem-based learning scenarios that focus on information and authentic stories gathered from our own experiences. These encounters range from those exemplified by teachers, parents, administrators, higher education professionals, and state leaders, with each representing events that occur in elementary, middle, and high school classrooms located in a variety of settings. We find that learning scenarios (Weber et al., 2014) have enormous appeal and are appropriate for professional development because they:

- can be read and discussed in a short amount of time;
- allow the reader to gain greater understanding through empathy;
- encourage an active response;
- encourage an analysis of multiple perspectives;
- illustrate active problem-solving strategies that can be modeled and used with participants;
- encourage reflection on various solutions, thereby opening doors to new possibilities; and
- provide resources for further exploration of issues related to the case. (pp. 1–2)

We have also discovered from our initial work that learning scenarios mirroring real-world problems ending in a dilemma engage the reader in a reflective analysis of teaching and learning (Weber et al., 2014).

The learning scenarios encourage a detailed analysis and critical reflection of the most current and prevalent issues in differentiated instruction including flipped classrooms, 21st-century thinking skills, and the CCSS. Note that all names have been changed in an effort to preserve the privacy of the individuals, schools, and communities portrayed in the case studies. In some cases, the attributes of several students have been combined to illustrate the complexity of student needs.

This book offers the opportunity for educators and stakeholders to examine differentiation in a variety of programming options such as enrichment in the classroom, cluster grouping, resource room/pull-out classes, full-time programs, special classes, special schools, acceleration, advanced placement, early college entrance, online learning, and dual enrollment. Readers may work in pairs or small groups to investigate and analyze the scenarios.

Who Might Benefit From Analyzing Case Studies Related to Differentiated Instruction?

Case studies provide an opportunity for both the prospective teacher and in-service teacher to begin anticipating issues related to modifying the curriculum and instruction for gifted learners. Specifically, those who may benefit include:

- Preservice teachers enrolled in general and special education coursework.
- In-service teachers enrolled in advanced and/or graduate level coursework.
- All educators (teachers, administrators, counselors, psychologists, support staff) enrolled in Gifted and Talented Endorsement, Certification, and/or Professional development coursework.
- Practitioners at any level of professional development, responding to cases through discussion, who may refine understanding, explore more in-depth, reflect on current practices, and extend their perspectives.
- Parents and community members who wish to learn more about students who are gifted and talented. (Weber et al., 2014, p. 3)

How Will Reading Case Studies Be Relevant to Your Educational Practice?

Tailored to meet the needs of gifted learners, each learning scenario helps the reader explore critical issues related to curriculum and instruction. Each includes the following components:

- modifying the content,
- modifying the process,
- modifying the product,
- modifying pre- and postassessments, and
- modifying the learning environment.

Each case focuses on reinforcing the NAGC-CEC Teacher Preparation Standards in Gifted and Talented Education and the NAGC-CEC Advanced Standards in Gifted Education Teacher Preparation (2013a, 2013b; see Appendices A and B), thus supporting professional development opportunities for all educators and stakeholders involved in the education of gifted learners.

Being able to assess effective practices is a crucial component for teachers becoming knowledgeable about how to work with gifted students.

Table 0.1 details the cases and their key issues for discussion and analysis.

Table 0.1.
A Matrix of Case Studies

	Title	Key Issue(s)
Chapter 3	Miss Parker	Meeting the needs of early childhood learners
	Jacob	Considering options for early entrance and subject acceleration
	Meredith	Addressing the needs of special populations
	Confucius Academy, Mandarin Language Immersion School	Implementing preassessment; employing successful strategies in a language emersion setting
	Paul	Differentiating for ADHD/special populations
	Leah	Addressing the needs of twice-exceptional middle school learners
	Ms. Goodman and Ms. Lane	Addressing the needs of twice-exceptional learners
	International Baccalaureate: Primary Years Programme	Implementing IB programs
	Ms. Renaldo	Utilizing the Gradual Release Model
	Miss Wendell, Lesson 1	Creating tiered assignments
	Miss Wendell, Lesson 2	Creating tiered assignments
	Edgewood Academy	Supporting a differentiated philosophy
	SPARK: Ms. Duncan's Flipped Classroom	Employing a flipped classroom
	Neehar and Nayan	Planning and scheduling for high school students
Chapter 4	Dr. Ochoa's Cluster Classroom	Implementing differentiation strategies
	Miss Swarma's Classroom	Developing math talent
	Academic Learning, Exploration, Resource, and Technology School (ALERTS): A Ninth-Grade Gifted Academy	Designing a special school
	Gifted in Poverty	Addressing the needs of special populations
	Gifted and Talented Students and the Next Generation Science Standards	Addressing the needs of special populations; implementing science standards
Chapter 5	Mr. Jonathon, Lesson 1	Differentiating lesson plans
	Mr. Jonathon, Lesson 2	Differentiating lesson plans
	Differentiating and Assessing Products With Menus	Using menus in lesson planning
	Mr. Randall and Natalie	Utilizing learning contracts

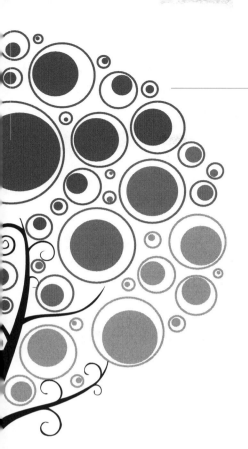

Chapter 1

Implementing Case Studies to Support High-Quality Professional Development

How Is Professional Development Part of Ongoing Learning?

Organizations, including schools, recognize the need to innovate as part of continuous improvement and to stay ahead of the rapid changes impacting schools. Innovative schools are open to change and are led by principals who have specific change facilitator styles, including concern for people shown in social and meaningful ways, organizational efficiency shown through trust in others, and strategic sense shown through vision and planning (Liu, Ritzhaupt, & Cavanaugh, 2013).

In these schools, innovative teaching practices are encouraged. Innovative teaching practices are more likely to flourish when particular supportive conditions are in place. These conditions include:

- ⊙ teacher collaboration focused on peer support and sharing teaching practices,
- ⊙ professional development centered on active and direct engagement of teachers in practicing and examining new teaching methods, and
- ⊙ a school culture with a common vision of innovation and support for new types of teaching. (Shear, Gallagher, & Patel, 2011, p. 12)

Features of Effective Professional Development

Research-based recommended content, contexts, and approaches to professional development have been proposed (Darling-Hammond, Wei, Andree, Richardson, & Orphanos, 2009) and codified in the National Staff Development Council Standards for Staff Development (2001). Key recommendations include:

- focus on teaching and learning;
- emphasis on specific content and learners;
- sustained, intense, and collaborative experiences, including with peers, mentors, and coaches;
- access to or development of teaching materials (learning designs);
- integration with curriculum, assessment and standards;
- learning embedded in the context of practice; and
- cycles of active learning and reflection.

These case studies can be used in a variety of ways to support professional or staff development as recommended above. They can support coursework related to preservice and in-service general education, special education, and gifted education. Other educators, such as administrators, counselors, psychologists, and support staff, as well as parents, can benefit from analyzing cases about differentiation. Required texts for these courses may lack real-world, authentic learning scenarios that engage the learner beyond the content presented in the book. This book of case studies supplements a variety of courses while providing educators and other stakeholders the opportunities for collaborative inquiry and learning. The cases can also be analyzed in a workshop format within the school setting, such as Professional Learning Communities (PLC).

As communities of practice, PLCs offer the benefit of professional collaboration, known to be among the most important contributors to effective professional learning (Jensen, 2014). Online PLCs afford educators anywhere with the opportunity to engage with colleagues who share a focus on improving practice detailed guidance (Sessums, 2014). Just as online learning programs have successfully differentiated learning for gifted students, online PLCs can effectively differentiate professional learning for their teachers. See the case of the Stanford University Education Program for Gifted Youth for a description and outcomes of this program (Ferdig, Cavanaugh, & Freidhoff, 2012). In recent years, online professional development has been used successfully to meet specific needs in a range of contexts. Both the literature base and practice support the use of online professional development for the following goals of:

- mentoring novice teachers (Dalgarno & Colgan, 2007),

- online courses and workshops for discrete knowledge and skill acquisition (Guldberg & Pilkington, 2006),
- online professional learning community (Sessums, 2009), and
- inquiry into effective teaching practice (Dana & Yendol-Hoppey, 2009).

Among the most promising and relevant forms of online professional development are Connected Learning Communities, which include:
- professional learning communities (PLCs),
- personal learning networks (PLNs), and
- communities of practice (CoPs).

Successful examples of Connected Learning Communities include:
- The Educator's PLN (http://edupln.ning.com),
- The Global Education Collaborative (http://www.globaleducation conference.com),
- EdChat Interactive (http://www.edchatinteractive.org/home),
- Edcamp (http://edcamp.wikispaces.com),
- The Nerdy Teacher (http://www.thenerdyteacher.com),
- Blogging About the Web 2.0 Connected Classroom (http://web20 classroom.blogspot.com), and
- Teacher Reboot Camp (http://teacherrebootcamp.com).

Online Possibilities for Reflective Educators

Online communities, mentors, and tools increasingly support formalized cycles of educator reflection known as action research or teacher inquiry (Dana, Dawson, Wolkenhauer, & Krell, 2012). Inquiry is the type of job-embedded intensive teacher-directed form of professional development advocated by researchers and professional organizations (Dana, Dawson, Wolkenhauer, & Krell, 2013). Online or blended teacher inquiry programs include peer mentoring, coaching, sharing of effective practices, and a focus on data from problems of practice. These virtual communities of reflection may occur in discussion forums, learning management systems, or specialized systems for teacher inquiry (Dawson, Cavanaugh, & Ritzhaupt, 2012). In such programs, attention must be given to the purposes and health of the community. The Community of Inquiry model (Garrison, Anderson, & Archer, 2010) is a useful framework to guide online professional learning so that it balances social presence, cognitive presence, and teaching presence.

How Do Case Studies Support High-Quality Professional Development?

The National Network of Eisenhower Regional Consortia and Clearinghouse stated:

> Effective professional development experiences provide opportunities for teachers to work with colleagues and other experts in professional learning communities to improve their practice. When continuous learning is a part of the school's norms and culture; teachers are rewarded and encouraged to take risks and to learn together. (as cited in Mundry, 2005, p. 14)

The analysis of a case study lends itself to a workshop format within the school setting, such as PLCs, thus empowering staff with decision-making strategies. Wiggins and McTighe (2006) emphasized the importance of focus for a PLC:

> For a school to be a model learning organization, all faculty members should be professional learners: They should engage in deep, broad study of the learning they are charged to cause. What works? What doesn't? Where is student learning most successful, and why? Effectively tackling these questions is what the "professional" in "professional practice" means. (para. 3)

The use of case studies in this setting provides an opportunity to change individuals' knowledge, understanding, behaviors, values, and beliefs. Consider collecting data during these meetings to guide personal professional growth as well as the professional development of the teachers. Case discussions and examination of student work have been shown to develop teachers' content knowledge and pedagogical reasoning skills and to increase student achievement (Barnett & Tyson, 1999). Finally, remember that professional development sustained over time is more closely linked to improved student learning than are short-term or one-time experiences (Birman, Desimone, Porter, & Garet, 2000).

The learning scenario presented in each case study provides an *introduction*, followed by a detailed *narrative* of a particular problem or set of issues related to teaching gifted and talented students. Each scenario narrative encourages reflection on the key issue or issues. The *things to consider* section of each case provides the reader with essential information for careful consideration before making a decision. Suggested steps for "solving" a problem-based learning scenario include the typical "who, what, when, where, why, and to what extent" process taught to classroom students.

The case studies encourage discussion and can be used in a variety of settings that employ differentiation. They offer opportunities for role-playing different parts in the scenario and promote interviewing. When only a portion of the case is presented, readers may "interview" another student or the instructor to extract information. Written or take-home assignments are provided as well. The NAGC-CEC Teacher Preparation Standards in Gifted and Talented Education and the NAGC-CEC Advanced Standards in Gifted Education Teacher Preparation can support a skill set related to making decisions about implementing high-quality curriculum and instruction for gifted learners. The *discussion questions*, *activities*, and *extensions* support the substance of these standards.

Discussion questions specifically encourage exploration of the issue or issues presented in the learning scenario. They encourage the reflection of personal and professional philosophies and may stimulate further investigations provided in the activities that follow. It is crucial that these questions be used to guide the direction of the discussion. A variety of questions particular to the case are provided, allowing the facilitator or reader to choose to answer some or all of them before proceeding to the activities and extensions. Although it is critical to maintain the integrity of a dilemma with various solutions possible, the reader or group must recognize that some solutions are more easily implemented or probable in given situations. Allowing adequate time to examine these questions helps to ensure that different perspectives and viewpoints are considered. While discussion questions particular to each case are included, a series of generic questions should also be considered. The following list from Weber et al. (2014) includes additional generic questions to consider:

- Who is the focus of the case study?
- What is the primary issue to be addressed?
- Is there a secondary issue?
- What cultural factors impact this case study (e.g., socioeconomic status, limited language proficiency, ethnicity, traditions, values/beliefs, family setting, community norms)?
- What other factors are relevant to the case study (e.g., evidence of special abilities, mental and physical health limitations or concerns, safety, learning differences, learning style, access to services, motivation, engagement, achievement)?
- With whom could you collaborate to resolve the issue(s)?
- What course of action would you recommend?
- What research supports your recommendation?

⊙ What additional information or resources would be helpful? (p. 8)

Use of such questions encourages the reader to take responsibility for the problem. Over a period of time, self-directed learning is encouraged and there is less scaffolding needed. *Activities* prompt further exploration of the issues involved in the case, while *extensions* provide an opportunity for the reader to apply understanding and insights related to the issue presented in another context, field, or situation. These extensions often provide an opportunity to generalize beyond the particular case. Choosing to participate in one or more of the activities and/or extensions ensures that insight into the topic is obtained. Suggestions for *additional readings* offer the facilitator and/or reader supplementary resources to broaden the concept for enhanced understanding.

Decision-making and problem-solving strategies to enhance a case study analysis are provided in *Exploring Critical Issues in Gifted Education* (Weber et al., 2014) and can also be useful tools when examining the cases in this book.

Facilitating Professional Development

You may decide that you are either going to be a facilitator of learning and lead a group discussion, participate as an individual in a group discussion, or participate in an online setting. As a facilitator of learning, whether you choose to conduct a PLC, or a 1–3 hour or full-day professional development workshop or supplement reading in coursework, your preparation and familiarity with the cases will enable you to lead the discussion for your group so that all participants benefit from the discourse. The following steps will help the facilitator run an effective professional development session:

1. Determine the learning environment that is conducive to the size of the room and number of participants (e.g., need for tables, participants working in pairs, small groups, or large groups). Decide if additional materials are needed such as a white board, chart paper, markers, etc.

2. Identify which NAGC-CEC Teacher Preparation Standards in Gifted and Talented Education and NAGC-CEC Advanced Standards in Gifted Education Teacher Preparation are most important to address based on the needs, readiness, and interests of the group. Select the cases that support the standards identified.

3. Read each case study thoroughly so you are familiar with all aspects of the case.

4. Understand the steps for a case study analysis.

5. Make sure each participant has a copy of this book and reads the case(s).

6. Determine which questions will be most helpful for discussion, which activities will be most appropriate for all or some of the participants, and which extensions will provide further insight and investigation for all, or some, of the participants. Note that as in any classroom there will be different levels of knowledge, skills, and understandings and you may have to adjust the pace, depth, and breadth of the discussions—in other words, differentiate for the learners.

7. Facilitate the case analysis for the participants. Being a good facilitator requires listening skills and observation skills, along with knowing when and where to ask questions and elicit further discussion. Be prepared to share additional resources if needed.

8. Assign a timekeeper to ensure that adequate discussion is appropriated and an opportunity for all to participate is considered.

Depending on which activities and/or extensions are selected, the time needed to complete them will depend on the depth and complexity required for the case. Final products may take you into the next session or may actually be shared and applied within the local school, district, or other appropriate venue at a later time.

> ## Suggested Format for a Session Agenda
>
> Introduction—5–10 minutes
> Reading the Case—10–15 minutes
> Applying a Case Study Analysis—35–45 minutes
> Reflection and Selection of Assignments and/or Extensions—10–15 minutes

How Can Technology Enhance Capacity for Differentiation In Education?

Multiple sources now address the use of technology not only in classrooms for the gifted, but also in the regular classroom, classrooms for twice-exceptional students, and students with disabilities. The purpose of technology for gifted students and ways to infuse technology as a tool for learning are explored in this book. On the back cover of *Using Media and Technology With Gifted Learners*, Siegle (2005) stated:

As technology has become a ubiquitous part of education in the 21st century, it is now imperative that students become technologically literate by knowing what technology is, how it works, and how it can be put to use to attain goals. Because of their capacity for depth and complexity, ability to transfer learning from one situation to another, fast processing, and inductive learning, gifted students are particularly adept at becoming technologically literate and putting technology to use to solve problems in novel ways.

What Siegle (2005) described is a tool for gifted learners, not the one answer to accommodate gifted students' independent study or research. As Jeffrey Shoemaker (2014) described in his blog, "The Roles of Technology and Social Media in the Gifted Classroom: An #oagctdchat Topic," "I see the role of technology as a tool for students to use" (para. 3). Shoemaker went on to say that just having 1:1 computers in the classroom does not mean that students will learn more, but that teachers can enhance learning by using a tool that engages gifted students. Shoemaker (2014) concluded with:

> In today's classroom technology and social media have a big role to play not only in communication, but in educational engagement. It is important to use technology in the classroom, but it must be used in a way that enhances your teaching not the only thing that teaches your students. (para. 14)

This case studies book does not focus on technology as the means of differentiation for gifted learners, but the cases do suggest uses of technology to enhance gifted students' learning and engagement in content, process, and products.

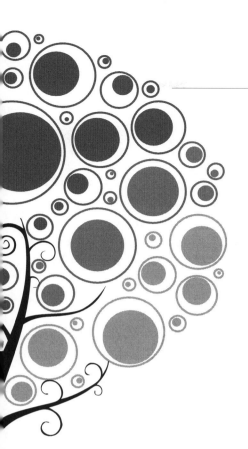

Chapter 2

Utilizing Case Studies to Promote Teacher Preparation Standards

Why Are the NAGC-CEC Teacher Preparation Standards in Gifted and Talented Education and NAGC-CEC Advanced Standards in Gifted Education Teacher Preparation Important?

The goal of professional development in gifted education should be to support all educators in helping every student achieve the highest level of learning and development. This is a paradigm shift in professional development from a focus on just improving teacher performance. In 2005, the National Network of Eisenhower Regional Consortia and Clearinghouse identified seven principles of effective professional development. Principle 3 states,

> Effective professional development experiences are research-based and use methods that mirror those used in the classroom. They engage teachers as adult learners in the learning approaches they will use with their students, e.g., starting from what teachers understand and building from there, and providing ample time for in-depth investigations, collaborative work, and reflection. (as cited in Mundry, 2005, p. 13)

The NAGC-CEC Teacher Preparation Standards in Gifted and Talented Education and the NAGC-CEC Advanced Standards in Gifted Education Teacher Preparation emphasize a strong knowledge base including a focus on the literature and theory in the field, reviews of the literature, and position papers. The research used is based on peer-reviewed studies using appropriate methodologies that emphasize a cause/effect focus and support replication of results. Promising practices and professional wisdom are also components supported in these standards. Aligning our cases with these standards provides educators an opportunity to expand their content and instructional repertoires with the intent on improving student growth.

NAGC has outlined the Knowledge and Skill Standards in Gifted and Talented Education for All Teachers (n.d.) to include:

1. Understand the issues in definitions, theories, and identification of gifted and talented students, including those from diverse backgrounds;
2. Recognize the learning differences, developmental milestones, and cognitive/affective characteristics of gifted and talented students, including those from diverse backgrounds, and identify their related academic and social-emotional needs; and
3. Understand, plan, and implement a range of evidence-based strategies to assess gifted and talented students, to differentiate instruction, content, and assignments for them (including the use of higher-order critical and creative-thinking skills), and to nominate them for advanced programs or acceleration as needed. (para. 3)

Johnsen (2012) writes about the standards in the field and their effects on professional competence. The standards can serve as benchmarks to guide training and professional development opportunities for preservice and in-service teachers. They provide direction for gaining expertise in meeting the needs of gifted learners. The standards are supported by research and emphasize the knowledge and skills to become an exemplary teacher in the field. Johnsen also reminds us that it is the students who reap the benefits of high standards for teachers. Those teachers who receive training tend to implement more differentiation strategies (like those supported in the standards) in their classroom.

Table 0.1 (p. 6) details the various topics related to differentiation occurring in various environmental settings. An analysis of the cases provides an opportunity for the reader to engage in these essential knowledge and skills outlined in the NAGC-CEC Teacher Preparation Standards in Gifted and Talented Education and the NAGC-CEC Advanced Standards in Gifted Education Teacher Preparation.

How Can Reflective Thinking Reinforce the Implementation of the Standards?

"Research has clearly demonstrated that the effects of the reflection improve teaching" (Danielson, 1996, p. 53). Danielson (2009) reminded us of the importance of fostering reflective thinking and suggested that such a skill is best promoted with colleagues. Providing dilemmas during professional development opportunities encourages educators to develop a reflective practice. Case studies provide an opportunity to analyze and study a problem, gain new knowledge (which may require further research), and recommend a sound decision, thus, resulting in something new learned. Danielson (2009) also suggested a series of prompts that would encourage educators to question their own classroom practices and would work well with the case studies presented. They include:

- What worked in this lesson? How do I know?
- What would I do the same or differently if I could reteach this lesson? Why?
- What root cause might be prompting or perpetuating this student behavior?
- What do I believe about how students learn? How does this belief influence my instruction?
- What data do I need to make an informed decision about this problem?
- Is this the most efficient way to accomplish this task? (para. 35)

Providing opportunities for reflective thinking should be a priority when working through the cases presented. Journal writing and dialogue or an interactive journal format provide an opportunity to expand thinking and stimulate awareness of personal values and beliefs. These formats may be used as a vehicle for further reflection or to be explored or connected to other issues at a later time. Most importantly, reflective thinking allows for consideration of the consequences of our actions on the teaching-learning process. Additional prompts for reflective thinking include:

- I want to improve . . .
- I have learned . . .
- This makes me realize . . .
- This is important because . . .
- This reminds me of . . .
- I used to think . . . but now I think . . .
- This makes me think . . .
- My long-term and short-terms goals for teaching and learning are . . .

- ⊙ Maybe . . .
- ⊙ I chose this task because . . .
- ⊙ I want to achieve . . .
- ⊙ This impacts my students' learning because . . .
- ⊙ I want to keep challenging myself . . .
- ⊙ I would do things differently . . .
- ⊙ When I revise, I will . . .
- ⊙ I now believe . . .

Reflection should be considered as an additional factor to assess growth of the educator in addition to improving learning outcomes of students. Areas to assess for growth may include pedagogical understanding, critical thinking, personal growth, and transformation learning (see Table 2.1). It is important to note that providing stimulating stems for reflection draws attention to the usefulness of the knowledge, skills, and dispositions relevant to the field. Assessment of this growth is the means for modifying tomorrow's instruction.

Emphasizing the use of reflective thinking with the case studies helps the reader (a) relate new knowledge to any prior understanding, (b) think in both abstract and conceptual terms, (c) apply specific strategies in novel tasks, and (d) understand their own thinking and learning strategies. Thus, reflective practice as a part of a case study analysis creates an atmosphere conducive to pedagogical understanding, critical thinking, personal growth, and transformational learning. Use of this rubric, along with the prompts suggested, fosters collegial learning and teaching and ensures a path that leads to professional growth for teachers and increasing learning for their students.

Table 2.1
Assessing for Growth

	Foundational	Transitional	Accomplished
Pedagogical Understanding	Uses a limited range of pedagogical approaches in practice. Recognizes that teacher standards link to practice.	Exhibits a wide range of effective pedagogical approaches in practice. Identifies the impact of teacher standards on practice.	Applies in practice or experience an understanding of learning theories. Links teacher standards to practice.
Critical and Creative Thinking	Limits critical and creative thinking to analysis only. Views experiences in isolation.	Thinks critically to analyze and judge, but with limited adaptation and originality. Recognizes the need to connect experiences.	Thinks critically and creatively, employing advanced levels for analyzing, judging, originality, and accepting/rejecting ideas. Connects experience to prior knowledge, coursework, and NAGC-CEC standards.
Personal Growth	Makes some references to research and connections about the impact on the classroom or professional setting. Able to identify area(s) for future development and improvement.	Makes references to best practices and some connections about the impact on the classroom or professional setting. Able to plan, identify, and articulate both short and long term goals; able to identify objectives needed to meet goals; able to identify strategies needed to meet goals.	Includes specific references to best practices and describes the impact on the classroom or professional setting. Able to assess growth over time and state future goals for teaching.
Transformational Learning	Becomes aware of own and others' assumptions. Recognizes the need to think in new ways.	Begins to question assumptions. Shows independent thinking.	Exhibits change in beliefs or attitudes thus contributing to an environment that encourages transformation. Exhibits self-directed learning that creates opportunities for transformation.

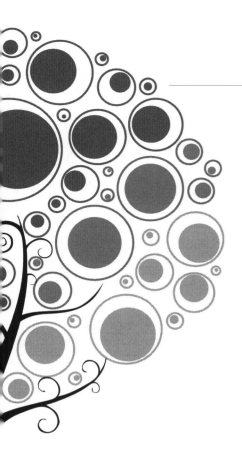

Chapter 3

Case Studies

Differentiated Instruction
in a Regular Classroom

These case studies explore issues related to differentiated instruction for gifted learners including special populations of gifted learners (e.g., twice exceptional, English language learners [ELL], children from poverty) in the regular classroom in early childhood, elementary, middle, and high school settings.

Miss Parker

Introduction

As a new teacher working in an inclusion classroom, there are many challenges to differentiating the curriculum, instruction, and assessment to meet the needs of diverse learners. Unpacking the standards means developing a better understanding of what you are teaching your students, but not necessarily how you are teaching your students. Follow Miss Parker as she develops a lesson on verbs, teaches her lesson, assesses her students, and finds that sometimes things don't go exactly as planned.

Miss Parker is a first-year teacher assigned to an inclusive first-grade classroom in a suburban school district. A number of children walk to school, ride their bikes, or are driven to school by their parents. Many parents are involved and a vital part of the school environment. Walking through the halls each day, one is likely to find a number of parents helping in various classroom and school settings, providing a strong support base for the teachers and staff. The Parent Teacher Organization (PTO) also has 90% parent involvement. The school is high achieving, receiving an "A" rating from the State Department of Education for the past several years. Also, the school is home to the Exceptional Student Education programs for the district, with more than 150 students in the programs offered.

There are a total of 783 students attending the school, with 4% of the student population identified as African American, 3% Hispanic, 3% Asian/Pacific Islander, 3% Multiracial, and less than 1% considered Alaskan. The remaining 86% of the student population is White/Non-Hispanic. Less than 1% of the students in the school are considered "limited English language proficient." Less than 1% of the student population participates in the free and reduced lunch programs that are offered by the school. The student to teacher ratio is 14:1.

Miss Parker's class is a mainstream first-grade class that contains 19 students, with one student who has a disability and is in a wheelchair, one student on an Individualized Education Plan (IEP) who has Asperger's syndrome, and two students identified as academically gifted. She is responsible for providing meaningful learning opportunities for all students in the classroom. This includes differentiating her instruction and assessment instruments to fit the needs of each and every diverse learner in the classroom. One of Miss Parker's lessons has the following objective from the CCSS, ELA-Literacy.L.1.1c: Use singular and plural nouns with matching verbs in basic sentences (e.g., He hops; We hop). (*Note.* The following lesson plan has been used by permission of Amanda Allen, former student intern, Cunningham Creek Elementary School, St. Johns, FL.)

Miss Parker introduces the lesson by telling students that they are going to learn about verbs and then play a game of charades to show how well they know how to use verbs. Students are asked the following questions:

- Who can tell me what a part of speech is?
- What parts of speech have we already learned about?
- How can we use parts of speech in our writing? Why are they important to our lives and how do they help us become better writers?
- What is a verb? How do we use it in our writing?

Students are then given an example of a verb—"run"—and asked: "What kind of word is 'run'? What is happening in a story when we read the word 'run'?" Students reply that "run" is an action word, and that verbs tell us what a person or thing in a story is doing. Students are then asked to provide examples. "Why would you call that word a verb? What makes it an action word?"

Singular nouns with a matching verb and plural nouns with a matching verb are listed on a chart with clarifications provided about plural versus singular. Students are asked to give examples of sentences using singular and plural nouns with matching verbs. For each example, students put a matching verb into a sentence, using a singular or plural noun, for example, "The dog runs."

Miss Parker asks, "What if we wanted to say more than one dog runs? How would we say that?" The children reply, "The dogs run" for a plural noun, because there would be more than one dog in that example.

Things to Consider

- » Some students require less time than others to master a particular understanding or skill.
- » Learners in classrooms vary in degree by their readiness, interest, and learning profile.
- » Opportunities need to be provided in order to support a diversity of learners and maximize their potential.
- » There are many strategies for differentiation that support a range of individual differences in the classroom.

The lesson proceeds with the students playing "Verbs Charades," with students taking turns picking a verb out of a bag and acting it out for the class. Students are called on to guess the action. For each guess, the guessing student puts the verb into a sentence, using a singular or plural noun to match the verb. The following verbs are used in the game:

- Run
- Walks
- Skips
- Jumps
- Blink
- Swims

⊙ Dance   ⊙ Wave   ⊙ Read
⊙ Stomp   ⊙ Sleep   ⊙ Sits
⊙ Eat   ⊙ Write   ⊙ Hop

Students are formatively assessed with a worksheet (see Figure 3.1). When Miss Parker reviews the worksheets, she finds that several students completely missed the target standard, while others had a partial understanding and a few completely mastered the standard. Some students did not seem to understand what the directions were asking of them.

Discussion Questions

1. Novice teachers may need help to design appropriate learning and performance modifications for individuals with gifts and talents that enhance creativity, acceleration, depth, and complexity in academic subject matter and specialized domains. What role does preassessment play in differentiating curriculum and instruction? How might the lesson on verbs have been developed differently with preassessment data?

2. Looking at the CCSS, why is this student outcome *important* for Miss Parker to address?

3. What does Miss Parker need to do next? Why?

4. What resources and materials would be helpful in making any revisions to the lesson?

5. How might tiered assignments be used to develop additional activities for students still struggling with mastery of the standard and for those students who have mastered the standard?

6. What other differentiation strategies might be used?

7. Was Miss Parker's assessment strategy appropriate? Why or why not? What issues need to be considered when choosing an assessment strategy? What strategy might you suggest?

Activities

1. Develop several tiered activities that would follow this lesson on using singular and plural nouns with matching verbs in basic sentences.

2. Research other differentiation strategies that might be appropriate to use in a subsequent lesson. Choose one and plan the next lesson for Miss Parker.

3. Create a tic-tac-toe menu with a variety of activities and products related to CCSS.ELA-Literacy Standard: Demonstrate command of the conventions of standard English grammar and usage when writing or speaking, or another appropriate standard.

Part One: Write two sentences using a singular noun and a matching verb.

1. _____

_____

2. _____

_____

Part Two: Write two sentences using a plural noun and a matching verb.

1. _____

_____

2. _____

_____

Figure 3.1. Miss Parker's formative assessment worksheet.

Extensions

1. In a discussion with a colleague, describe how this lesson or one similar to it could be integrated with other subject areas to impact student learning on a deeper level.
2. Develop a plan of action for differentiating a unit of study in an area that students have had mixed results in mastery. Research various strategies for differentiation. Identify possible pre- and postassessment strategies for the unit. Implement your plan and evaluate the results. Share your findings with a colleague.
3. Research various menu options. Create several for your classroom use.
4. Choose 8–12 video clips related to differentiation (from http://www.youtube.com/user/BERStaffDevelopment/videos). Make a list of key points that you have learned and identify ways to share them colleagues.

Additional Readings

Adams, C. M., & Pierce, R. L. (2006). *Differentiating instruction: A practical guide to tiered lessons in the elementary grades.* Waco, TX: Prufrock Press.

Adams, C. M., & Pierce, R. L. (2010). *Differentiation that really works: Strategies from real teachers for real classrooms, grades 3–5.* Waco, TX: Prufrock Press.

Adams, C. M., & Pierce, R. L. (2011). *Differentiation that really works: Strategies from real teachers for real classrooms, grades K–2.* Waco, TX: Prufrock Press.

Colangelo, N., & Davis, G. A. (Eds.). (2002). *Handbook of gifted education* (3rd ed.). Boston, MA: Allyn & Bacon.

Heacox, D. (2002). *Differentiating instruction in the regular classroom: How to reach and teach all learners, grades 3–12*. Minneapolis, MN: Free Spirit Publishing.

Heacox, D. (2009). *Making differentiation a habit: How to ensure success in academically diverse classrooms*. Minneapolis, MN: Free Spirit Publishing.

Hughes, C. E., Kettler, T., Shaunessy-Dedrick, E., & VanTassel-Baska, J. (2014). *A teacher's guide to using the Common Core State Standards with gifted and advanced learners in the English language arts*. Waco, TX: Prufrock Press.

Johnsen, S. K., & Kendrick, J. (Eds.). (2005). *Language arts for gifted students*. Waco, TX: Prufrock Press.

Kingore, B. (2004). *Differentiation: Simplified, realistic, and effective*. Austin, TX: Professional Associates Publishing.

National Association for Gifted Children. (n.d.). *Gifted education practices*. Retrieved from http://www.nagc.org/resources-publications/gifted-education-practices

Pierce, R. L., & Adams, C. M. (2004). Tiered lessons: One way to differentiate mathematics instruction. *Gifted Child Today, 27*(2), 58–65.

Roberts, J. L., & Inman, T. F. (2009). *Strategies for differentiating instruction: Best practices for the classroom*. Waco, TX: Prufrock Press.

Smutny, J. F., & von Fremd, S. E. (2004). *Differentiating for the young child: Teaching strategies across the content areas, PreK–3*. Thousand Oaks, CA: Corwin Press.

Tomlinson, C. A. (Vol. Ed.). (2004). Differentiation for gifted and talented students. In S. M. Reis (Series Ed.), *Essential readings in gifted education series: Vol. 5*. Thousand Oaks, CA: Corwin Press.

VanTassel-Baska, J. (2003). *Curriculum planning and instructional design for gifted learners*. Denver, CO: Love Publishing.

Jacob

Introduction

Young gifted and talented learners and the extent of their needs may be difficult to assess. This case study introduces Jacob, a highly gifted 4-year-old, who is offered early entrance to kindergarten. A supportive team considers his needs, appropriate methods for differentiated instruction, and future placement options.

Jacob and his family have recently moved to Hillcrest City. At 4, Jacob is intellectually curious and eager to begin school. Before moving, his former preschool teacher encouraged Jacob's parents to explore options for early entrance to school. Jacob's mother contacts a local school and learns that a comprehensive assessment of cognitive functioning, personal characteristics, learning preferences, and interests is required. She submits the required student background information form and a letter from her son's former preschool teacher to initiate the process. A week later, the school secretary calls to schedule a meeting for Jacob with the Early Entrance Evaluation Team.

While the school psychologist, a kindergarten teacher, and a first-grade teacher interview Jacob in one room, his mother completes a checklist of behaviors in another. The team meets with Jacob for 75 minutes, completing the Observed Social Behaviors Form and the Vineland Adaptive Behavior Scale—Second Edition, a test of fine and gross motor skills. They describe Jacob as "small in stature but surprisingly mature and independent" and document the ease with which Jacob separated from his mother, his expansive vocabulary, keen sense of humor, and apparent passion for space science. Although the team did not assess Jacob's reading skills, their report includes a notation that he has, by his own admission, "been reading for a very long time." When asked how he learned to read, he sheepishly responded, "I just knew."

Following protocol, the school psychologist administers the Wechsler Preschool and Primary Scale of Intelligence™–Fourth Edition (WPPSI™–IV) to measure Jacob's cognitive abilities. When the team meets to review the data, the psychologist reports that Jacob's WPPSI score of 149 places him in the highly gifted range and far exceeds the district's minimum of 130 for early entrance. The team uses the data obtained to complete the Iowa Acceleration Scale (IAS; 3rd Edition). After reviewing the IAS findings, they conclude Jacob is an excellent candidate for early entrance to kindergarten. When the psychologist calls Jacob's parents, they're thrilled to learn their son qualifies for early entrance to kindergarten and relieved to know his educational needs will soon be addressed.

Things to Consider

» Requests for early entrance to kindergarten or first grade are initiated by parents and are appropriate for approximately 1% of the population.

» Successful early entrance is dependent on a child's developmental readiness and exceptional academic ability when compared to chronological peers.

» Decisions for early entrance should be made after careful assessment of a child's cognitive, developmental, and social and emotional abilities.

» An intelligence quotient, commonly referred to as an IQ, represents a score derived from a standardized test designed to assess intelligence. Individuals who score in the highly gifted range, 145–159 on IQ tests, represent approximately >1% of the population.

When Jacob enters school in the fall, his teacher, Miss Albert, quickly discovers he reads fluently and is able to properly print his first and last name. Jacob accurately copies words with appropriate spacing and is able to write simple sentences. When asked how high he can count, he replies, "to infinity." He pauses for a moment and inquires if she would like him to count by 5s or 10s, because it would take a long time. He shares his personal preference for counting by 10s.

After Jacob's first day, Miss Albert wonders how she can provide him with the appropriate level of challenge and still meet the diverse instructional needs of the other 21 students in her classroom. She pulls Jacob's records and reviews them once again. She questions Jacob's placement in her class and realizes, at 4 years old, he is nearly 18 months younger than most of his classmates.

The next morning, Miss Albert requests that Mrs. Laing, the school's literacy coach, help to administer the Dynamic Indicators of Basic Early Literacy Skills Next (DIBELS Next) assessments to each of the students in Miss Albert's classroom. Over the next 2 days, they administer the sequence of one-minute measures that function as indicators of phonemic awareness, alphabetic principle, accuracy, and fluency with connected text, reading comprehension, and vocabulary. Miss Albert hopes the data will help her determine the range of student needs within her classroom, and help inform instruction. The data from her class identifies nine students in need of significant intervention to reach grade-level proficiency, six scoring mid-range, four above average, and Jacob. Jacob's scores are perfect in each area and far beyond any student with whom she's worked with previously.

To better understand his ability and recommend the appropriate level of text complexity, Mrs. Laing assesses Jacob using The Lexile® Framework for Reading. Miss Albert and Mrs. Laing reason the quantitative method based on individual words and sentence lengths will provide a Lexile measure that can be used to determine Jacob's current and stretch Lexile bands. When Jacob scores a 695L (a score consistent with midyear fifth-grade students in the 25th–75th percentile), Miss Albert is both surprised and concerned. Some of the books in Jacob's Lexile range—*The Boxcar Children* (Warner, 1977), *Holes* (Sachar, 2000), and *Because of Winn-Dixie* (DiCamillo, 2000)—do not seem content-appropriate for a child his age. Although there is not a direct correspondence between a specific Lexile measure and specific grade level, Figures 3.2 and 3.3 indicate typical Lexile Reader measures by grade and typical text measures by grade, respectively.

At Mrs. Laing's suggestion, Miss Albert requests a conference with the principal and the gifted and talented coordinator to discuss how Jacob's instructional needs can be best supported. The first-grade teacher and the school psychologist who originally tested Jacob are invited to join the discussion. All agree that Jacob is intellectually ready for more challenging work but question the advisability of an additional grade-level acceleration. They create a plan in which Miss Albert will replace the kindergarten ELA and mathematics curriculum with the first-grade curriculum. The first-grade teacher offers enrichment ideas, and Mrs. Laing shares a leveled reading list for highly able readers. They agree to meet again in 2 weeks to monitor Jacob's progress. That evening, Miss Albert calls Jacob's parents to share the team's recommendations. Jacob's parents are grateful for Miss Albert's willingness and ability to differentiate the curriculum for their son. They agree Jacob is too young for an additional grade-level acceleration at this time.

Things to Consider

Gifted readers typically:
» read early and may be self-taught,
» have an expansive vocabulary,
» read for pleasure and for information,
» have an advanced level of comprehension,
» think and process information at an accelerated pace, and
» read and perform at least two levels above their chronological peers on assessments.

Two weeks later, Miss Albert confirms the first-grade curriculum materials are more appropriate and Jacob begins reading books selected from a fourth-grade reading list. She also states that on occasion, he seems tired and overwhelmed by the noise and activity on the playground. He, at one juncture, fell asleep during the afternoon and wet his pants.

Over the next few months, Miss Albert remains in close contact with Jacob's parents and meets frequently with the first-grade teacher and psychol-

Grade	Reader Measures, Mid-Year 25th percentile to 75th percentile (IQR)
1	Up to 300L
2	140L to 500L
3	330L to 700L
4	445L to 810L
5	565L to 910L
6	665L to 1000L
7	735L to 1065L
8	805L to 1100L
9	855L to 1165L
10	905L to 1195L
11 and 12	940L to 1210L

Figure 3.2. Typical Lexile Reader measures by grade. From *Lexile-to-Grade Correspondence* by The Lexile® Framework for Reading, 2015, retrieved from https://www.lexile.com/about-lexile/grade-equivalent/grade-equivalent-chart. Copyright 2015 by MetaMetrics. Reprinted with permission.

Grade	Text Demand Study 2009 25th percentile to 75th percentile (IQR)	2012 CCSS Text Measures
1	230L to 420L	190L to 530L
2	450L to 570L	420L to 650L
3	600L to 730L	520L to 820L
4	640L to780L	740L to 940L
5	730L to 850L	830L to 1010L
6	860L to 920L	925L to 1070L
7	880L to 960L	970L to 1120L
8	900L to 1010L	1010L to 1185L
9	960L to 1110L	1050L to 1260L
10	920L to 1120L	1080L to 1335L
11 and 12	1070L to 1220L	1185L to 1385L

Figure 3.3. Typical text measures by grade. From *Lexile-to-Grade Correspondence* by The Lexile® Framework for Reading, 2015, retrieved from https://www.lexile.com/about-lexile/grade-equivalent/grade-equivalent-chart. Copyright 2015 by MetaMetrics. Reprinted with permission.

ogist to discuss Jacob's progress. By the end of the first semester, Jacob seems well adjusted to school. He excels in his classwork and is popular among his classmates.

In the spring, Miss Albert, the gifted and talented coordinator, the principal, the first-grade teacher, and the psychologist all meet to create a written acceleration plan and discuss Jacob's classroom placement for the next year. They discuss the options available within the district: a traditional first-grade classroom with or without subject acceleration; whole-grade acceleration; placement in one of the district's third-, fourth-, or fifth-grade cluster classrooms; or placement in one of the building's combined classrooms—either grade 1 and 2 or grade 3 and 4.

Discussion Questions

1. In what ways has Miss Albert differentiated Jacob's curriculum? Has she been able to address all his instructional needs? Why or why not?
2. What tools beyond DIBELS can Miss Albert use to monitor Jacob's progress?
3. Is the Lexile Reading Framework a suitable indicator of Jacob's reading level and appropriate reading materials? Why or why not? Are other options available?
4. Where do the needs of gifted learners fit into an RtI model?
5. Which setting do you recommend for Jacob's fall placement (i.e., a traditional first-grade classroom with or without subject acceleration; whole-grade acceleration; placement in one of the district's third-, fourth-, or fifth-grade cluster classrooms; or placement in one of the building's combined classrooms—either grade 1 and 2 or grades 3 and 4)? Why?
6. The CCSS were created to establish clear, consistent guidelines for what every K–12 student should know and be able to do in mathematics and ELA. In what ways might Jacob and other gifted learners be impacted by the CCSS?

Activities

1. Prepare an outline of a unit of study on animals and their habitats for Jacob and his classmates. Indicate how the unit will be differentiated for Jacob, as well as his classmates, who may be significantly below grade level. You may choose to plan for a combined grade 1 and 2 classroom setting or a traditional classroom. At your instructor's discretion, you may choose to alter this activity for another grade level or thematic topic.

2. With a partner, select six books of varying levels among Lexile measures to explain the effects of seasons on animals, plants, and people appropriate for lower-elementary students. Create a tic-tac-toe menu indicating activities with varying levels of challenge and products. Describe how the menu will be used in class and how the students will be assessed.

3. Research the Schoolwide Enrichment Model-Reading (SEM-R) and discuss one of the following in a 500-word essay: In what ways can the SEM-R address the diverse instructional needs in a district that has adopted the RtI philosophy? How can SEM-R be used to differentiate instruction for twice-exceptional students (who are intellectually gifted and have a specific learning disability) or ELLs in elementary settings?

4. How might eBooks be used to supplement Jacob's reading choices? Create a list of various resources that provide eBooks for gifted and advanced readers.

Extensions

1. Use the CCSS for ELA to explore text complexity and select four books for an advanced reader based on readability, appropriate vocabulary, and sentence structure. Write a 500-word essay to support your selections based on the criteria above. At the discretion of your instructor, complete the assignment by selecting books for a twice-exceptional 9-year-old student with a Lexile measure of 400L or 1,000L.

2. Research ways in which classroom teachers can assess and support the mathematical interest and talent in elementary students. Create an annotated bibliography of six to eight resources that can be used to extend and enrich mathematical thinking. Justify each selection and how it can be utilized.

Additional Readings

Assouline, S. G., Colangelo, N., Heo, N., & Dockery, L. (2013, April). High-ability students' participation in specialized instructional delivery models: Variations by aptitude, grade, gender, and content area. *Gifted Child Quarterly, 57,* 135–147. doi:10.1177/0016986213479654

Brulles, D., Saunders, R., & Cohn, S. J. (2010). Improving performance for gifted students in a cluster grouping model. *Journal for the Education of the Gifted, 34,* 327–350.

Cavanaugh T. W., & Weber, C. L. (2014). Gifted students and advanced readers. In T. W. Cavanaugh (Ed.), *Ebooks for elementary school* (pp. 167–175). Santa Barbara, CA: ABC-CLIO.

Cukierkorn, J. R., Karnes, F. A., Manning, S. J., Houston, H., & Besnoy, K. (2007). Serving the preschool gifted child: Programming and resources. *Roeper Review, 29,* 271–276. doi:10.1080/02783190709554422

Eyre, D. (2007). Structured tinkering: Improving provision for the gifted in ordinary schools. *Gifted & Talented International, 22*(1), 31–38.

Gadzikowski, A. (2013). *Challenging exceptionally bright children in early childhood classrooms.* St. Paul, MN: Redleaf Press.

Haslam-Odoardi, R. (2010). Gifted readers and libraries: A natural fit. *Teacher Librarian, 37*(3), 32–36.

Housand, A., & Reis, S. M. (2008). Self-regulated learning in reading: Gifted pedagogy and instructional settings. *Journal of Advanced Academics, 20,* 108–136. doi:10.4219/jaa-2008-865

Kingore, B. (2002). Reading instruction for the primary gifted learner. *Understanding Our Gifted, 15,* 12–15. Retrieved from http://www.bertiekingore.com/readinginstruction.htm

Little, C. A., & Hines, A. H. (2006, Fall). Reading after school: Exploring interests, emphasizing strengths, and expanding horizons. *Teaching for High Potential,* 3–4.

McGee, C. D., & Hughes, C. E. (2011). Identifying and supporting young gifted learners. *Young Children, 66,* 100–105.

MetaMetrics. (2015). *The Lexile Framework for reading: Matching readers with texts.* Retrieved from https://www.metametricsinc.com/lexile-framework-reading

Minnesota Department of Education. (2013). *Early entrance into kindergarten: Comprehensive evaluation guidance.* Retrieved from http://education.state.mn.us/MDE/SchSup/Kindergarten/index.html

National Governors Association Center for Best Practices, & Council of Chief State School Officers. (2010). *Common Core State Standards for English language arts.* Washington, DC: Author.

NGSS Lead States. (2013). *Next generation science standards: For states, by states.* Washington, DC: The National Academies Press.

Reis, S. M., & Boeve, H. (2009). How academically gifted elementary, urban students respond to challenge in an enriched, differentiated reading program. *Journal for the Education of the Gifted, 33,* 203–240.

Reis, S. M., Eckert, R. D., McCoach, D. B., Jacobs, J. K., & Coyne, M. (2008). Using enrichment reading practices to increase reading fluency, comprehension, and attitudes. *Journal of Educational Research, 101,* 299–315.

Reis, S. M., & Fogarty, E. A. (2006). Savoring reading schoolwide. *Educational Leadership, 64*(2), 32–36.

Reis, S. M., McCoach, D. B., Coyne, M., Schreiber, F. J., Eckert, R. D., & Gubbins, E. J. (2007). Using planned enrichment strategies with direct instruction to improve reading fluency, comprehension, and attitude toward reading: An evidence-based study. *The Elementary School Journal, 108,* 3–23. doi:10.1086/522383

Rogers, K. B. (2002). *Re-forming gifted education: Matching the program to the child.* Scottsdale, AZ: Great Potential Press.

VanTassel-Baska, J. (2013). *Using the Common Core State Standards for English language arts with gifted and advanced learners.* Waco, TX: Prufrock Press.

Walpole, S., & McKenna, M. C. (2007). *Differentiated reading instruction: Strategies for the primary grades.* New York, NY: Guilford Press.

Weber, C. L., & Cavanaugh, T. W. (2006, fall). Promoting reading: Using ebooks with gifted and advanced readers. *Gifted Child Today, 29*(4), 56–63.

Westphal, L. E. (2013). *Differentiating instruction with menus for the inclusive classroom: Language arts, grades K–2.* Waco, TX: Prufrock Press.

Meredith

Introduction

Although more than 40% of all public school students in the U.S. are educated in rural settings, their school districts are often underfunded and typically unable to provide the rigorous educational opportunities gifted learners require. Rural gifted learners are commonly isolated geographically from pools of intellectual peers. Recognizing and responding to the unique needs of gifted learners requires schools to provide students with differentiated learning and counseling services. Although whole-grade acceleration is often the easiest and most cost effective method to address those needs, the decision to do so should only be made after carefully considering all aspects of the student's learning situation.

This case introduces the education professional to the challenges of meeting the needs of gifted learners in rural settings. In this complex case, a highly gifted learner named Meredith is moving from an urban, full-time gifted program to a rural community.

Meredith is an African American female in the seventh grade. She is the only child in a single parent household. She attends Jefferson Academy (JA), a full-time, urban middle school program for highly gifted students. At the end of the school year, Meredith and her mother, Susan, will move to Clarkston, a rural community located 85 miles away. Susan, a single mother and recent MBA graduate, will become the manager of a local grain elevator. Both mother and daughter are eager to experience a country-style life.

A recent census found Clarkston's population of 1,177 is comprised of 86% White and 13% Hispanic residents. African American, Asian, and American Indian residents total 1% of the community. Less than 20% of the adults have attended a postsecondary institution. Most residents either are farmers, construction workers, or employed in healthcare or with the local school district.

The Clarkston School District (CSD) serves 329 students among grades K–12, with 48% qualified to receive free and reduced lunch. The experienced staff at CSD is dedicated to their students. Although outdated, the school maintains the K–6 and 7–12 class buildings. The school buildings are adjacent to each other and share a common cafeteria and daily schedule. A federal grant provided funds to purchase new computers and white boards for all classrooms last year.

> ## Things to Consider
>
> Small schools have both challenges and opportunities for meeting the diverse needs of their students.
>
> » Although classes are often small, teachers more easily address specific student needs when they have the time to individualize instruction.
>
> » Opportunities to accelerate by grade or subject may be easier to facilitate due to the close proximity of buildings and flexible schedules.
>
> » Gifted learners may feel recognizably isolated from their age mates.
>
> » Staff, technology, and curriculum resources may be limited by available resources and funding.
>
> » Geographic isolation may make opportunities for enrichment, academic competition, and mentorships difficult to attain.
>
> » Many rural students are severely disadvantaged from the lack of advanced educational opportunities and exposure to the arts.

Susan describes her daughter as physically and socially mature for her age. Meredith, identified as a highly gifted student in second grade, was exposed to academic parity with her chronological peers throughout her urban programs. Meredith is an independent, self-motivated student who has consistently demonstrated high levels of achievement. She has a 4.5 grade point average, has been accelerated in mathematics, and will complete her ninth-grade honors algebra class before the move. She is a voracious reader, a conscientious student, and has earned the respect of her classmates and teachers. Meredith is also very active. She enjoys playing basketball and she has earned a black belt through national karate competitions.

In preparation for the move, Meredith's mother met with the JA Principal, Ms. Walsh, to discuss the transfer of her records and recommendations for grade-level placement within the CSD. All parties understand that many changes will occur with the move and the level of services Meredith currently receives in her former school will be unavailable at her new school. After a thorough review of Meredith's records and consultation from JA's gifted service coordinator and the school psychologist, Ms. Walsh recommends full-grade acceleration for the fall. She believes acceleration is the only option that will continue to foster academic growth and support Meredith's social and emotional needs. Susan and Meredith are comfortable with the recommendation. They have requested that a letter stating the same be included with records forwarded to the Clarkston School District.

CSD principal, Mr. Smyth, has reviewed Meredith's files and recommendations from JA. Although admittedly inexperienced with full-grade acceleration, he has denied the request. Mr. Smyth is willing to place Meredith as an eighth grader into 10th-grade mathematics, but feels full-grade acceleration could be detrimental during her transition to the new school and community.

Discussion Questions

1. Is Meredith a good candidate for full-grade acceleration? Why or why not? What tools are available to inform the decision-making process?
2. What data and other information typically informs placement when a student moves from one district to another? What additional information should be considered when a student moves from a district providing full-time gifted services to a district with limited or no services?
3. What are some of the barriers and solutions with providing a challenging and appropriate education for gifted learners living in rural communities?
4. What are some of the likely social and emotional issues Meredith will face as she makes a transition to living in a rural setting and attending a new school? What is the responsibility of the school to assist in the transition? How might a school social worker or counselor help?
5. What are some of the advantages for gifted students living in rural areas?

Activities

1. Research some models of services, which incorporate online learning opportunities for students living in rural or isolated areas. Create a 5-minute presentation outlining the advantages and disadvantages of online learning for rural students, or create a graphic organizer to help staff and students determine if a student is a good candidate for online learning.
2. Review talent development websites to determine the location of the nearest site for students in your state. Prepare a one- to two-page paper in which you discuss the opportunities and advantages of participating in a talent search program. Explain how a gifted student living in a rural setting might benefit from testing and participation in a summer program. Discuss the potential social and emotional impact of the experience on rural students.
3. The NAGC Pre-K–Grade 12 Gifted Education Programming Standard 4: Learning Environment addresses the needs for gifted learners to access learning environments that foster personal and social responsibility, multicultural competence, and interpersonal and technical communication skills for leadership in the 21st century to ensure specific student outcomes. Select one of the five competencies and cre-

ate a plan for Meredith's transition to Clarkston School District. Your plan should indicate how you would use evidenced-based practices to monitor success of the plan.

4. The school believes it to be in the best interest of Meredith to have her remain in her age-appropriate grade. Create a scenario that defines how Meredith's needs are met in the regular classroom. The scenario may include single subject acceleration.

5. Create a scenario that defines how Meredith's needs are met through grade-level acceleration. The scenario should address how Meredith's academic progress will be monitored and her social and emotional needs will be met.

6. Role-play a follow-up discussion that might take place between Mr. Smyth and Susan.

7. Review high school graduation requirements in your state and create an "ideal" educational plan to share with Meredith and her mother. The plan should use a combination of school-based, online, credit by exam, and summer enrichment opportunities.

Extensions

1. Review your state's statute on graduation requirements. Does the state permit a district to award high school credit for classes or coursework completed prior to high school entrance? Can a student complete a required course through independent study, online, or during the summer? Summarize your findings in a one-page document to share with your colleagues.

2. Design a professional development plan for K–12 teachers working in a rural setting that addresses common characteristics and classroom issues for gifted and highly able learners. Include recommendations for ongoing training.

3. Design a professional development workshop on differentiated instruction for K–12 teachers. Create an outline for the training and questions to discuss about practices.

Additional Readings

Cash, R. M. (2011). *Advancing differentiation: Thinking and learning for the 21st century*. Minneapolis, MN: Free Spirit Publishing.

Dixon, F. A., & Moon, S. M. (Eds.). (2015). *The handbook of secondary gifted education* (2nd ed.). Waco, TX: Prufrock Press.

Gentry, M., Rizza, M. G., & Gable, R. K. (2001, spring). Gifted students' perceptions of their class activities: Differences among rural, urban, and suburban student attitudes. *Gifted Child Quarterly, 45*, 115–129. doi:10.1177/001698620104500205

Heacox, D. (2009). *Making differentiation a habit: How to ensure success in academically diverse classrooms.* Minneapolis, MN: Free Spirit Publishing.

Howley, A., Rhodes, M., & Beall, J. (2009). Challenges facing rural schools: Implications for gifted students. *Journal for the Education of the Gifted, 32,* 515–536.

Howley, C. B. (2009). The meaning of rural difference for bright rednecks. *Journal for the Education of the Gifted, 32,* 537–564.

Kordosky, D. (2010). *Rural gifted students: Victims of public education.* Indianapolis, IN: Dog Ear Publishing.

Lewis, J. D. (2009). *The challenges of educating the gifted in rural areas.* Waco, TX: Prufrock Press.

Northey, S. S. (2005). *Handbook on differentiated instruction for middle and high schools.* Larchmont, NY: Eye on Education.

VanTassel-Baska, J. (2005). *Acceleration strategies for teaching gifted learners.* Waco, TX: Prufrock Press.

Winebrenner, S. (2005). *Differentiating content for gifted learners in grades 6-12* [CD-ROM]. Minneapolis, MN: Free Spirit Publishing.

Confucius Academy, Mandarin Language Immersion School

Without question, the issue investigated most often in research on language immersion education is students' ability to perform academically on standardized tests administered in English. This question emerges again and again in direct response to stakeholder concerns that development of a language other than English may jeopardize basic schooling goals, high levels of oral and written communication skills in English, and grade-appropriate academic achievement. The research response to this question is longstanding and consistent: English-proficient immersion students are capable of achieving as well as, and in some cases better than, non-immersion peers on standardized measures of reading and math.

—Tara Williams Fortune (2015),
"What Research Tells Us About Immersion"

Introduction

Language immersion schools are often appealing to families who value second-language acquisition and search for academic rigor. While character-based languages may afford additional challenges, gifted and talented students attending immersion schools may still require differentiated instruction. These unique students typically learn at an accelerated pace and often exhibit deeper understanding than many of their classmates. Preassessment, the hallmark of differentiated instruction, is essential to assessing prior knowledge and determining appropriate learning targets. In this case, Mr. Liú discovers the importance of preassessment and the range of student understanding within his second-grade classroom.

Confucius Academy is a full immersion, Mandarin Chinese public charter school. The K–8 school focuses on academic rigor, language, and culture immersion in Mandarin Chinese. Of the 730 students who attend the school, 50% identify as Asian, 41% as White, 3% as Hispanic, 5% as Black, and 1% as two races. Confucius Academy has a 17:1 student to teacher ratio, and 5% of the students qualify for free or reduced lunch. Many of the students are the children of academics, business executives, or other professionals. The school is well resourced and has an active parent group.

The director of curriculum and instruction ensures the content delivered in Mandarin covers all state standards and components of the Core Knowledge Sequence, building both knowledge and Mandarin fluency. Confucius

In mathematics, 87% met or exceeded state standards:
- Does Not Meet Standards: 5.2%
- Partially Meets Standards: 7.8%
- Meets Standards: 28.8%
- Exceeds Standards: 58.2%

In reading, 79.6% met or exceeded state standards:
- Does Not Meet Standards: 10.6%
- Partially Meets Standards: 12.5%
- Meets Standards: 44.6%
- Exceeds Standards: 32.3%

In science, 74.8% met or exceeded standards:
- Does Not Meet Standards: 9.7%
- Partially Meets Standards: 15.5%
- Meets Standards: 51.6%
- Exceeds Standards: 23.2%

Figure 3.4. Previous year's student testing results.

Academy's young and energetic staff works tirelessly to create and maintain a high-quality program for their students. Mandarin language acquisition begins in kindergarten and builds throughout the K–8 student experience:

- Grades K–1: Full immersion in Mandarin Chinese in core subject areas of mathematics, science, social studies, and language arts. Art, physical education, music, and computer classes are taught in English.
- Grades 2–4: Full immersion in Mandarin Chinese in core subject areas plus six class periods per week (approximately 300 minutes/week) in ELA. Chinese is now integrated into art, physical education, music, and computer classes.
- Grades 5–8: Approximately 50% English and 50% Chinese among all subject areas throughout the week. Chinese classes include mathematics (leveled), Chinese language arts, Chinese conversation, social studies, music, and orchestra. English classes include mathematics (leveled), science, social studies, ELA, art, computer, and physical education.

Students in all grades consistently earn high ratings on required state tests. Of students tested during the previous year, 87% met or exceeded state standards in mathematics. The results of student testing are shown in Figure 3.4.

Mr. Liú's Assessment

Mr. Liú has been teaching fifth grade for 3 years and is a native Mandarin speaker. He has earned the respect of his colleagues and he is well liked by the students. Mr. Liú has designed many of the common assessments used by his grade-level colleagues and frequently shares new strategies at staff meetings. In the spring, when he learns a second-grade teacher will retire, he applies and receives the transfer to a new classroom within the school. To prepare for his new assignment he spends much of the summer familiarizing himself with the CCSS and his new curriculum. He outlines each of his units for the school year and works to design preassessments for each. He learns that his new grade-level colleagues do not use common assessments and is anxious to learn more about the strategies they use.

Mr. Liú and his students are working on the grade 2 measurement and data standard. They will soon begin a unit on telling time. In CCSS.Math.Content.2.MD.C.7 students are required to tell and write time. During a grade-level meeting, Mr. Liú asks his colleagues Mrs. Neu, Miss Guō, and Miss Zhāng what preassessments they use for the unit.

Mrs. Neu uses discussion as an informal preassessment during her class's morning meeting. A few days prior to beginning the unit on time, she asks her students:

- ⊙ What time is it now?
- ⊙ How do you know what time it is?
- ⊙ At what time will we go to lunch?

Mrs. Neu gauges instructional readiness by student response and plans her lessons accordingly.

Miss Guō uses a worksheet with six blank clock faces. She instructs her students to indicate specific hours by drawing hands on the clocks. She observes the speed at which students complete the task and then checks for accuracy.

Miss Zhāng prefers to give her students worksheets with pictures of nine analog clocks showing hands in a variety of positions. She gives the students 10 minutes to label the times. She then reviews the papers to determine student understanding. She typically discovers a few students who aren't familiar with analog clocks and a few who can correctly identify the time on every image.

Mr. Liú reflects on the preassessment methods shared by his colleagues. He sees some merit in each, but feels they offer limited evidence of understanding. He is aware his students have varying skill levels in all subjects and wonders if the information he'll gain from preassessment methods his colleagues use will be sufficient.

Mr. Liú considers the options available and the diverse needs of his students. During the first weeks of school, three students demonstrate ability to learn at a faster rate than their classmates. Chen, Lilly, and Alice complete their assignments accurately and efficiently. In the hallway and during free time, he witnesses evidence of their expansive vocabulary in English and in Mandarin. Lilly and Alice are twins and working with them is challenging. On two separate occasions, Mr. Liú reprimands Lilly for smirking when her peers make errors. He reprimands Alice for her impatience with classmates who are slow to answer questions. Although they clearly prefer to work together, Mr. Liú reprimands and separates Chen, Lilly, and Alice in the classroom and for all group work. He reasons that by strategically placing them in the classroom, they can assist other students who may struggle from time to time. Reluctantly, at the request of their mother, he agrees to replace reading materials for the twins with more challenging texts. Early completion of mathematics work has, on occasion, earned them additional free reading time.

Things to Consider

» Classroom work completed early should always be reviewed for accuracy and gaps in knowledge before curricular extensions or enrichment opportunities are assumed appropriate.
» Early and accurate completion may be an indication students are capable of more challenging work.
» Gifted and talented students typically need fewer repetitions to master a new skill.
» Gifted and talented learners may benefit from curriculum compacting, so they can move through the curriculum at an accelerated pace.

Mr. Liú decides to create his own preassessment for the unit on time. A week prior to beginning the new unit, Mr. Liú gives each student a blank sheet of paper. He tells his class they should note everything they know about time. The students seem excited and eager to begin.

As he walks around the class, Mr. Liú notices several students drawing clock faces with hands labeling the hours and minutes. Two students draw clock faces that indicate quarter and half hours. One student draws a digital clock on a microwave and a mobile phone. Another draws clock faces and shows the equivalent time on digital clocks. While passing Chen's desk, the student appears to be writing an extensive explanation. His paper is filled with characters and it includes an illustration that does not appear to be a clock. Chen is engrossed in his work and does not notice Mr. Liú.

Following class, Mr. Liú sits at his desk and reviews the preassessment. He begins to sort the papers, checking first for accuracy and second for evidence of deeper understanding. Alice has drawn and labeled clocks that indicate when she wakes up, waits for the bus, eats lunch, returns home, and when she goes to bed. Lilly's paper is messy, appears hurried, and is incomplete. Other children in the class have drawn clocks that are either missing numbers or inaccurately labeled. The most common error among the students is the confusion of the "big hands" and "little hands."

When Mr. Liú reads Chen's paper, he is not able to categorize Chen's work. It far exceeds the expectations, even when compared with the work of his former fifth-grade students. Chen has accurately described characteristics of digital and analog clocks. He has also described how a sundial indicates the time of day by the position of the sun. Chen's illustrations also show a rough outline of the U.S. with labeled time zones. Chen includes a notation, explaining that when he calls his grandmother, who lives in California, at 3 p.m. Central Standard Time, it is 1 p.m. on the Pacific Coast.

Discussion Questions

1. Mr. Liú's classroom is unique in many ways. What are his greatest opportunities and challenges?
2. Mr. Liú has chosen to separate his most advanced students. Is this a good idea? Explain your answer.
3. In what ways can instruction be differentiated in a language immersion classroom?
4. What are the strengths and limitations of the three types of preassessments described by Mr. Liú, Mrs. Neu, Miss Guō, and Miss Zhāng?
5. What lesson or lessons should Mr. Liú plan next?

Activities

1. Use the CCSS to design a preassessment and outline a unit of study for a grade level of your choice. Share and solicit feedback from grade-level colleagues or similar preservice teachers.
2. Identify learning targets for a unit lesson and design a pre- and postassessment for your students. If you are a preservice teacher or a teacher without a current assignment, select the grade level and subject you would like to teach.
3. Using the "jigsaw technique," create a cooperative learning activity for a classroom in which students are arranged in groups and each group member is assigned a different piece of information. Group members will join with members of other groups to research or share ideas about the information. Members will then return to their original groups to "piece together" the information and share new understandings.

Identify the grade level, learning target, and information for a group of five.

Extensions

1. Create a 5–10 minute webinar in which you discuss preassessment and three potential strategies for the grade level of your choice. Select examples relating to your current assignment or the grade you hope to teach.
2. Contact a language immersion school in your area and ask to observe a classroom during a period of instruction. Identify strategies that mirror or differ from traditional classrooms. Meet with the teacher afterward to discuss challenges unique to the classroom setting. Share your observations with your classmates.

Additional Readings

Bialystok, E., Peets, K. F., & Moreno, S. (2014). Producing bilinguals through immersion education: Development of metalinguistic awareness. *Applied Psycholinguistics, 35,* 177–191. doi:10.1017/S0142716412000288

Cash, R. M. (2011). *Advancing differentiation: Thinking and learning for the 21st century.* Minneapolis, MN: Free Spirit Publishing.

Center for Applied Linguistics. (2011). *Directory of foreign language immersion programs in U.S. schools.* Retrieved from http://webapp.cal.org/Immersion

Cohen, A. D. (2011). *Strategies in learning and using a second language* (2nd ed.). New York, NY: Taylor & Francis.

Cohen, A. D. (2012). Comprehensible pragmatics: Where input and output come together. In M. Pawlak (Series Ed.), *New perspectives on individual differences in language learning and teaching* (pp. 249–261). doi:10.1007/978-3-642-20850-8_16

Core Knowledge Foundation. (2015). *Core knowledge.* Retrieved from http://coreknowledge.org

Fortune, T. W. (2015). *What research tells us about immersion.* Retrieved from http://asiasociety.org/education/chinese-language-initiatives/what-research-tells-us-about-immersion

Heacox, D. (2009). *Making differentiation a habit: How to ensure success in academically diverse classrooms.* Minneapolis, MN: Free Spirit Publishing.

Hoh, P.-S. (2005). The linguistic advantage of the intellectually gifted child: An empirical study of spontaneous speech. *Roeper Review, 27,* 178–185.

Ikeda, M., & Takeuchi, O. (2006). Clarifying the differences in learning EFL reading strategies: An analysis of portfolios. *System, 34,* 384–398. doi:10.1016/j.system.2006.04.007

Jiang, X., & Cohen, A. D. (2012). A critical review of research on strategies in learning Chinese as both a second and foreign language. *Studies in Second Language Learning and Teaching, 2,* 9–43.

Johnsen, S. K., & Sheffield, L. J. (Eds.). (2013). *Using the Common Core State Standards for mathematics with gifted and advanced learners.* Waco, TX: Prufrock Press.

Johnson, D. T. (2000). *Teaching mathematics to gifted students in a mixed-ability classroom.* Retrieved from http://www.educationoasis.com/resources/Articles/teaching_gifted_math.htm

Leaver, B. L., & Shekhtman, B. (2002) Principles and practices in teaching superior-level language skills: Not just more of the same. In B. L. Leaver & B. Shekhtman (Eds.), *Developing professional-level language proficiency* (pp. 3–33). New York, NY: Cambridge University Press.

National Governors Association Center for Best Practices, & Council of Chief State School Officers. (2010). *Common Core State Standards for English language arts.* Washington, DC: Author.

National Governors Association Center for Best Practices, & Council of Chief State School Officers. (2010). *Common Core State Standards for mathematics.* Washington, DC: Author.

Nicolay, A.-C., & Poncelet, M. (2013). Cognitive advantage in children enrolled in second-language immersion elementary school program for three years. *Bilingualism: Language and Cognition, 16,* 597–607. doi:10.1017/S1366728912000375

Paul

Twice-exceptional learners are students who have evidence of the potential for high achievement capability in areas such as specific academics; general intellectual ability; creativity; leadership; and/or visual, spatial, or performing arts AND also have evidence of one or more disabilities as defined by federal or state eligibility criteria such as specific learning disabilities; speech and language disorders; emotional/behavioral disorders; physical disabilities; autism spectrum; or other health impairments, such as ADHD.

—Susan Baum (2012), "What's in a Name? Defining and Reifying Twice-Exceptional Education"

Introduction

To appropriately differentiate instruction, educators are required to determine the instructional readiness, learning profile, and interests of students within their classrooms. Reviewing student academic histories, test results, observations, work samples, and interest inventories provides important information but may not be adequate. Other factors, such as health, home environment, poverty, truancy, family duress, abuse, and neglect impact student performance, but may not be readily apparent. Investing the time and effort to learn as much as possible about students within their classroom allows educators to diagnose critical needs and plan for multitiered systems of support.

Paul is 8 years old and lives on a reservation with his maternal grandfather, John. Paul's father is deceased and Paul's mother, Jane, is a recovering alcoholic. Depressed and struggling to remain sober, Jane relinquished custody of Paul to her father just before Paul's second birthday. Diabetes, high blood pressure, liver problems, poor eyesight, and expanding memory issues prevent John from working. He cares deeply for his grandson and does his best to provide a stable home environment despite all of the challenges. Over the past 11 years, Jane has been in and out of addiction treatment programs. She began drinking at 14, dropped out of school, and was pregnant by the age of 17. She was a heavy alcohol user and experienced frequent blackouts during her first two trimesters of pregnancy, but managed to stay healthy during the final months. She relapsed 2 months later during the strain of caring for her fussy infant. Although currently stronger, her energy is totally consumed by her job and recovery.

> ## Fetal Alcohol Syndrome
>
> The results of prenatal exposure to alcohol range from Fetal Alcohol Syndrome (FAS), the leading cause of preventable mental retardation in the United States, to other fetal alcohol effects causing lifelong disruptions in cognitive, linguistic, and social development. This range of effects is referred to as Fetal Alcohol Spectrum Disorders (FASD). The most common birth defect associated with FASD is central nervous dysfunction, and children prenatally exposed to alcohol may present with cognitive, behavioral, and psychological dysfunction, resulting in lifelong disabilities. Abnormal cognitive functioning manifests in a variety of domains, including mathematical deficiency, difficulty with abstract concepts such as time and space, and inability to see the relationship between cause and effect, as well as comprehension and memory deficits. FASD is a physical disability with behavioral symptoms often demonstrated by poor attention and concentration skills, impaired judgment, hyperactivity, and impulsivity (Malbin, 2002; Streissguth & Kanter, 1997).

On her "good days," when Jane isn't working, she visits John and Paul. She enjoys cooking for them and attempts to organize the small home in which they live. She'd like to help more often, but the disarray in which she finds the home unnerves her, and she is exhausted by Paul's endless questions and energy. Although small and physically immature, Paul is generally healthy and happy. He is inquisitive, imaginative, and has an abundance of physical energy. He is popular among his classmates at Oak Tree Elementary, where he is well known for his sense of humor and practical jokes. His inclination to bounce when he walks has earned him the nickname of "Springer."

Paul loves spending time with his grandfather and other tribal elders. Late nights listening to stories are often followed by late mornings, so Paul frequently misses the bus to school. When this occurs, his grandfather allows him to stay home. Paul's grandfather knows how difficult it is for Paul to sit still in school and remembers Jane's brothers had similar problems before dropping out years ago.

Paul is happiest while roaming the reservation and observing all the wildlife that inhabit the tribal land. He likes to carry a sketchbook and can sit for hours making detailed drawings of the animals and birds. Members of his community admire his sketches that cover the living room walls of his grandfather's house. When prompted, Paul contributes meaning to his drawings by offering dramatic stories from the perspective of the wildlife.

Things to Consider

The Child Abuse Prevention and Treatment Act (CAPTA), U.S. Public Law 93-247, has been revised and expanded many times since it was first introduced in 1974. The law provides funding to states in support of prevention, assessment, investigation, prosecution, and treatment activities. Also included are grants to public agencies and nonprofit organizations for demonstration programs and projects that protect children under the age of 18. In addition to funding, CAPTA identifies mandatory reporters. Teachers, principals, other school personnel, social workers, and healthcare providers are among the many professionals identified as mandatory reporters of child abuse and neglect. Abuse is defined as the imminent risk of serious harm, death, serious physical or emotional harm, sexual abuse, or exploitation. Emotional abuse is defined as a sustained, repetitive pattern of behavior that demonstrably impairs a child's emotional development or sense of self-worth, including constant criticism.

The law defines neglect as the failure to provide for a child's basic needs. This may include: physical neglect, such as the lack of appropriate supervision or the failure to provide necessary food, shelter, or medical care; educational neglect, such as the failure to educate a child or attend to the child's special education needs; emotional neglect, such as the inattention to a child's emotional needs; or exposure to domestic violence. Excessive corporal punishment is also legally considered a form of neglect (Child Welfare Information Gateway, 2011).

Miss Jenkins, Paul's second-grade teacher, is concerned about Paul's truancy but is actually relieved when he's not in class. She feels guilty about the situation but is unsure how to handle Paul. He has a tendency to disrupt the class with his humor and captivating stories. Miss Jenkins is also confused by Paul's uneven performance in her classroom. Although he receives high scores on math fact quizzes, he struggles to read. This seems very unusual to her, given his high verbal ability. Knowing his tendency to take over, she's learned not to use round robin reading activities on days when he's at school. When she does, Paul makes a show of rubbing his eyes and finding the words on the page. To the delight of his classmates, he normally changes the paragraph he's been assigned to read. When this occurs, she finds it difficult to redirect her class of 28 students.

Oak Tree Elementary School has adopted the Response to Intervention (RtI) model for monitoring student growth. The teachers administer the AIMSweb© universal screening assessment for mathematics and reading three times a year to gauge progress toward year-end goals. Paul's second-grade performance is assessed in the fall and it indicates he is above grade level in mathematics but significantly below in reading. Comparing the current with the previous year's diagnostic series, Miss Jenkins sees little if any growth. Paul's records also indicate the one-on-one intervention prescribed during the previous year was discontinued after Paul failed to attend school on the majority of dates for which he was scheduled to meet with the reading specialist. The records indicate the family has no phone and does not respond to mailed requests for conferences. Miss Jenkins does consider requesting an additional reading assessment by the school's RtI team, but is reluctant with Paul's history of truancy and his unresponsive guardian.

Still puzzled by the discrepancies between Paul's performances in mathematics and reading, Miss Jenkins schedules a meeting with a special education colleague. As the two review Paul's cumulative file, it becomes apparent that more information is needed. The special education teacher agrees that given his verbal ability and success in mathematics, Paul's performance in reading is significantly lower than expected. She wonders aloud if Paul may be twice exceptional. The special education teacher explains that twice-exceptional students are gifted students with other learning differences. Miss Jenkins is surprised to learn that it is possible for gifted learners to have significant learning issues, such as dyslexia and ADHD.

Characteristics of Twice-Exceptional Students

Twice-exceptional students may:

- » often struggle to learn basic skills;
- » show high verbal abilities but extreme difficulties with written language expression;
- » have co-occurring differences in reading and/or math;
- » experience reading problems due to cognitive processing deficits;
- » exhibit strong observation skills but deficits in memory skills;
- » excel in real-world problem solving and have outstanding critical thinking and decision-making skills;
- » demonstrate strong observation skills but have difficulty with memory skills and often independently develop compensatory skills;
- » show attention deficit problems but may concentrate for long periods in areas of interest;
- » have strong questioning attitudes and may appear disrespectful when questioning information, facts, etc., presented by teachers;
- » display unusual imagination, frequently generating original and, at times, rather "bizarre" ideas
- » be extremely divergent in thought, appearing to daydream when generating ideas;
- » be unwilling to take risks with regard to academics but take risks in nonschool areas without consideration of consequences;
- » use humor to divert attention from school failure, to make fun of peers, or to avoid trouble;

Characteristics of Twice-Exceptional Students, continued

» appear immature because they may use anger, crying, withdrawal, etc., to express feelings and to deal with difficulties;

» require frequent teacher support and feedback in deficit areas but be highly independent in other areas;

» appear stubborn and inflexible;

» be sensitive regarding disability area(s) or highly critical of themselves and others, including teachers; or

» express concern about the feeling of others even while engaging in antisocial behavior (Idaho State Department of Education, 2010, pp. 5–8; National Education Association, 2006, pp. 7–8).

Things to Consider

Attention Deficit Hyperactivity Disorder (ADHD) is the most common behavioral disorder of childhood, and is marked by a constellation of symptoms including immature levels of impulsivity, inattention, and hyperactivity (American Psychiatric Association, 1994). The National Institutes of Health declared ADHD a "severe public health problem" in its consensus conference on ADHD in 1998. In the ongoing dialogue about ADHD in gifted children, three questions often arise. Are gifted children over-diagnosed with the disorder? In what ways are gifted ADHD children different from gifted children without the disorder and from other ADHD children? Does the emerging research suggest any differences in intervention or support?

There are three subtypes of ADHD: predominantly inattentive type, predominantly hyperactive/impulsive type, and combined type. The combined type is most common and best researched. The DSM-IV states that to meet criteria for a diagnosis of Combined Type ADHD, a child must meet at least six of the nine criteria from both lists and exhibit significant impairment in functioning. Symptoms must occur in more than one setting, have been present for at least six months, and have been present before the age of seven. It is important to note that a child who meets the criteria but doesn't exhibit significant impairment is not diagnosed with the disorder. The subjective determination of what constitutes significant impairment is one of several factors that contribute to the controversy regarding diagnosis and treatment, especially in gifted children. (Neihart, 2003, para. 1–2)

Discussion Questions

1. In what ways do Paul's home life and family history impact his instructional readiness?

2. Is Miss Jenkins required to file a report under CAPTA? Why or why not?

3. In what ways does Paul appear to be twice exceptional? What are his strengths and challenges?

4. What clues are provided by Paul's behavior that might indicate further assessment is needed? What concerns do you have? Why?
5. What strengths does Paul have? What can be done to develop his interests and talents?
6. What role does culture play in Paul's case? Are there common issues among American Indian students that should be considered? If so, what are they?

Activities

1. Read and synthesize three articles on ADD or ADHD in a 250–500 word paper.
2. Write a lesson plan for a grade level of your choice that includes modifications for twice-exceptional students and for gifted students.
3. With a classmate, create a scenario in which a classroom teacher discusses student achievement, behavior, and needed intervention with the guardian of an at-risk student. Your scenario should include realistic data and evidence of the need for an intervention. Role-play the scenario in front of your colleagues.

Extensions

1. Research strategies for working with students who have confirmed or suspected fetal alcohol syndrome. Create a PowerPoint that indicates scientifically based interventions to share with licensed or preservice teachers.
2. Create and upload an informational presentation about teaching gifted ADHD or gifted ADD students on YouTube or Slideshare.
3. Conduct two separate interviews, one with a special education teacher and another with a teacher of gifted students. Ask each of the teachers to discuss their experiences working with twice-exceptional students and their three most successful strategies. Share the results with your classmates.

Additional Readings

Baldwin, S., & LeBlanc, R. (2005). *Teaching students with Fetal Alcohol Spectrum Disorder: A resource guide for Florida educators.* Retrieved from http://www.fldoe.org/core/fileparse.php/7690/urlt/0070099-fetalco.pdf

Baum, S. (Vol. Ed.). (2004). Twice-exceptional and special populations of gifted students. In S. M. Reis (Series Ed.), *Essential readings in gifted education series: Vol. 7.* Thousand Oaks, CA: Corwin Press.

Besnoy, K. D. (2006). *Successful strategies for twice-exceptional students.* Waco, TX: Prufrock Press.

Finlay, G. H., & Sorenson, A. L. (1995). *What educators need to know about having students with Fetal Alcohol Syndrome and fetal alcohol effects in the classroom: Issues, identification, intervention & instructional strategies.* Charlottesville, VA: The Curry School of Education, University of Virginia. Retrieved from http://files.eric.ed.gov/fulltext/ED385039.pdf. (ED385039)

Fuchs, D., Mock, D., Morgan, P. L., & Young, C. L. (2003). Responsiveness-to-intervention: Definitions, evidence, and implications for the learning disabilities construct. *Learning Disabilities Research & Practice, 18,* 157–171. doi:10.1111/15405826.00072

Fugate, M. C., Zentall, S. S., & Gentry, M. (2013, October). Creativity and working memory in gifted students with and without characteristics of Attention Deficit Hyperactive Disorder: Lifting the mask. *Gifted Child Quarterly, 57,* 234–246. doi:10.1177/0016986213500069

Gentry, M., & Fugate, C. M. (2012). Gifted Native American students: Underperforming, under-identified, and overlooked. *Psychology in the Schools, 49,* 631–646. doi:10.1002/pits.21624

Harwood, M., & Kleinfeld, J. S. (2002). Up front, in hope: The value of early intervention for children with Fetal Alcohol Syndrome. *Young Children, 57*(4), 86–90.

Johnsen, S. K. (2005). *Identifying gifted students: A step-by step guide.* Waco, TX: Prufrock Press.

Kaufmann, F. A., & Castellanos, F. X. (2000). Attention-Deficit/Hyperactivity Disorder in gifted students. In K. A. Heller, F. J. Mönks, R. J. Sternberg, & R. F. Subotnik (Eds.), *International handbook of giftedness and talent* (2nd ed., pp. 621–632). Kidlington, Oxford, England: Elsevier Science.

Neihart, M. (2008). Identifying and providing services to twice exceptional children. In S. I. Pfeiffer (Ed.), *Handbook of giftedness in children: Psycho-educational theory, research, and best practices* (pp. 115–138). New York, NY: Springer.

Silverman, L. K. (2002). Gifted children with learning disabilities. In N. Colangelo & G. A. Davis (Eds.), *Handbook of gifted education* (3rd ed., pp. 533–546). Boston, MA: Allyn & Bacon.

Leah

Introduction

Gifted and talented learners with learning disabilities are often difficult to identify. These unique learners have remarkable strengths in one or more areas and significant weaknesses in others. According to Baum (2004), these students can be grouped into three categories: students identified as gifted who also have subtle learning disabilities; students identified as having a learning disability, but are not identified as gifted; and unidentified students whose giftedness and learning disabilities mask each other so that the student functions at or slightly below grade level.

Leah's case study introduces an 11-year-old student and past participant in an elementary gifted program with reading difficulties. Leah's teachers are surprised when her parents express concerns about the discrepancy between their daughter's efforts and achievement.

Leah comes from an intact middle class family living in a small Midwestern community. Her father is an electrical engineer, and her mother is an elementary school teacher. The family values education and begins dinner each evening by asking the children about their school day. If time allows, the conversation typically turns to current events.

At 11, Leah is arguably one of the most well-liked girls in the sixth grade. Friends describe her as smart, cute, and fun. They envy her ability to get along with everyone—popular kids, smart kids, jocks, and nerds all like Leah. She skis competitively, has a great voice, and knows the lyrics to "all" the songs. Last year, when Leah qualified for the Midwest Junior Championship Ski Trials, the sidelines were filled with family and friends. Although classroom work isn't easy for Leah, she loves attending school. She likes the interaction with her classmates and enjoys several of her classes. She finds science interesting, especially class demonstrations and experiments. She actively participates in social studies and language arts class discussions, but finds keeping up with the reading to be an ongoing challenge. Choir is her favorite and math has become increasingly difficult for her.

Things to Consider

» Expectations for middle school students are not the same as elementary students. Sixth graders typically experience increased homework and reading assignments upon entering middle school.
» Study skills and time management are learned behaviors.

Teachers enjoy Leah in class, describing her as a "respectful and conscientious student." Comments shared by teachers during conferences and on report cards indicate Leah's assignments are thorough and on time. Although group work, experiential learning, and projects are particular strengths for Leah, classroom and achievement test scores are typically in the average to below-average range. This is somewhat surprising given her third-grade Cognitive Abilities Test (CogAT) score of 129 and past participation in the elementary gifted program.

Although Leah's mother is worried about her daughter, colleagues at school have confirmed with assurance that Leah is a "great kid, doing just fine." When Leah admits during her sixth-grade conference that homework can, at times, seem overwhelming, her teachers are surprised. They assume her contributions to class discussions reflect a wide range of knowledge and above-average reading ability. They aren't aware that Leah reads very slowly, often re-reading passages many times for basic comprehension. They have no idea how hard she works or how frustrated she is about schoolwork.

With an eye on the future, Leah's parents are concerned her test scores and grades aren't an accurate indication of their daughter's ability. As an educator, Leah's mother is aware her daughter may have some deficits in key components that prevent comprehension of increasingly rigorous texts. Both parents worry about state assessments required for graduation and college entrance exams.

Leah realizes she spends far more time on her homework than her peers and is beginning to wonder if something is wrong. She is exhausted and discouraged by late nights of study. Once confident, she now questions her own capabilities, and if she'll be allowed to take the enriched and accelerated courses that interest her.

At the request of Leah's family, a special needs assessment is conducted to determine if Leah has all compensatory components required for reading. During a preliminary interview with Leah, the team notes she is a highly verbal, articulate, and uses advanced vocabulary appropriately. She presents herself as an intelligent and pleasant young lady who is clearly frustrated by issues with homework. When the team reviews Leah's records and discovers a descending pattern of achievement, they determine further investigation is needed. They begin with reading assessments. In addition to assessing Leah's speed at which she reads, the assessment team looks closely at Leah's ability to read strategically, understand complex vocabulary and text, and write clearly and coherently. The team uses the Gray Oral Reading Tests to assess Leah's reading efficiency. They suspect that Leah has trouble with visual scanning, processing (looking from the board to her paper), and working memory. The results are somewhat surprising:

- Reading rate: 5%

- ⦿ Fluency rate: 9%
- ⦿ Comprehension rate: 75%

The discrepancy between Leah's reading rate and comprehension rate is much greater than anticipated. They note the discrepancy and Leah's difficulties with spelling and sequencing, which make problem solving and note taking difficult. Further, Leah's difficulties with sequencing, working memory, and reading also impact her ability to complete numerical operations and story problems in math.

> The International Dyslexia Association (2013) identified the following as common characteristics in twice-exceptional individuals:
> » Superior oral vocabulary
> » Advanced ideas and opinions
> » High levels of creativity and problem-solving ability
> » Extremely curious, imaginative, and questioning
> » Discrepant verbal and performance skills
> » Clear peaks and valleys in cognitive test profile
> » Wide range of interests not related to school
> » Specific talent or consuming interest area
> » Sophisticated sense of humor (para. 2)

Leah's parents tell the team they have worked with Leah for years to overcome areas of relative weakness. Leah's mother has taught Leah to use visual clues and mnemonics to memorize information. Leah's father helps Leah understand abstract concepts by relating them to real-life problems. They wonder aloud why the district uses manipulatives in problem solving at the elementary level but not in middle school mathematics classrooms.

When the team shares their assessment findings with Leah's parents, they note many of Leah's weaknesses are consistent with those found in dyslexic students. They recommend consultation with a dyslexia specialist. Leah's parents are surprised but relieved to know that their daughter has received a thorough assessment and that a diagnosis may lead to a solution.

What Is Dyslexia?

Dyslexia is characterized by difficulties with accurate and/or fluent word recognition and by poor spelling and decoding abilities. These difficulties typically result from a deficit in the phonological component of language that is often unexpected in relation to other cognitive abilities and the provision of effective classroom instruction. Secondary consequences may include problems

> **What Is Dyslexia?, continued**
>
> in reading comprehension and reduced reading experience that can impede growth of vocabulary and background knowledge. (International Dyslexia Association, 2002, para. 1)

Discussion Questions

1. What is Leah's greatest school challenge? As she moves through the school system are the challenges she faces likely to increase or decrease? Why or why not?
2. In what ways can classroom teachers modify the curriculum to address the needs of twice-exceptional students with reading difficulties? Should the grading rubric be modified as well? Why or why not?
3. How does reading instruction at the secondary level differ from reading instruction for elementary students? Do students learn to read or read to learn? Explain.
4. What type of assessment is likely to provide the most accurate picture of Leah's strengths and relative weaknesses? Why? What conversation, if any, would you have with Leah prior to assessment?
5. Should twice-exceptional students be allowed to take accelerated classes? Why or why not?
6. How would professional development training help classroom teachers identify a twice-exceptional student?

Activities

1. Working with a partner, plan a lesson on a topic of mutual interest that meets the diverse range of instructional needs within a heterogeneous classroom. Identify the learning goal and outcomes for your plan.
2. Research dyslexia to learn about effective instructional strategies for working with dyslexic elementary or secondary students. Share your findings in a product of your choice with your classmates.
3. Using a format of your choice, create a slide presentation in which you identify common reading issues for elementary or secondary students. Share the presentation with classmates or upload to a public slide sharing website.
4. Meet with a reading specialist to discuss strategies to increase reading speed and comprehension. Meet with a gifted education specialist to discuss school services for twice-exceptional students. Write a summary of each conversation.

Extensions

1. Using a state standard or CCSS standard, create a lesson plan in which students may choose from several modalities to learn about a topic in science or social studies. Post your lesson on a teacher-sharing site. Your plan should identify the standard, learning target, and an assessment rubric.
2. Plan and record a webinar that raises awareness of twice-exceptional learners. Share your webinar with your colleagues or classmates.
3. Create an annotated bibliography of current research in literacy that focuses on gifted learners with reading problems.
4. Read two articles on any of the following systematic and explicit instructional methods: structured literacy, simultaneous multisensory reading, or explicit phonics. Write a 250–500 word essay in which you compare and contrast the methods of instruction. With prior instructor approval, you may substitute another instructional method or review a specific product.

Additional Readings

Besnoy, K. (2006). *Successful strategies for twice-exceptional students.* Waco, TX: Prufrock Press.

Catts, H. W., Hogan, T. P., & Adlof, S. M. (2005). Developmental changes in reading and reading disabilities. In H. W. Catts & A. G. Kamhi (Eds.), *The connections between language and reading disabilities* (pp. 23–36). Mahwah, NJ: Lawrence Erlbaum Associates.

Colorado Department of Education. (2012). *Twice-exceptional students gifted students with disabilities: Level 1: An introductory resource book* (4th ed.). Retrieved from http://www.cde.state.co.us/sites/default/files/documents/gt/download/pdf/level_1_resource_handbook_4th_ed_10-2-12.pdf

Compton, D. L., Fuchs, D., Fuchs, L. S., Elleman, A. M., & Gilbert, J. K. (2008). Tracking children who fly below the radar: Latent transition modeling of students with late-emerging reading disability. *Learning and Individual Differences, 18,* 329–337. doi:10.1016/j.lindif.2008.04.003

Johnsen, S. K. (2005). *Identifying gifted students: A step-by step guide.* Waco, TX: Prufrock Press.

Johnson, E. S., Smith, L., & Harris, M. L. (2009). *How RTI works in secondary schools.* Thousand Oaks, CA: Corwin Press.

Leach, J. M., Scarborough, H. S., & Rescorla, L. (2003). Late-emerging reading disabilities. *Journal of Educational Psychology, 95,* 211–224. doi:10.1037/0022-0663.95.2.211

McCallum, R. S., Bell, S. M., Coles, J. T., Miller, K. C., Hopkins, M. B., & Hilton-Prillhart, A. (2013). A model for screening twice-exceptional students (gifted with learning disabilities) within a response to intervention paradigm. *Gifted Child Quarterly, 57,* 209–222. doi:10.1177/0016986213 500070

McGregor, T. (2007). *Comprehension connections: Bridges to strategic reading.* Portsmouth, NH: Heinemann.

Moats, L. C., & Dakin, K. E. (2007). *Basic facts about dyslexia and other reading problems.* Baltimore, MD: International Dyslexia Association.

National Education Association. (2006). *The twice-exceptional dilemma.* Retrieved from http://www.nea.org/assets/docs/twiceexceptional.pdf

Rakow, S. (2011). *Educating gifted students in middle school: A practical guide* (2nd ed.). Waco, TX: Prufrock Press.

Robb, L. (2003). *Teaching reading in social studies, science, and math: Practical ways to weave comprehension strategies into your content area teaching.* New York, NY: Scholastic.

Salembier, G. B. (1999). Scan and run: A reading comprehension strategy that works. *Journal of Adolescent and Adult Literacy, 42,* 386–394.

Solis, M., Ciullo, S., Vaughn, S., Pyle, N., Hassaram, B., & Leroux, A. (2012). Reading comprehension interventions for middle school students with learning disabilities: A synthesis of 30 years of research. *Journal of Learning Disabilities, 45,* 327–340. doi:10.1177/0022219411402691

Swanson, H. L., & Deshler, D. (2003). Instructing adolescents with learning disabilities: Converting a meta-analysis to practice. *Journal of Learning Disabilities, 36,* 124–135.

Torgesen, J. K., Houston, D. D., Rissman, L. M., Decker, S. M., Roberts, G., Vaughn, S., . . . Lesaux, N. (2007). *Academic literacy instruction for adolescents: A guidance document from the Center on Instruction.* Retrieved from http://www.centeroninstruction.org/academic-literacy-instruction-for-adolescents-a-guidance-document-from-the-center-on-instruction

Torgesen, J. K., & Miller, D. H. (2009). *Assessments to guide adolescent literacy instruction.* Retrieved from http://www.centeroninstruction.org/files/Assessment%20Guide.pdf

Walpole, S., & McKenna, M. C. (2007). *Differentiated reading instruction: Strategies for the primary grades.* New York, NY: Guilford Press.

Winebrenner, S. (2003). Teaching strategies for twice-exceptional students. *Intervention in School and Clinic, 38,* 131–137.

Ms. Goodman and Ms. Lane

Introduction

Ms. Goodman is a coordinator of gifted services for an urban district. Ms. Lane is a fourth-grade regular education classroom teacher. The district recently received a transfer student who has severe emotional and behavioral problems, but has also been identified as gifted. The student is currently being evaluated for appropriate services.

Luiz, who is of Hispanic descent, has just been adopted by a single father. Although his adoptive father, Mr. Rodriguez, was aware of Luiz's emotional and behavioral disorder (EBD), he did not realize the extent of its severity. Luiz was abandoned at birth and was in several foster homes, never staying in one home for any great length of time. He was relocated to a new home because he was unable to "fit it." He was also deemed uncontrollable. Mr. Rodriguez is a professional in the community and wants to provide the best possible home situation for Luiz. He is extremely interested in Luiz's welfare. He has met with the coordinator of gifted programs, Ms. Goodman, and the fourth-grade regular education classroom teacher, Ms. Lane. Figures 3.5 and 3.6 provide information about the school's enrollment.

Luiz first came to Ms. Goodman's attention when she was contacted by the principal. At that meeting, previous school data were provided and reviewed. A second meeting was held to discuss various options and included Ms. Goodman, Ms. Lane, and Mr. Rodriguez. Ms. Goodman was also invited to meet and observe Luiz in the classroom.

Ms. Goodman's Observations

Luiz has problems controlling his behavior. He is disruptive in class and can barely sit still. He exhibits ADHD characteristics. He calls out frequently. He says mean things to the other children in the class. He is not interested in what the teacher is teaching. He takes his pencils and scribbles across the pages of his notebook. He seems angry. His test scores indicate he has an above-average/gifted ability but he does not work up to his potential. Luiz was identified with EBD. I am concerned about placing Luiz in the gifted program until he is able to better gain control of his emotions.

Ms. Lane's Observations

I am frightened of Luiz and so are the other children. I am afraid that he will do something to harm himself, them, or even me. He has run away from home a few

Ethnic Group	Number of Students Enrolled
White	288
Black	72
Multiracial	51

Figure 3.5. Enrollment by ethnic group.

	Disabled Enrollment (%)	Nondisabled Enrollment(%)
This school	21.5	78.5
State average	16	83.8

Figure 3.6. Disabled and nondisabled enrollment.

times. He does have an IQ score above 130, as indicated on a nationally normed test. Somehow, he has been able to compensate for his lack of focus and gains what he needs to learn from reading books. His adoptive father is very supportive and anxious to provide for his new son. Luiz seems to respond better to male figures. He is only interested in topics of his choosing. He has a short attention span regarding anything else.

Luiz's Observations

I don't know how to act around the other students. They seem silly and boring. I want to be left alone. Almost everyone makes me angry. I can't seem to control my thoughts or feelings. I just feel mad most of the time. I do like my new dad though. I hope that I don't do anything that will make him want to send me away. I would rather stay home all day and read my books on space and play computer games. Science is my favorite subject. I wish I could just stay home and spend time with my new dad. School is a waste of my time.

Mr. Rodriguez's Observations

I was so excited to adopt Luiz. I know that Luiz has some serious behavior problems, but he is such a smart boy. His education is very important to me and I want to participate in his school activities. I work full-time but want Luiz to know that I will be here if he needs me. Parenting a child is new to me so I need any guidance the school can offer.

Things to Consider

» Gifted students with emotional and behavior problems are not often referred for gifted programs, or they are exited from gifted programs because of their behavior. They may also experience periods of underachievement (Reid & McGuire, 1995).
» Gifted students with emotional and behavior problems may become disengaged with school.

When Mr. Rodriguez met with the school staff, he inquired about Luiz's participation in the pull-out program for gifted students. The staff wonders which placement would best meet Luiz's cognitive, social, and emotional needs. Should he be placed temporarily in the gifted program to see how he does? Or, instead should the district consider placement in a program for students with an emotional and behavioral disorder?

Discussion Questions

1. What are the major and minor issues in this case?
2. What would an IEP for Luiz include?
3. What concerns are raised regarding Luiz's cognitive, social, and emotional needs?
4. What curricular and instructional implications arise from Luiz's needs?
5. What should the school do next?
6. What long-term plans need to be developed for a continuum of services?
7. What role does collaboration and inclusion play in any future decisions related to Luiz's placement?
8. What can Mr. Rodriguez do at home to nurture Luiz's giftedness?

Activities

1. Role-play the next meeting to include Luiz, Ms. Goodman, Ms. Lane, Mr. Rodriguez, and the school's principal.
2. Develop an intervention plan for Luiz.
3. Compile a list of the most recent research related to meeting the needs of gifted children with emotional or behavioral disorders. Provide a summary to colleagues.
4. Which differentiation strategies might be effective with Luiz? Justify your choices in a class discussion.
5. Create a bumper sticker that emphasizes the affective needs of gifted learners.

Extensions

1. Develop a chart identifying curricular and instructional implications for twice-exceptional children.
2. Develop a plan of action for working with parents of twice-exceptional learners.
3. What does the research tell us about the correlation between motivation and learning to achievement gains? Make a summary of your findings.
4. Explore the concerns related to the misidentification of ADHD in gifted children. Create a pamphlet to help guide parents and educators about these concerns.
5. Identify various resources in your area to support parents and teachers in meeting the needs of twice-exceptional children and share them on your school's website.
6. What, if any, is the connection of Dabrowski's overexcitabilities with gifted children who exhibit emotional or behavioral disorders? Present your findings in a discussion with a colleague.

Additional Readings

Baum, S. M., Olenchak, F. R., & Owen, S. V. (1998). Gifted students with attention deficits: Fact and/or fiction? Or, can we see the forest for the trees. *Gifted Child Quarterly, 42,* 96–104. doi:10.1177/001698629804200204

Cross, T. L. (2005). *The social and emotional lives of gifted kids: Understanding and guiding their development.* Waco, TX: Prufrock Press.

Garland, A. F., & Zigler, E. (1999). Emotional and behavioral problems among highly intellectually gifted youth. *Roeper Review, 22,* 41–44. doi:10.1080/02783199909553996

Neihart, M., Pfeiffer, S. I., & Cross, T. L. (2016). *The social and emotional development of gifted children* (2nd ed.). Waco, TX: Prufrock Press.

Probst, B. (2007, January/February). When your child's second exceptionality is emotional: Looking beyond psychiatric diagnosis. *2e Twice Exceptional Newsletter, 20,* 1–24.

Robinson, A., Shore, B. M., & Enersen, D. L. (2007). *Best practices in gifted education: An evidence-based guide.* Waco, TX: Prufrock Press.

Silverman, L. K. (1993). *Counseling the gifted and talented.* Denver, CO: Love Publishing.

Webb, J. T., Amend, E. R., Webb, N. E., Goerss, J., Beljan, P., & Olenchak, F. R. (2005). *Misdiagnosis and dual diagnosing of gifted children and adults: ADHD, Bipolar, OCD, Asperger's, depression, and other disorders.* Scottsdale, AZ: Great Potential Press.

International Baccalaureate: Primary Years Programme

Introduction

International Baccalaureate (IB) offers three levels of programming: Primary Years Progamme (PYP), Pre-K through grade 5; Middle Years Programme (MYP), grades 6 through 10; and Diploma Programme (DP), grades 11 through 12. IB requires programmes to follow specialized guidelines. PYP curriculum guidelines require a Program of Inquiry (POI). Activities are developed from the POI and are based on IB's six transdisciplinary themes: Who We Are, Where We Are in Place and Time, How We Express Ourselves, How the World Works, How We Organize Ourselves, and Sharing the Planet (International Baccalaureate Organization [IBO], 2014), and a central idea that must be included in teachers' Planners (unit plans). Teachers have the freedom to add personal creativity and to address specialized learning needs of their students in the lessons.

PYP years end with Exhibition, the students' presentations of research that is the culmination of their learning experiences at the IB-PYP campus.

IB expects that gifted students will not be clustered in one classroom and that all students participate in the activities and strategies teachers include in unit plans.

This case looks at a campus POI and excerpts from a fifth-grade Planner to show how students prepare for fifth-grade Exhibition. It also illustrates ways in which gifted students' meet learning standards within an IB classroom.

De Leon Primary Years Programme Elementary School

De Leon Elementary School is one of 20 schools in the district, with 450 students in prekindergarten through fifth grade. The school has long been recognized as high achieving by the state's department of education. It is a neighborhood school that accepts transfers when space is available. Although most of the students are from the surrounding neighborhood, there are approximately 30 students who are bused from a high-poverty area of the district and 10 students who have transferred for the IB program.

De Leon is ranked as Recognized by a statewide system that only has one level above that designation, Exemplary. Figure 3.7 illustrates De Leon Elementary's demographic composition.

The majority of the teaching staff remains at De Leon because of its IB designation. The principal has been on the campus for 22 years, first as a teacher, then assistant principal. The campus has a very involved parent organization that volunteers for anything the faculty requests.

Ethnicity	Enrollment
African American	20%
White	41%
Hispanic	36%
Other	3%
Total enrollment	450

Figure 3.7. De Leon Elementary demographics.

Kindergarten Through Grade 5

Each grade level introduces and develops students' learning through transdisciplinary themes with a central idea built on each inquiry. Each PYP campus is required to develop a POI organized by the six transdisciplinary themes (IBO, 2014). From the POI, each grade level creates a Planner (unit plan) for their grade. The Planner includes inquiry through Form, Function, Causation, Connection, Change, Perspective, Responsibility, and Reflection (IBO, 2014). As stated in the introduction, all students in each classroom participate in the same activities. Differentiation for the gifted occurs through strategies, pacing, and products.

Table 3.1 is an example POI for Where We Are in Place and Time.

Things to Consider

» Often students believe learning for a test as proof of learning. This perception has an effect on their academic growth. PYP Exhibition offers an alternative to demonstrate learning.

» IB offers inquiry learning for students' inquiry with a wider lens of global studies.

» PYP teachers who meet individual student needs must have time and support for planning.

Fifth Grade

PYP students must present an Exhibition during fifth grade. This presentation is a culmination of individual and/or group research into a subject of their choosing. De Leon PYP asks students to present their products to all students in their school during Exhibition Day, as well as to parents and the community during the evening. Even though all fifth graders complete a group and/or individual research project, De Leon PYP gifted students are asked to explore their subject individually and to include a "So What?" and "How?" that takes their learning beyond what, where, and when to why each student chose

Table 3.1
POI for Where We Are in Place and Time

Programme of Inquiry	Grade Level	Central Idea	Lines of Inquiry	Concepts
Where We Are in Place and Time: An inquiry into orientation in place and time, personal histories; homes and journeys; the discoveries, explorations, and migrations of humankind; the relationships between the interconnectedness of individuals and civilizations, from local and global perspectives.	K	People make their homes in different places and in different ways.	• The similarities and differences of homes • Necessity of homes • Types of homes	• Function • Causations • Change
	1	My home is part of the world community.	• Comparison of homes around the world • Parts of my neighborhood and community • Relationships to communities around the world	• Form • Function • Connection
	2	Evidence of the past links one's personal history to others past and present.	• Connection of past, present, and future • Interpreting guidelines and family trees • Geographic connection	• Function • Connection • Perspective
	3	Through time people journey to new destinations to explore the world.	• Development of maps and globes for travel • Human travel past and present • Compare and contrast modes of transportation	• Change • Connection • Perspective
	4	People immigrate for a variety of reasons and have an impact on their new homeland.	• Reasons for immigration • Responsibility of citizenship • Effects of immigration	• Causation • Perspective • Responsibility
	5	Individuals can make a difference within communities.	• Causes and effects of a global program • Possible solutions to a global problem	• Causation • Connection • Responsibility • Perspective • Reflection

Adapted from "Programme of Inquiry" by Mountainview Elementary School, 2010–2011, retrieved from http://www2.wacoisd.org/mountainview/ib_schools.htm. Copyright 2010 by Mountainview Elementary School. Adapted with permission.

his or her subject, how their learning influenced them, and how their project may impact others.

Table 3.2 details excerpts from the fifth-grade Planner (unit plan), by Morgan, Canham, and Gibson (personal communications, April 14, 2014), teachers at Mountainview Elementary in the Primary Years Programme, that illustrate how the POI guides learning for the PYP culminating experience, Exhibition.

IB requires that teachers and students reflect on this experience after Exhibition. At this time, students complete a set of questions to guide their reflection. Teachers infuse students' thoughts with their insights to refine the Exhibition experience as they plan for next year's students and Exhibition.

Discussion Questions

1. In what ways does the fifth-grade example of IB curriculum approximate best practice for gifted learners?
2. Does the POI facilitate learning for gifted students? If so, in what ways? If not, why not?
3. Which elements of an IB unit plan could you include in your unit plan? How?
4. What types of preassessment could have been included in the fifth-grade unit plans?
5. What specific guidance could a fifth-grade teacher give to gifted students as they prepare for Exhibition?
6. Do the fifth-grade Exhibition and IB curriculum facilitate the affective needs of gifted learners? If so, in what ways? If not, why not?
7. Reference the IB learner profile on the IBO website (http://www.ibo.org). In what ways would the profile facilitate the learning nature and needs of the gifted?
8. From the POI in this case and information from http://www.ibo.org, in what ways does PYP accommodate lifelong learning about global issues?

Activities

1. Research International Baccalaureate PYP, MYP, and/or DP. Create a KWL chart for yourself before initiating your research. After completing your research, describe what new learning occurred for you through a narrative or graphic organizer.
2. Develop a differentiated lesson for a gifted student based on one of the POI examples included in this case.

Table 3.2
Transdisciplinary Theme: Where We Are In Place and Time

Central Idea
Individuals can make a difference within a community.
Summative Assessment Tasks
Students are grouped according to self-selected topics or gifted students select their topic for an individualized study. Research is based on the central idea. Students create a presentation, write a description of their topic with research, provide sketches of their presentation board or outline of technology-based presentation, practice their presentation, work cooperatively in groups or share ideas through peer evaluations, and make public presentations.
Evidence of Connection Between Central Idea and Transdisciplinary Theme
Students learn about other cultures. Their research gives evidence of their understanding of their place in the community and the world at large as well as how they relate to their community and around the world.

Examples of Topics Chosen for Research	
• What is child labor?	• How is the panda habitat different from other habitats?
• How can we help white tigers?	• What are some ways to prevent cardiovascular disease?

3. Create a lesson plan for one grade level of your choice that helps students explore a global issue. Include details about how the global issue relates to their campus and in their city or state.

4. Research competitions available for PYP students. Select one competition to infuse into a unit plan.

5. Develop a math, science, social studies, or an English/language arts/reading center for one of the transdisciplinary themes described in this case. Include a narrative about a student, his or her learning needs, and expected learning outcomes.

Extensions

1. Compare and contrast a POI with your district's scope and sequence or curriculum guide for gifted.

2. Visit an IB classroom, PYP, MYP, or DP. Prepare a synopsis of your visit.

3. Create a presentation to a community or school group that discusses the advantages and disadvantages of instituting an IB program on your campus.

Additional Readings

Hertberg-Davis, H., Callahan, C. M., & Kyburg, R. M. (2006). *Advanced placement and International Baccalaureate programs: A fit for gifted learners*

(RM06222). Storrs: University of Connecticut, The National Research Center on the Gifted and Talented.

Kitsantas, A., & Miller, A. D. (2015). *Characteristics and context of Primary Years Programme (PYP) students' self-efficacy and self-regulatory development.* Retrieved from http://www.ibo.org/globalassets/publications/ib-research/pyp/pyp-self-efficacy-full-report-en.pdf

Roberts, J. L., & Boggess, J. R. (2012). *Differentiating instruction with centers in the gifted classroom.* Waco, TX: Prufrock Press.

Sizmur, J., & Cunningham, R. (2012). *International Baccalaureate Middle Years Programme (MYP) in the UK.* Slough, Berkshire: National Foundation for Educational Research. Retrieved from http://www.ibo.org/globalassets/publications/ib-research/ibmyp-finalnferreport-plus supplementaryanalyses.pdf

Skrzypiec, G., Askell-Williams, H., Slee, P., & Rudzinski, A. (2014). *International Baccalaureate Middle Years Programme (MYP): Student social-emotional well-being and school success practices.* Retrieved from http://www.ibo.org/globalassets/publications/ib-research/myp/socialemotionalfinalreport.pdf

Westphal, L. E. (2011). *Ready-to-use differentiation strategies, grades 3–5.* Waco, TX: Prufrock Press.

Ms. Renaldo

Introduction

Many states are implementing various standards for accountability purposes. As districts require teachers to transition to new standards (e.g., CCSS), instructional models are sometimes also mandated as a way to teach to the new standards. Teachers may struggle with all of the new requirements but still maintain their focus on meeting the needs of the diverse learners in their classrooms. Ms. Renaldo is one such teacher. See how Ms. Renaldo implements the "Gradual Release Model" (Pearson & Gallagher, 1983) and determines if it could be adapted to meet the needs of high-ability and gifted learners.

Cyprus Oaks Elementary School

Cyprus Oaks Elementary School is located in an urban district in a populous southern state. The elementary school is public and serves approximately 1,200 students in grades K–5. The school's vision statement suggests that Cyprus Oaks is dedicated to actively engaging all students, regardless of discipline or special needs, in order to achieve academic success and reach their full potential as students and members of a community. Cyprus Oaks Elementary has consistently earned an "A" statewide school grade and has also been honored with the Five Star School Award, Golden School Award, Red Carpet School Award, Little Red School House Award, and a state School Recognition Award.

Cyprus Oaks Elementary School has an astounding number of the mores of the community instilled into its curriculum. Teachers at Cyprus Oaks are dedicated to their students and they are constantly working to inspire their students. The school portrays a sense of community amongst the teaching and office staff, the students, and the parents. The school also emphasizes the importance of parent involvement to increase the success of the students. It achieves this by sending home Parent Teacher Association (PTA) information, classroom newsletters, opportunities to volunteer at the school, and planners and folders that the parents have to sign, indicating awareness of their child's progress and behavior at school. Additionally, the halls are also full of student work and the school's mission. For example, the fourth-grade team consistently displays student work throughout the hallway and in the classroom to promote a sense of achievement, while also identifying the standard aligned with the lesson.

The school constantly collaborates in a variety of settings to focus on the school's improvement plan. Monthly steering meetings are held to provide each grade-level representative an opportunity to discuss his or her grade level's goals and concerns, and then communicate the information with his or her grade level at the monthly grade-level meeting. Each subject area also collaborates weekly to share ideas and plan lessons. Lastly, faculty meetings are held monthly to discuss achievements and apprehensions regarding the school's improvement plan.

Students at Cyprus Oaks Elementary School

At Cyprus Oaks Elementary School, more than half of the student population is White and approximately one quarter of the population is African American. The student population also includes Hispanics, Asian/Pacific Islanders, and students identified as two or more races. Approximately 35% of the school population is eligible for free or reduced breakfast and lunch programs. Cyprus Oaks also caters to students with IEP plans, providing services in all exceptional areas including special needs, speech and language services, ELL services, and gifted education. These services offer strategies that help gifted learners, help students overcome deficits, and provide individualized programs to meet specific needs with experienced teachers who focus on the education of Exceptional Student Education (ESE) students. Furthermore, the majority of the ESE students are placed in an inclusion classroom setting with collaborative help from the general education and ESE teacher.

The Classroom Setting

Ms. Renaldo has been placed in a fourth-grade reading/language arts classroom. The fourth-grade students consist of a homeroom class of 22 students and switch with another teacher's class of 21 students. The homeroom class is an inclusion class that includes five ESE students, two ELL students, and three gifted students. In total, there are 13 boys and 9 girls. The switch class consists of one ELL student, one student with an emotional and behavioral disorder, and four gifted students. In this class, there are 12 boys and 9 girls. Furthermore, there is a mixture of various learning styles present in the two classes. Many of the students are visual and kinesthetic learners and Ms. Renaldo makes sure to include visual models and provide the directions that are both visual and verbal. She also includes hands-on class, group, and independent activities to meet the needs of her students.

When the Reading Baseline Curriculum Guide Assessment was given to the students during the first week of school, only five students mastered 50% or more of the 14 reading standards tested. A majority of the students only mastered 3 of the 14 standards while three students did not master any of the standards. A majority of the students in both of the classes are below level in their reading skills with only the gifted students reading above grade level.

Because all fourth graders in the state will be assessed in writing, Ms. Renaldo has focused her next week's lessons to develop her students' writing skills. The district has recently adopted the "Gradual Release of Responsibility Model" (Pearson & Gallagher, 1983), which requires that the teacher, by design, transition from assuming "all the responsibility for performing a task . . . to a situation in which the students assume all of the responsibility" (Duke & Pearson, 2002, p. 211). The gradual release of responsibility model of instruction has been documented as an effective approach for improving writing achievement (Fisher & Frey, 2003), thus Ms. Renaldo has designed her lesson plans implementing this method (see Table 3.3).

She still needs to consider what additional modifications she will make to her lesson so that her gifted students will be challenged in writing. Although Ms. Renaldo has attended several district-wide professional development workshops on this model, she still struggles with providing challenging options within the frameworks of the model for her gifted learners.

Things to Consider

» Instructional models need to be able to meet the needs of diverse learners in a classroom.
» Modifications to lessons provide opportunities for learners with unique needs to be challenged or supported.
» Districts need to provide professional development opportunities for teachers implementing district and/or state mandates so that teachers are prepared to meet the needs of all learners in their classrooms.

Discussion Questions

1. Which characteristics of the school community support excellence in teaching?
2. Can one instructional approach meet the needs of various learners in a classroom? Why or why not?
3. How might the lesson be different if you change the order of the release of responsibility? Would the lesson be more appropriate for gifted learners? Why or why not?
4. What resources and materials would be helpful in making revisions to meet the needs of Ms. Renaldo's gifted students?
5. How might tiered assignments or another strategy for differentiation be used to develop additional activities for students still struggling with mastery of the standard and those students who have already mastered the standard?

Table 3.3
Ms. Renaldo's Writing Lesson Plan

<table>
<tr><td rowspan="8">Planning</td><td colspan="2" align="center">Benchmark</td></tr>
<tr><td colspan="1">State Standard: LA.4.4.1.1 The student will write narratives based on real or imagined ideas, events, or observations that include characters, setting, plot, sensory details, a logical sequence of events, and a context to enable the reader to imagine the world of the event or experience.

Common Core State Standard: W.4.3 Write narratives to develop real or imagined experiences or events using effective technique, descriptive details, and clear event sequences.</td><td>Objectives
Students will be able to generate ideas from multiple sources and choose a topic based on personal experiences.</td></tr>
<tr><td>Assessment
"Begin with the end in mind." How will you know whether your students have made progress toward the objective? How and when will you assess mastery?</td><td>Essential Question(s)
A higher order question that is directly derived from the benchmark, introduced at the beginning of the lesson, discussed throughout the lesson, and answered by students at the end of the lesson to show understanding of the concepts taught.</td></tr>
<tr><td>Students will write a small moment story in their writer's notebook demonstrating mastery of the skill (choosing a topic).</td><td>How can I choose a story topic that focuses on one small moment?</td></tr>
<tr><td>Higher Order Questions (3–5)
What questions will be answered to provoke higher order thinking and include moderate to high complexity levels? What would the ideal student response be for each question?</td><td>Vocabulary
Essential vocabulary that should be introduced and/or reviewed.</td></tr>
<tr><td><ul><li>What is the difference between a focused and unfocused story?</li><li>What small moment are you writing about?</li><li>What makes your story focused?</li><li>How can you make your story more focused?</li><li>How can writing about a small moment make your writing more interesting?</li></ul></td><td><ul><li>Small moment: A specific and small event in time (e.g., a big moment can be a story about your trip to the beach, but a small moment can be just about your favorite part of that trip to the beach).</li><li>Zoom in: When you focus or move in closer to something (e.g., when someone moves a camera lens to zoom-in on a specific object).</li><li>Focused versus unfocused: When all of your attention is centered on something specific versus unspecific, when your attention is not centered on something specific (e.g., when a student is giving all of his attention to the teacher, he is considered focused. When a student is staring out the window when a teacher is teaching, he is considered unfocused).</li></ul></td></tr>
</table>

<table>
<tr><td rowspan="2">Lesson Cycle</td><td colspan="1" align="center">Introduction</td></tr>
<tr><td>1. Introduce the essential question(s).
2. Present a slice of watermelon (with seeds) to the class.
3. Discuss the metaphor of the slice of watermelon representing a big topic and the seeds represent small moments within that big topic.<ul><li>The slice of watermelon represents a big topic or idea such as a day at the beach.</li></ul></td></tr>
</table>

Table 3.3, continued

Lesson Cycle	• Each seed within the watermelon or big topic represents small moments or events that happen within the big topic such as building a sand castle at the beach or snorkeling in the ocean water.
	
	4. Introduce and discuss the vocabulary.
	  • Use the seeds to provide a visual representation of a *small moment*.
	  • Use a magnify glass as a visual representation of *zoom in* and *focused versus unfocused*.

Modeling ("I Do")
- Explicitly model exactly what students are expected to do during shared practice, guided practice and eventually during independent work.
- Conduct a think aloud.
- Model the use of a graphic organizer or interactive journal entry.

1. Tell students that writers make their stories more interesting when they "zoom in" and focus on a small, specific moment in time.
2. Discuss how a small moment starts and ends in the same place/location; focuses on one thing or event; includes details including adjectives, feelings, and characters; and has a beginning, middle, and end.
3. Model writing a small moment (seed story) entry in a writer's notebook.
4. Conduct a brainstorming to list details of a trip to the beach (watermelon story).
5. Write a small moment story focusing on just one activity that happened on the trip to the beach (seed story).
6. Explain how zooming in on a small moment (a seed in the watermelon) helps the reader see and feel what you experienced, whereas writing about a big topic (a watermelon story) simply summarizes what happened.

Guided Practice "We Do"
- Provide students support while they try doing what was modeled to them.
- Guide students to independent practice by providing an opportunity to work in small groups and practice what was taught during the guided portion of the lesson.
- Encourage student engagement through peer interaction.
- Incorporate the use of collaborative strategy in small groups.
- Perform checks for understanding.

1. Present the small moment anchor chart.
2. Explain and model the activity.
  - Read a sticky note with a big topic written on it.
  - Write a small moment (1–2 sentences) related to the big topic on a blank sticky note.
  - Stick the big topic sticky note in the correct spot on the anchor chart and the small moment sticky note in the correct spot on the anchor chart.

3. Place students in small groups and give each group a sticky note with a big topic written on it.
4. Have students work in small groups to complete the activity as modeled by the teacher.
5. Monitor and provide feedback and encouragement to students during the activity.
6. After the activity, review and conduct a discussion about the activity.

Independent Practice "You Do"
- Allow students the opportunity to independently practice what was learned throughout the lesson.
- Pull small groups or individuals for more intensive support.
- Assign students independent work that is directly aligned with the "I DO," "WE DO," and "THEY DO" portions of the lesson.
- Provide above-level students with extended practice through the use of higher level activities.

- Students who need extra support will work in a small group with the teacher to write a small moment story about an activity/event they did at the beach in their writer's journal. Some students will be provided a graphic organizer to plan out their story.
- Students who are working on level and independently will write a small moment story about an activity/event they did at the beach in their writer's journal.

Table 3.3, continued

Lesson Cycle	• Students who need to be challenged or finish early will begin brainstorming small moment ideas for various big topics on a narrative writing prompt chart.
	Close • Wrap up the lesson and help students organize the information learned in to a meaningful context. • Have students reflect on or answer the Essential Question. • Help students connect today's learning to their bigger goal in the course.

	1. Have students turn to their shoulder partner and share their small moment so everyone has a chance to share.
	2. Share a few of the students' small moment stories to the class. Ask higher order questions:
	  • What makes your story focused?
	  • How can you make your story more focused?
	  • How can writing about a small moment make your writing more interesting?
	  • What is the difference between a focused and unfocused story?
	
	3. Refer back to the essential question and how it applies to real-life experience.

Note. The lesson plan has been used by permission of Erika Florez, former student intern, Mandarin Oaks Elementary School, Jacksonville, FL.

6. What higher order questions related to the topic can be asked of the gifted students?

7. In what ways can Ms. Renaldo provide enrichment to her gifted learners?

Activities

1. How might you scaffold the essential question to increase its rigor? Provide several examples.

2. What modifications can Ms. Renaldo make to the content, process, product, and/or learning environment to meet the needs of her gifted learners? Revise the lesson plan with the changes.

3. List various activities for independent practice by completing the following "Students who need to be challenged or finish early will . . ."

4. Create a series of lessons that incorporate the "Gradual Release Model" (Pearson & Gallagher, 1983). After implementing the lessons, write a reflection on what went well and what you would change if you were to teach these lessons again.

5. Design a writing lesson implementing the RAFT (Role, Audience, Format, and Topic) writing strategy in a different subject area, such as science or social studies. View the video at https://www.youtube.com/watch?v=OLJ_32y6lR0 to learn about RAFT.

Extensions

1. Research the "Gradual Release of Responsibility Model" (Pearson & Gallagher, 1983). Conduct a Plus, Minus, Interesting (PMI) to determine if this model is appropriate for gifted learners.

2. Review Kaplan's Depth and Complexity Model. Use the 11 components as a springboard to make changes to this lesson or one of your own. Complete a planning chart with your suggestions.

3. Check out "Tips for Parents: Writing and the Gifted Child," available at http://www.davidsongifted.org/db/Articles_id_10376.aspx. Create a set of tips for your students' parents on writing or any other topic or subject area.

4. Develop a plan of action for differentiating a unit of study in an area that students have had mixed results in mastery. Research various strategies for differentiation. Identify possible pre- and postassessment strategies for the unit. Implement your plan and evaluate the results. Share your findings with a colleague.

5. Research various menu options. Create several for your classroom use.

6. Choose 8–12 video clips related to differentiation (available at http://www.youtube.com/user/BERStaffDevelopment/videos). Make a list of key points that you have learned and identify ways to share them with colleagues.

Additional Readings

Collins, N. D., & Cross, T. L. (1993). Teaching the writing process to gifted and talented students. *Gifted Child Today, 16*(3), 22–23.

Hughes, C. E., Kettler, T., Shaunessy-Dedrick, E., & VanTassel-Baska, J. (2014). *A teacher's guide to using the Common Core State Standards with gifted and advanced learners in the English language arts.* Waco, TX: Prufrock Press.

Miller, L., & Lubkert, E. (2012). *Language arts for gifted learners.* Waco, TX: Prufrock Press.

Smith, K. J. (2014). From pop-up books to Shakespeare: Writing as problem solving across the grade levels. *Gifted Child Today, 37*(4), 223–234. doi:10.1177/1076217514544028

VanTassel-Baska, J., Zuo, L., Avery, L. D., & Little, C. A. (2002). A curriculum study of gifted-student learning in the language arts. *Gifted Child Quarterly, 46,* 30–44. doi:10.1177/001698620204600104

Miss Wendell, Lesson 1

If an optimal educational match is achieved, the child will realize that school is an exciting and challenging place that fosters curiosity, thinking, imagination, and friendships. (as cited in Kottmeyer, 2014, para. 1)

Introduction

Miss Wendell is a kindergarten teacher with a very diverse group of learners. The district requires that all teachers differentiate their curriculum and instruction to meet the needs of their students. As a new teacher, Miss Wendell is modifying her assignments because she knows that her students have come to school with a variety of knowledge, skills, and experiences. She knows that if she does not provide different activities some of her students will be bored and some will misbehave. She wants to provide challenging activities that require every one of her students to learn something new. Meet Miss Wendell and her class as she modifies her lesson on Dr. Seuss.

Miss Wendell is a kindergarten teacher working at a school in a suburban district. Mountain Creek Elementary (MCE) has earned the Department of Education's "A" school designation every year since 1998. Mountain Creek Elementary has also received various recognition awards and grants that are only given to schools that consistently are high performers or that show significant gains in achievement. Mountain Creek Elementary is the home for Exceptional Student Education (ESE) programs for the district. Miss Wendell's kindergarten class is welcoming, and filled with a variety of educational decorations, student work, and bright colors. The class of 17 students sits in three assigned tables in groups of four or more. There is a carpet in the front of the room where students go for most of their group instruction. They use the rug area to read as a class and for circle time. Miss Wendell uses many "hands up," "pair up," and "share up" activities with students for recalling information and participating in class discussions. Seatwork is given but mostly for either assessment purposes or group assignments. There are eight girls and nine boys in the classroom.

Although there are a few students with special needs who require intervention, there is one student, Brian, who has been tested and diagnosed with autism. Miss Wendell uses techniques such as preferential seating, extended time, and teacher assistance as needed so Brian can be successful in and out of the classroom. There are several students who have not been labeled, but are struggling academically. One student, Matt, is below grade level and is having a difficult time academically. He needs significant support/assistance in all activities. Another student, Keri, seems to be on grade level, however, she struggles with fluency and comprehension in reading. She is a slow worker and tends to use recess time or free center time to finish her work. Another student, Ernesto, is an English for Speakers of Other Languages (ESOL) student from Honduras. Although he speaks English, his home language is Spanish. Ernesto seems to be on grade level, however, he struggles with staying seated and has a constant need for recognition. There are four students, Nick, Mason, Gabe, and Sophia, who consistently achieve at grade level and beyond.

Things to Consider

» Children need activities at school, which encourage them to exercise their minds and use creative thinking and problem-solving skills.

» Tiered assignments demand different levels of mastery and provide different degrees of complexity.

» The idea behind tiered activities is that all students, regardless of differences in ability, skill, and experience, can focus on the same learning objective.

» Achievement gains are encouraged when students who are struggling, on grade level, or advanced receive instruction and activities in a tiered format.

In celebration of Dr. Seuss's birthday, Miss Wendell developed a lesson using *The Cat in the Hat* (Seuss, 1957). She thought about the diverse needs of the learners in her classroom and used the plan in Table 3.4 for her lesson.

Discussion Questions

1. Are the activities tiered? Why or why not?
2. Do the activities presented meet the needs of Miss Wendell's diverse classroom, including those students with gifts and talents by engaging them in meaningful and rigorous learning activities and social interactions? How do you know?
3. What are the strengths of this lesson? The weaknesses?
4. What changes might make the activities more or less challenging?
5. What other information would be helpful to know about Miss Wendell's classroom? Why?
6. How many tiers or groups of students do you have in your own classroom? How do you group your own students?

Activities

1. Evaluate the video "How does tiering benefit teachers" (LEARN NC, n.d.; available at http://www.learnnc.org/lp/multimedia/15818) and read the "Rethinking the role of the teacher" segment found at

Table 3.4
Miss Wendell, Lesson 1

Lesson Topic/ Subject/Grade Level	Rhyming words/language arts/ kindergarten.
Common Core State Standard	RF.K.2.a. Recognize and produce rhyming words.
Objective	Students will hear the similarities in the words through rhymes. Students will be able to identify rhyming words and will be able to make up their own rhyming words.
Vocabulary	• **Word family:** A group of words that have the same pattern of vowels and constants. • **Rhyme:** Words that sound alike by having the same ending sound. • **Vowel:** A, E, I, O, U, and sometimes Y. • **Consonant:** A letter in the alphabet that is not a vowel.
Engagement/Hook	Students will be called by table colors to the carpet to watch a Brain Pop Jr. video (available by subscribing at http://www.brainpop.com/educators/community/bp-topic/) on rhyming words. Stop the video periodically to check for the students' comprehension.
Opening	Ask the students to raise their "quiet hands" if they know the meaning of a rhyme. "What if I told you all that by the end of the day you all will be Rhyme Masters! So listen up if you want to be a Master!" I will then ask students if they can tell me what a rhyme is or why we need rhymes. I am looking for an answer similar to a rhyme is a word that has an ending sound like another word's ending (cat, hat, mat, tree, bee, see, etc.). I will call on students to come up with some rhyming words of their own. Before we begin reading *The Cat in the Hat* by Dr. Seuss (1957), I will ask that as I am reading the book, students are to put their fingers on their noses if they hear a rhyming word. After reading two pages, I will stop and we will review the rhyming words they heard. I will continue until the book is finished or the class becomes restless.
Guided Practice	"Now, let's look at our worksheets to see what we are going to do today. Blue table (struggling students) will be working on a Time to Rhyme worksheet where you cut out four different pictures and paste them into the correct spots where they would fit for rhyming words (e.g., fish-dish). Once you have finished coloring then you may cut out the pictures to glue in the correct spots. Red and yellow tables (on grade level) will be working on a Rhyme Time With Dr. Seuss worksheet. This group will have 15 words (e.g., ring, Sam, bat, hat, clam) you must cut out and glue under the appropriate columns of hat, ham, and thing. Green table (above grade level) will be picking five rhyming words and write them on the lines in the shape of the cat's hat. When you are finished, you are to write five sentences with the five rhyming words you chose and then color your hat." (Figure 3.8 is an example of one student's work.)
Closing	Students will be called back to the carpet to review rhyming words. We will review how some rhyming words are made up for silly words and others are actually real words.
Evaluation	I will be periodically checking to see if all students have their fingers on their noses because they heard rhyming words. Students will also be evaluated on their accurate completion of worksheets assigned.

Note. This lesson plan has been used by permission of Heather McDonald, former student intern, Cunningham Creek Elementary School, St. Johns, FL.

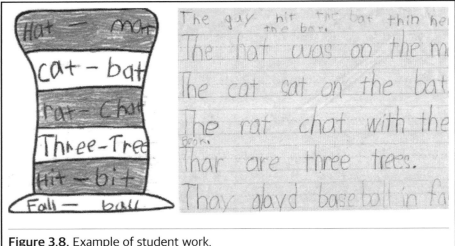

Figure 3.8. Example of student work.

LEARN NC (n.d., para. 2; available at http://www.learnnc.org/lp/editions/every-learner/6680). In a class discussion, address the following questions: What do you believe is the role of the teacher? How can tiering benefit you?

2. Create an activity for a fourth higher level tier.
3. Generate a list of additional ideas for differentiated lessons related to rhyming words.

Extensions

1. Are certain differentiation strategies more effective with certain students? What needs to be considered during the decision-making process for lesson planning? Create a flow chart outlining the process.
2. "Responsive teaching is flexible teaching." What does this mean to you? Share your thoughts in a discussion with colleagues.
3. What does the research tell us about the correlation between motivation and learning to achievement gains? Make a summary of your findings.
4. What role do learning contracts play in Response to Intervention (RtI)? Read a talk on RtI for gifted students, available at http://www.rtinetwork.org/professional/rti-talks/transcript/talk/24 (Coleman, 2010).

Additional Readings

Adams, C. M., & Pierce, R. L. (2011). *Differentiation that really works: Strategies from real teachers for real classrooms, grades K–2*. Waco, TX: Prufrock Press.

Hertzog, N. B. (2008). *Early childhood gifted education*. Waco, TX: Prufrock Press.

National Association for Gifted Children. (n.d.). *Young bright children*. Retrieved from http://www.nagc.org/resources-publications/resources-parents/young-bright-children

Olszewski-Kubilius, P., Limburg-Weber, L., & Pfeiffer, S. (2003). *Early gifts: Recognizing and nurturing children's talents*. Waco, TX: Prufrock Press.

Smutny, J. F., & von Fremd, S. E. (2004). *Differentiating for the young child: Teaching strategies across the content areas, K–3*. Thousand Oaks, CA: Corwin Press.

Smutny, J. F., Walker, S. Y., & Meckstroth, E. A. (1997). *Teaching young gifted children in the regular classroom: Identifying, nurturing, and challenging ages 4–9*. Minneapolis, MN: Free Spirit Publishing.

Tomlinson, C. A., & Moon, T. R. (2013). *Assessment and student success in a differentiated classroom*. Alexandria, VA: ASCD.

Westphal, L. E. (2013). *Differentiating instruction with menus for the inclusive classroom: Language arts, grades K–2*. Waco, TX: Prufrock Press.

Miss Wendell, Lesson 2

Introduction

Continue following Miss Wendell as she modifies her lesson on Abraham Lincoln and President's Day to meet needs for her kindergartners. The district requires that teachers differentiate their curriculum and instruction to meet the needs of their students. As a new teacher, Miss Wendell is modifying her assignments because she knows that her students have come to school with a variety of knowledge, skills, and experiences. She knows that if she does not provide different activities some of her students will be bored and some will misbehave. She wants to provide challenging activities that require every one of her students to learn something new.

Miss Wendell is a kindergarten teacher working at a school in a suburban district. Mountain Creek Elementary (MCE) has earned the Department of Education's "A" school designation every year since 1998. Mountain Creek Elementary has also received various recognition awards and grants that are only given to schools that consistently are high performers or that show significant gains in achievement. Mountain Creek Elementary is the home for Exceptional Student Education (ESE) programs for the district. Miss Wendell's welcoming kindergarten classroom is filled with a variety of educational decorations, student work, and bright colors. The class of 17 students sits in three assigned tables in groups of four or more. There is a carpet in the front of the room where students go for most of their group instruction. They use the rug area to read as a class and for circle time. Miss Wendell uses many "hands up," "pair up," and "share up" activities with students for recalling information and participating in class discussions. Seatwork is given but mostly for either assessment purposes or group assignments. There are eight girls and nine boys in the classroom.

Although there are a few students with special needs who need intervention, there is one student, Brian, who has been tested and diagnosed with autism. Miss Wendell uses techniques such as preferential seating, extended time, and teacher assistance as needed so Brian can be successful in and out of the classroom. There are several students who have not been labeled, but are struggling academically. One student, Matt, is below grade level and is having a difficult time academically and needs significant support/assistance in all activities. Another student, Keri, seems to be on grade level, however, she struggles with fluency and comprehension in reading. She is a slow worker and tends to use recess time or free center time to finish her work. Another student, Ernesto, is an ESOL student from Honduras. Although he speaks English, his home language is Spanish. Ernesto seems to be on grade level however, he struggles with staying seated and has a constant need for recognition. There are four students, Nick, Mason, Gabe, and Sophia, who consistently achieve at grade level and beyond.

Things to Consider

» Managing a differentiated classroom requires a variety of approaches.
» Teachers benefit from developing lessons that meet the needs of diverse learners.
» Grouping strategies are critical to enhancing instruction in a differentiated classroom.

In celebration of President's Day, Miss Wendell developed a lesson focusing on Abraham Lincoln. She thought about the diverse needs of the learners in her classroom and used the plan in Table 3.5 for her lesson.

Discussion Questions

1. What is the most important thing to teach in this lesson? Why?
2. Are the activities differentiated? Why or why not?
3. Are Miss Wendell's grouping strategies appropriate for this lesson? How can you tell?
4. What other graphic organizer could Miss Wendell use with her class?
5. In what ways would you change the content of the lesson for advanced and gifted learners? The process(es) of the lesson? The products of the lesson? The learning environment?
6. Do the activities provide an accurate assessment of the standard? Why or why not?
7. How might you differentiate the assessment strategies for advanced and gifted learners?
8. How do students benefit from teachers developing activities that meet the needs of diverse learners in their classrooms?

Activities

1. Develop a list of questions related to this topic or a similar topic that could be asked of students at different levels.
2. How does the preassessment of facts differ from the preassessment of concepts or big ideas? Develop a preassessment tool for assessing *concepts* to be used with this lesson or a lesson of your choice. Consider your response to this question as you develop your instrument.
3. Create a learning menu of activities to support this objective or another social studies objective for one of more ability levels of learners.

Table 3.5
Miss Wendell, Lesson 2

Lesson Topic/ Subject/Grade Level	Abraham Lincoln and President's Day/social studies/ kindergarten.
Common Core State Standard	SS.K.A.2.2. Recognize the importance of celebrations and national holidays as a way of remembering and honoring people, events, and our nation's ethnic heritage.
Objective	The kindergarten social studies student will demonstrate knowledge of Abraham Lincoln and President's Day so that, after participating in a lesson about Abraham Lincoln and President's Day, they can correctly identify and state facts in a KWL chart.
Vocabulary	• **President:** A leader who is elected. • **Memorial:** Something that honors an important person or event. • **Abolish:** To end. • **Assassinate:** To kill an important person.
Engagement/Hook	Students will be called by table colors to the carpet to watch a Brain Pop Jr. video (available by subscribing at http://www.brainpop.com/educators/community/bp-topic) on Abraham Lincoln. Stop the video periodically to check for the students' comprehension.
Opening	Ask the students to raise their "quiet hands" if their dad, mom, or grandparents have an important job to go to every day. "Raise your hand if you have ever had an important job, such as cleaning your room, walking the dog, feeding the cat, etc. Today we are going to learn about a man who had a very important job to do. His name is Abraham Lincoln and he looks like this (show a picture of Mr. Lincoln). Does anyone know what Abraham Lincoln's job was called? Being a President of the United States means being a leader and making decisions for the whole country. Some cities celebrate Abraham Lincoln with parades and celebrations. We celebrate Abraham Lincoln by having a holiday from school with county and federal offices being closed including no mail being delivered. We have two presidents who have birthdays in February and we celebrate both of them. Does anyone know who they are? Let's fill out a KWL chart of what we know, what we want to know, and what we have learned with our lesson today. Think of something you know about Abraham Lincoln and I will write it down on the sticky note and place it on the "K" column of our chart. Now what do we want to know about Abraham Lincoln? I will add those to the "W" column of our chart." Then, I will read the book *Young Abraham Lincoln, Log Cabin President* (Woods, 1992) and stop frequently to ask questions to check for understanding. Students will be dismissed to return to their color-coded tables.
Guided Practice	"Now, let's look at our worksheets to see what we are going to do today. Blue table (struggling students) will be working on a worksheet connecting the letters from A to Z to form a picture of Abraham Lincoln as a boy. Red and yellow tables (on grade level) will color pictures and organize the three pages into a book. Each student will read aloud the story (He was born in a log cabin. He read by a fire. He became our 16th president.). Green table (above grade level) will write facts from a story picture about Abraham Lincoln." As children are finishing, I will be asking them to share facts for me to write on sticky notes to later add to the "L" column on our KWL chart.
Closing	Students will be called back to the carpet. We will finish our KWL chart about Abraham Lincoln. Students will share their thoughts from the sticky notes added to the chart. Students will also complete a President's Day ABC order worksheet.
Evaluation	Students will be evaluated on their accurate completion of worksheets assigned, the group KWL chart, and President's Day worksheet.
Enrichment	Blue tables and red/yellow tables will receive an Abraham Lincoln word search. The green table will receive a worksheet with the prompt "If I were president I would . . . "

Note. This lesson plan has been used by permission of Heather McDonald, former student intern, Cunningham Creek Elementary School, St. Johns, FL.

4. Create several versions of a game about President's Day for various levels of students.

5. Design a learning center with differentiated activities about "celebrations" or another appropriate theme related to national holidays for your grade level and students' needs.

Extensions

1. Review video clips of differentiated classrooms. Make a grid with categories such as managing a differentiated classroom, implementing differentiation strategies, implementing differentiation models, applying grouping strategies, implementing differentiated assessment, etc. What differentiation techniques are being implemented? List those observed in the various video clips. Discuss your observations with others.

2. Develop a list of guiding questions and/or activities that could be used with any of the differentiation video clips. Use the questions and activities to provide an in-service with educators.

3. What are the greatest challenges in implementing a differentiated classroom, especially for young children? Research various approaches to these challenges and report your findings in a KWL chart.

4. Create a checklist of teacher behaviors that support differentiation.

5. When students are engaged in motivating activities, learning is more likely to be successful. Create a bumper sticker with a similar quote that supports the need for differentiation.

Additional Readings

Adams, C. M., & Pierce, R. L. (2011). *Differentiation that really works: Strategies from real teachers for real classrooms, grades K–2.* Waco, TX: Prufrock Press.

Hertzog, N. B. (2008). *Early childhood gifted education.* Waco, TX: Prufrock Press.

National Association for Gifted Children. (n.d.). *Young bright children.* Retrieved from http://www.nagc.org/resources-publications/resources-parents/young-bright-children

Olszewski-Kubilius, P., Limburg-Weber, L., & Pfeiffer, S. (2003). *Early gifts: Recognizing and nurturing children's talents.* Waco, TX: Prufrock Press.

Smutny, J. F., & von Fremd, S. E. (2004). *Differentiating for the young child: Teaching strategies across the content areas, K-3.* Thousand Oaks, CA: Corwin Press.

Smutny, J. F., Walker, S. Y., & Meckstroth, E. A. (1997). *Teaching young gifted children in the regular classroom: Identifying, nurturing, and challenging ages 4-9.* Minneapolis, MN: Free Spirit Publishing.

Tomlinson, C. A., & Moon, T. R. (2013). *Assessment and student success in a differentiated classroom.* Alexandria, VA: ASCD.

Westphal, L. E. (2013). *Differentiating instruction with menus for the inclusive classroom: Language arts, grades K–2.* Waco, TX: Prufrock Press.

Edgewood Academy

Introduction

Edgewood Academy, a small independent school, has committed to provide professional development and training to help its faculty implement differentiation in its school. Learn more about the decision-making process, planning, and follow-through necessary to implement differentiation as you follow this school in its endeavor.

Edgewood Academy, an independent school founded in 1970, has approximately more than 300 students in grades Pre-K (beginning with age 3) through grade 6 and about 45 faculty and staff members. The school is dedicated to empowering students to achieve academic excellence by fostering lifelong global skills and community stewardship. The school offers a variety of curricular experiences to meet the diverse needs and interests of their students, such as STEAM (science, technology, engineering, arts, and math) classes, global studies, foreign language classes including Spanish and Mandarin Chinese, extracurricular afterschool activities including sports and visual and performing arts programs, and service learning options. In their curriculum mapping, the school consults the CCSS, yet they are not necessarily the driving force of the curriculum. The school also considers national standards as they prepare their students for any future settings they may encounter after graduating from the school.

Edgewood Academy has an admissions process and enrolls a variety of students including those who are classified by the formal state definition of "gifted," with a focus on superior intellectual development. The faculty and administration realize that because of the diverse cognitive levels of its student population there is a need to implement teaching strategies that ensure the academic and social/emotional development of students who are capable of learning above grade level. They decide to consult with an expert in the field of gifted education to outline professional development strategies, including large-group instruction workshops, book studies, and grade-level meetings for putting differentiation into practice. Edgewood Academy decides to focus on three main issues:

- What support do teachers need in order to develop and/or reflect upon their philosophy about differentiation? How does a school develop a philosophy about differentiation?
- What professional development strategies can help promote the implementation of differentiation in the classroom?
- What factors might influence the implementation of differentiation?

> **Things to Consider**
>
> » Planning and carrying out professional development related to differentiation for teachers is key to successful implementation.
> » A plan for implementing differentiation must include input from the faculty in order to create a learning community that respects individual differences.
> » Because change can create uncertainty and stress in a faculty, administrative support is essential if curricular modifications and faculty growth are going to take place.

It was important to develop a professional development plan that would empower the teachers in their own classrooms and ultimately the school. Oftentimes, differentiation is associated with just instructional strategies. Edgewood Academy believed it was important to develop its own differentiation philosophy. All training sessions needed to emphasize that teachers develop a working vocabulary related to differentiation. Faculty and administration needed to speak with parents, children, and others using language commonly found in the field. When the teachers were asked informally about the definition of *differentiation*, oftentimes they associated differentiation with providing individualized instruction. The plan for professional development would provide various opportunities to enhance the teachers' understanding of this concept, in addition to providing strategies that support a differentiated classroom. A design for implementing differentiation included input from the faculty in order to create a learning community that respects individual differences. A needs assessment was administered to determine what the teachers knew about differentiation and what they need to know. The data collected reinforced not only the necessity for the faculty to learn about the strategies but for continued support and mentoring during the implementation process.

Discussion Questions

1. How do you define *differentiation*?
2. What does "differentiation is a philosophy" mean?
3. Why is it important to identify a personal philosophy for differentiation?
4. Why do teachers and others working with gifted learners need professional development?
5. What are some of the issues, positive and negative, with implementing differentiation in classrooms?
6. Are there differences in the needs of public schools versus independent schools in meeting the needs of gifted learners? If so, what are they?
7. What professional development strategies could be implemented?

Activities

1. Create a needs assessment about differentiating the curriculum and instruction and administer it to a group of teachers. Using the results, identify a list of topics and strategies for a brown bag lunch, a focus for a PLC in your school, or another strategy for professional development.
2. Make a list of your own professional development goals for working with diverse learners. Develop a plan to meet these goals.
3. Role-play a staff meeting where professional development related to supporting a differentiated classroom is the focus of the agenda.
4. What resources are needed to support differentiated classrooms? Prioritize a list.

Extensions

1. Research the components of effective professional development. Summarize your findings in a paper. What did you learn about professional development that you did not know before this research?
2. In what ways can you support effective professional development in your school? Develop a presentation to share your suggestions with administrators.
3. Review at least three different tools for assessing teachers' ability to implement differentiation. Create a chart exhibiting the strengths and weaknesses of each one.
4. How might professional development be tiered for different teachers? Brainstorm a list of topics from novice to expert and develop a training session for one or more of the topics.
5. Select any book of interest for a professional development book study. Develop study questions to guide the review of the book. Lead a book study in your school or organization based on your work.

Additional Readings

Association for Supervision and Curriculum Development. (1994). *Challenging gifted learners in the regular classroom*. Alexandria, VA. Author. [Video staff development set]. Retrieved from http://shop.ascd.org

Association for Supervision and Curriculum Development. (1997). *Differentiating instruction*. Alexandria, VA. Author. [Video staff development set]. Retrieved from http://shop.ascd.org

Association for Supervision and Curriculum Development. (2002). *At work in the differentiated classroom*. Alexandria, VA. Author. [Video staff development set]. Retrieved from http://shop.ascd.org

Association for Supervision and Curriculum Development. (2003). *Instructional strategies for the differentiated classroom 1–4*. Alexandria, VA. Author. [Video staff development set] Retrieved from http://shop.ascd.org

Association for Supervision and Curriculum Development. (2004). *Instructional strategies for the differentiated classroom 5–7*. Alexandria, VA. Author. [Video staff development set]. Retrieved from http://shop.ascd.org

Association for Supervision and Curriculum Development. (2008). *Differentiated instruction in action program 1: Elementary school*. Alexandria, VA. Author. [DVD]. Retrieved from http://shop.ascd.org

Association for Supervision and Curriculum Development. (2008). *Differentiated instruction in action program 2: Middle school*. Alexandria, VA. Author. [DVD]. Retrieved from http://shop.ascd.org

Association for Supervision and Curriculum Development. (2008). *Differentiated instruction in action program 3: High school*. Alexandria, VA. Author. [DVD]. Retrieved from http://shop.ascd.org

Kingore, B. (2004). *Differentiation: Simplified, realistic, and effective*. Austin, TX: Professional Associates Publishing.

Roberts, J. L., & Inman, T. F. (2009). *Strategies for differentiating instruction: Best practices for the classroom*. Waco, TX: Prufrock Press.

Tomlinson, C. A. (1995). *How to differentiate instruction in mixed-ability classrooms: A professional inquiry kit*. Alexandria, VA: ASCD.

Tomlinson, C. A. (1999). *The differentiated classroom: Responding to the needs of all learners*. Alexandria, VA: ASCD.

VanTassel-Baska, J. (2003). Content-based curriculum for high-ability learners: An introduction. In J. VanTassel-Baska, & C. A. Little (Eds.), *Content-based curriculum for high-ability learners* (pp. 1–23). Waco, TX: Prufrock Press.

Weber, C. L., Johnson, L., & Tripp, S. (2013). Implementing differentiation: A school's journey. *Gifted Child Today, 36*(3), 179–186. doi:10.1177/1076217513486646

Winebrenner, S. (2001). *Teaching gifted kids in the regular classroom* (Rev. ed.). Minneapolis, MN: Free Spirit Publishing.

SPARK: Ms. Duncan's Flipped Classroom

Introduction

This case details the story of Ms. Duncan's flipped cluster classroom with funds from a grant. The teacher's objective was to spark learning for all her students, both gifted and mixed-ability learners. The grant provided access to technology to allow students more time to think critically and creatively during the school day.

This case explores the flipped concept in an innovative project that seeks to accommodate all learners and provides access for all students regardless of socioeconomic status (SES) and availability of technology in the home.

Ms. Duncan

Ms. Duncan teaches in a self-contained cluster classroom with mixed-ability and gifted students, including 12 students identified as gifted, six students whose state standardized scores are in the average range, and four students whose scores are slightly below average. In a district with 90% of the students identified as low SES, 86% of Ms. Duncan's students are identified as low SES. Of the 12 identified as gifted, four are Hispanic, four are White, two are Asian, and two are African American. Three of the average and below-average students are Hispanic, three are White, one is Asian, and three are African American.

In order to write for a grant, Ms. Duncan researched a new idea that she had been reading about, the flipped classroom. She read,

> In essence, 'flipping the classroom' means that students gain first exposure to new material outside of class, usually via reading or lecture videos, and then use class time to do the harder work of assimilating that knowledge, perhaps through problem-solving, discussion, or debates. (Brame, 2013, p. 1)

Her research led her to the works of Walvoord and Anderson (1998). She found that their model includes the idea that students gain information about content prior to class discussions so that deeper thinking processes are given in classroom discussions about content. Students are assigned work via technology prior to class thus allowing for actual face-to-face class time that is more productive. Walvoord and Anderson (1998) reflect that feedback during class time clears up misunderstandings orally so that extensive written feedback after the fact is unnecessary.

Ms. Duncan's research gave her an idea. She decided to try something new. Her class of 22 students needed, well, a spark. One Friday she told the students that they were going to flip their classroom. They asked if they were going to turn their chairs and desks upside down. Were they going to do flips or stand on their heads? "No," she replied, "but you will have to wait until Monday to flip." All day they guessed and pondered how they would flip a whole classroom.

Ms. Duncan applied for and received the flipped classroom grant that would provide her class with 1:1 laptops for school and home use.

The Grant Application

The grant application asked for a rationale, objectives, benefits, and expected outcomes. In her rationale, Ms. Duncan stated that teachers often focus on struggling students, even in a cluster classroom. Ms. Duncan realized that much of her time was devoted to struggling students and that her gifted students needed opportunities to engage on a deeper and more complex level of thinking and production. She proposed that the learning would be more engaging for all students through the expansion of the learning time that was available to students at home or in afterschool care. Ms. Duncan believed that if the introduction to learning was outside the classroom, time in class could allow students to focus on synthesis, creativity, problem solving, and critical thinking, when she would be available to provide productive feedback on their thinking and projects.

Her objectives were to raise achievement scores on the state standardized testing with technology that allowed her to flip her classroom, to provide equal access for learning to all students with 1:1 technology that would be used at school and at home, and to provide other cluster classroom teachers with a creative and innovative model of technology as well as higher level thinking and learning.

As a pilot program for gifted students and their teachers in cluster classrooms, the project could provide baseline information about a flipped cluster classroom. Although not a structured research study, anecdotal and journal information, along with surveys from parents and students and pre-/postassessments, would offer insight on ways to create and continue teaching, as well as learning, in the flipped environment.

Expected outcomes were listed as growth on the state standardized testing, survey information from students and parents about both the flipped classroom and the technology provided, and evaluations of projects evidenced through a state-defined rubric that incorporated elements from the CCSS.

Ms. Duncan received 25 laptops, programs to support videos and PowerPoints, and 25 4G Internet cards with AT&T service. The laptops were formatted and security settings were added.

After learning she had received the grant, she sent a letter home to parents describing the project and asking them to attend a meeting to explain the flipped process, her expectations of the students, and her plans for their learning.

All students were represented at the parent/guardian meeting. Those attending were excited to learn about the flipped classroom and, after myriad questions, assured their full participation in the project.

Things to Consider

» Preassessment should be a key component of any classroom with all learners, including gifted learners.
» A flipped classroom must ensure that all students have access to basic knowledge and comprehension required for critical and creative thinking.
» Flipped work must meet various learning styles and needs of all students in the class.

SPARK's Structure

Following the parent/guardian meeting, Ms. Duncan was ready to start her project, which she named "SPARK." She planned the first week of the project with this timeline:

- **Day 1:** Students receive laptops and practice with the computer programs provided. Ms. Duncan includes both a video she develops explaining their new process and a PowerPoint that provides the same information.
- **Day 2:** Students practice completing a flipped lesson like those they will be doing at home in the future. They watch a video of Ms. Duncan introducing the CCSS related to U.S. Westward Expansion. Ms. Duncan includes a short pre-/postassessment for before and after the video. The assessment is a KWL chart asking what they already know, what they want to learn, and what they learned. Her purpose is to determine appropriate grouping and projects designed for each group or student. Ms. Duncan sends students home with the laptops so that they can watch the video again and add to their KWL chart.
- **Day 3:** Ms. Duncan groups students according to the preassessment and begins the study of Westward Expansion. At the end of the day, she shares another video clip about the next day's information and discussion.

- **Day 4:** The first day of their real flipped lesson includes evaluation of students' experience with and continuance of their assigned projects. Students repeat the process of the flipped lesson at their homes that night.
- **Day 5:** Each group or individual presents what they have learned and any part of their projects that are complete. Ms. Duncan evaluates their learning and begins preparing for her flipped classroom the next week. The next week's flipped information will include videos and PowerPoints to further determine the best venue for recognizing the variety of her students' learning styles.

Preassessment. Ms. Duncan gave the students a laminated KWL chart so that students could modify their chart as needed. Days 3 and 4 also included a preassessment before the video lecture started. The lecture was programmed to start after students completed the preassessment.

Videos for lecture. Ms. Duncan prepared three videos for the students to watch. The first one introduced the lesson on Westward Expansion, the second revolved around explorers, and the third included early cities that developed along the major rivers.

Students' projects. After Ms. Duncan assessed learning through the preassessment, the KWL chart, and daily work on projects, she assigned projects through a tiered assignments board. All assignments included Bloom's applying, analyzing, evaluating, and creating. Gifted students were given problem-based scenarios that asked students to think critically and creatively. She built project choices around the Western hemisphere themes found in the CCSS for fifth grade.

Discussion Questions

1. Did Ms. Duncan adequately prepare her students for the flipped classroom? Why or why not?
2. In what ways will the flipped classroom meet the diverse needs of Ms. Duncan's students?
3. Was Ms. Duncan justified in receiving funding for her classroom? If so, list reasons. If not, explain.
4. How can a flipped classroom be used in a class with all gifted students?
5. What are the pros and cons of starting a flipped classroom?
6. Which core content areas are better suited to being flipped? Can all core content areas be flipped? Discuss the pros and cons of the flipped classroom for each content area.

7. Which venues for flipped lessons are more appropriate for your students: video clips, PowerPoints, Prezis, or others?

Activities

1. Prepare a presentation for parents to explain a flipped classroom approach.
2. Prepare a PowerPoint or video for a flipped lesson.
3. Develop a 3x3 menu for the students to complete after a flipped lesson.
4. Develop and apply for a grant to institute a flipped classroom for your class or one grade level on your campus.

Extensions

1. Research other ways technology can enhance learning. Describe at least three ways with narrative or graphic representation.
2. Explore research in professional journals that address other means of using 1:1 technology in the classroom. Find at least three articles and prepare a synopsis of each.
3. Create a compendium of grants that could fund 1:1 technology in a classroom or campus. Share your findings with other teachers and or administrators.

Additional Readings

Anderson, L. W., & Krathwohl, D. (Eds.). (2001). *A taxonomy for learning, teaching, and assessing: A revision of Bloom's taxonomy of educational objectives.* New York, NY: Longman.

Berrett, D. (2012, February 19). How 'flipping' the classroom can improve the traditional lecture. *The Chronicle of Higher Education.* Retrieved from http://chronicle.com/article/How-Flipping-the-Classroom/130857

Bransford, J. D., Brown, A. L., & Cocking, R. R. (2000). *How people learn: Brain, mind, experience, and school* (Expanded ed.). Washington, DC: National Academy Press.

Crouch, C. H., & Mazur, E. (2001). Peer instruction: Ten years of experience and results. *American Journal of Physics, 69,* 970–977. doi:10.1119/1.1374249

Deslauriers, L., Schelew, E., & Wieman, C. (2011). Improved learning in a large-enrollment physics class. *Science, 332,* 862–864. doi:10.1126/science.1201783

Fitzpatrick, M. (2012, June 24). Classroom lectures go digital. *The New York Times.* Retrieved from http://www.nytimes.com/2012/06/25/us/25iht-educside25.html

Hake, R. R. (1998). Interactive-engagement versus traditional methods: A six-thousand-student survey of mechanics test data for introductory physics courses. *American Journal of Physics, 66,* 64–74. doi:10.1119/1.18809

Lage, M. J., Platt, G, J., & Treglia, M. (2000). Inverting the classroom: A gateway to creating an inclusive learning environment. *The Journal of Economic Education, 31,* 30–43.

Mazur, E. (2009). Farewell, lecture? *Science, 323*(5910), 50–51. doi:10.1126/science.1168927

Novak, G. M., Patterson, E. T., Gavrin, A. D., & Christian, W. (1999). *Just-in-time teaching: Blending active learning with web technology.* Upper Saddle River, NJ: Prentice Hall.

Pashler, H., McDaniel, M., Rohrer, D., & Bjork, R. (2008). Learning styles: Concepts and evidence. *Psychological Science in the Public Interest, 9,* 105–119. doi:10.1111/j.1539-6053.2009.01038.x

Pasisis, G. (2015). *The flipped reading block: Making it work: How to flip lessons, blend technology, and manage small groups to maximize student learning.* New York, NY: Scholastic.

Siegle, D. (2014, January). Technology: Differentiating instruction by flipping the classroom. *Gifted Child Today, 37*(1), 51–55. doi:10.1177/1076217513497579

SparkNotes. (2015). *Westward expansion, 1807-1912.* Retrieved from http://www.sparknotes.com/history/american/westwardexpansion/study.html

Neehar and Nayan

Introduction

Selecting and scheduling appropriate courses is a challenging process for all high school students. For gifted learners with multipotentiality, scheduling is a particularly arduous process. Neehar and Nayan, who are new to the U.S., must consider required and rigorous classes, opportunities to develop their artistic interests, and family expectations in preparation to attend selective universities.

Neehar and Nayan are 14-year-old twin sisters. They were born in New Delhi, India. They moved to the U.S. 2 years ago with their family. In the fall, they will attend Washington High School, a high-performing school located in a Midwestern community that is home to a world famous medical center. Their father is a medical doctor who has been accepted into a prestigious fellowship program within the department of orthopedic and reconstructive surgery. Their mother has joined the affiliated medical school staff as a visiting professor. She will teach part-time as she continues her research in immunopathology. Both parents received medical training at Johns Hopkins University, and they are highly regarded within their respective fields. They returned to the U.S. for additional training, but that decision was made to both expand their research interests and expose their daughters to Western culture. They hope the experience will prepare Neehar and Nayan for prestigious universities in the U.S.

Neehar and Nayan's maternal grandparents are former university professors who live with the family. The grandparents manage the household and care for the girls when the parents are unavailable. They accompanied the family to the U.S., set up the household, and continuously help the family acclimate to their new home. They speak fluent English, are strong disciplinarians, and are clearly devoted to their granddaughters.

While considering the temporary relocation to the U.S., the family contacted several public and private schools, inquiring about the educational options available for the girls. After careful deliberation, they chose Washington High School (WHS), which is consistently listed as one of the top high schools in the U.S. The family was assured via e-mail and Skype conversations that the girls will receive a challenging and appropriate education.

Prior to the move, Neehar and Nayan were successful students at a competitive private school in New Delhi modeled after an exclusive school in England. They are fluent in Hindi, French, and English. Their academic records indicate high grades in science and in mathematics. Neehar has recognition from a math team and as a semifinalist in the Carnatic vocal category from the National Music Competition in Singapore. She hopes to become a medical doctor and follow her father's path as a surgeon. Nayan is more social than her sister and is a talented artist. Although she receives good grades, she is more interested in sketching and painting than her schoolwork. Her recent explorations in other media have heightened her interest in art.

The school counselor at WHS schedules a conference to meet the girls and register them for fall classes. The family soon learns that WHS offers a wide range of courses and learning experiences. The course catalog details a variety of traditional course options, surpassing the family's expectations. The girls are surprised to discover a number of alternative learning experiences are available. In addition to traditional coursework, educational experiences for WHS students may be remote to the school campus and even involve part-time employment and community service to others. The alternative learning experiences include independent studies, online courses, mentor programs, tutor programs, and concurrent credit/dual enrollment programs at technical or 4-year colleges.

To their surprise, the counselor explains the district's ability to allow course credit by assessment in extracurricular activities, activities outside of school, previous learning, and other experiences that meet approved academic standards. The family learns that in order to be awarded credit, a student must complete an application and submit supporting evidence to the principal's office. They are encouraged when they learn evidence may include letters of support, oral or written tests, interviews and performances, or demonstrations assessed by district staff or others knowledgeable in the state standards. They discover the girls will need to earn at least a "B" on the cumulative course assessment to receive credit for any required courses.

WHS students must earn 43 semester credits in grades 9–12. Students in grade 9 must register for eight credits each semester. Students in grade 10 must register for six credits each semester. Students in grades 11 and 12 must register for at least five credits each semester. The counselor provides the girls with a chart summarizing the requirements for graduation (see Figure 3.9). She notes that even though the family will return to India before graduation, state law requires all high school students make progress toward earning a diploma.

WHS students may choose to enroll in enriched courses. Options include opportunities to take honors courses and dual enrollment courses. Dual enrollment courses are those in which students may earn both high school and college credit and include Advanced Placement (AP) program or College Level Examination Programs (CLEP) in some states. The school's extensive list of AP courses, for which college credit may be awarded through examination, and enriched courses are listed in Figure 3.10.

Course Type	Credits	Notes
Mathematics	6	Algebra, geometry, and coursework in probability and statistics
Science	6	Physics, biology, and two additional semester credits
Language Arts/English	8	Language arts 9 or Pre-AP English 9, English 10 or Pre-AP English 10, U.S. Literature, and two additional semester credits
Social Studies	7	Geography, U.S. Government, U.S. History, World History or European History, and Economics
Arts	2	Coursework in visual arts, music, theater, dance, or media
Health	1	
Physical Education	2	
Elective credits	11	
Total Required Credits	43	

Figure 3.9. Required credits, courses for WHS graduation.

AP Accounting	AP Biology	AP Calculus (AB/BC)	AP Chemistry
AP Comparative Government AP	AP Computer Science	AP Economics (Micro/Macro)	AP Environmental Science
AP European History	AP French Language and Culture	AP German V	AP Human Geography
AP Latin V	AP Literature 12	AP Physics	AP Psychology
AP Spanish V	AP Spanish VI: Literature	AP Statistics and Trigonometry	AP Studio Art
AP U.S. Government	AP U.S. History	Enriched Biology	Enriched Chemistry
Enriched French IV	Enriched German IV	Enriched Physics 9	Enriched Sociology
Enriched Spanish IV	Enriched Psychology	Pre-AP English 9	Pre-AP English 10

Figure 3.10. WHS enriched and accelerated courses.

The counselor explains blended learning and how courses in this format differ from traditional courses. The girls discover that blended learning is a combination of face-to-face learning and online learning. As the mother listens to the conversation, she thinks this sounds perfect for Neehar, whose self-discipline and motivation serve her well, but not necessarily for Nayan, whose love of sketching sometimes interferes with her homework.

Things to Consider

Successful online students typically:
» are independent learners,
» are motivated,

```
Things to Consider, continued
```
» are self-disciplined,
» are organized and able to manage responsibilities,
» are proficient readers and communicators,
» have dependable technology,
» have good computer skills,
» understand and abide by netiquette,
» are at ease in cyberspace, and
» know when and how to ask for assistance.

To help the girls consider all their options, the counselor provides the course catalog and several worksheets to aid the planning process. She explains the book's format and provides samples of typical courses selected at each grade level and the mathematics sequence. She schedules the girls for placement exams that week, along with a follow-up appointment to discuss the results and proceed with registration. The girls leave with instructions to review all options, prepare a wishlist of six courses per semester and, if interested, a zero hour class. When their parents ask about zero hour classes, they are informed these extra classes are optional and offered before the regular school day begins. Ambitious students who have difficulty taking all the classes they want within their regular schedules often utilize zero hour classes.

That evening, the family reviews the many options available to the girls. The parents and grandparents are pleased by the robust selection of STEM-related courses. Nayan is encouraged by the variety of visual and performing arts courses, but Neehar worries about the upcoming math placement test. She hopes to qualify for courses labeled Sequence 4, Honors B, but is unsure if her studies in India have prepared her for the rigor of classes at WHS. The family considers the mathematics sequence (see Figure 3.11), the course options in the course catalogue (see Table 3.3), and the course-planning worksheet (see Table 3.4).

Discussion Questions

1. What information in addition to the placement tests should inform Neehar and Nayan's class registration?
2. In what ways will culture impact Neehar and Nayan's experience at WHS?
3. What special accommodations should be made for students who arrive in the U.S. and enroll in high school classes? Are accommodations universal or do they differ in response to culture and experience? Explain your answer.

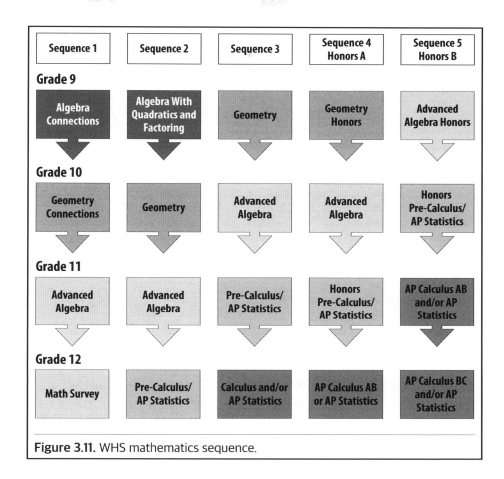

Figure 3.11. WHS mathematics sequence.

4. In what ways will Neehar's and Nayan's experiences differ from WHS's foreign exchange students?

5. WHS has a wide array of enriched, honors, and accelerated classes. How can the school ensure that students are placed in the appropriate class levels? Should achievement alone determine placement? What role does motivation play in the decision-making process?

6. With plans for returning to India in 2 years, what possible benefits would Neehar and Nayan obtain from registration in AP or other dual enrollment classes and/or early entrance to college? Given their current interests will the girls benefit equally? Explain your answer.

7. Do enriched, honors, and accelerated high school classes constitute a gifted high school program? Why or why not?

8. In what ways can extracurricular and summer programs benefit gifted and highly able learners?

Table 3.6
WHS Courses and Course Numbers

Performing and Visual Arts	Semester 1	Semester 2
Dance	1543	2543
Band*	1544	2544
Zero Hour Jazz Band*	1544 a	2544 a
Choir	1545	2545
Show Choir*	1545 a	2545 a
Zero Hour Varsity Choir*	2500	3500
Orchestra*	1546	2546
Ceramics 1	1547	2547
Ceramics 2	1548	2548
Ceramics 3	1549	2549
Ceramics 4	1550	2550
Photography 1	1551	2551
Photography 2	1552	2552
Photography 3	1553	2553
Photography 4	1554	2554
Digital Photography 1	1555	2555
Digital Photography 2	1556	2556
Drawing and Painting 1	1557	2557
Drawing and Painting 2	1558	2558
Drawing and Painting 3	1559	2559
Drawing and Painting 4	1560	2560
AP Studio Art Drawing, 2D Design*	1561	2561
AP Studio Art Drawing, 3D Design*	1562	2562
Business	**Semester 1**	**Semester 2**
Marketing	1600	2601
College Level Accounting	1602	2602
DECA 1*	1603	2603
DECA 2*	1604	2604
Personal Finance	1605	2605
Foundations in Business	1606	2606
Business Internship	1607	2606
Engineering and Technology	**Semester 1**	**Semester 2**
Engineering Fundamentals*	1701	2701
Engineering Design Studio*	1702	2702
Civil Engineering and Architecture*	1703	2703

Table 3.6, continued

Engineering and Technology, *continued*	Semester 1	Semester 2
AP Computer Science*	1704	2704
Aerospace Engineering*	1705	2705
Maker Space*	1706	2706
Zero Hour Maker Space*	ZM1	ZM2
English	**Semester 1**	**Semester 2**
Pre-AP English 10	1800	2800
US Literature and Composition*	1801	2801
AP Literature and Language*	1802	2802
World Literature: Junior Seminar	1803	2803
World Literature: Senior Seminar	1804	2804
Film and Literature	1805	2805
Creative Writing	1806	2806
Communications	1807	2807
Public Speaking	1808	2808
Print and Broadcast Journalism	1809	2809
Family and Consumer Science	**Semester 1**	**Semester 2**
Interior Design	1901	Not offered
Child Psychology	1902	2902
Psychology of Relationships	1903	2903
Food and Nutrition	1904	2904
International Foods	Not offered	2905
Advanced Foods	1906	Not offered
Fashion Design	1907	2907
English as a Second Language *(ESL students only, placement upon assessment)*	**Semester 1**	**Semester 2**
ESL Skills 1-2*	1000	2000
ESL Skills 3*	1001	2001
ESL Skills 4*	1002	2002
ESL Skills 5*	1003	2003
ESL Literacy*	1004	2004
ESL Resource*	1005	2005
Science	**Semester 1**	**Semester 2**
Biology	1300	2300
Enriched Biology	1301	2301
AP Biology*	1302	2302
Chemistry	1303	2303
Enriched Chemistry	1304	2304

Table 3.6, continued

Science, *continued*	Semester 1	Semester 2
AP Chemistry*	1305	2305
AP Environmental Science*	1306	2306
Physics	1307	2307
Enriched Physics	1308	2308
AP Physics*	1309	2309
Special Education Services	**Semester 1**	**Semester 2**
Alternative Reading*	1201	2201
Alternative Mathematics*	1202	2202
Alternative Science*	1203	2203
Alternative Resource*	1204	2204
ASD Resource*	1205	2205
English Lab*	1206	2206
Mathematics Lab*	1207	2207
U.S. History Lab*	1208	2208
Adapted Physical Education*	1209	2209
Study Support*	1210	2210
Job Training*	1211	2211
Work Experience*	1212	2212

*Courses require prior approval.

Note. Students who are interested in online course work, independent study, internships, mentorships, and/or college courses not offered on campus should schedule a conference with the Academic Dean no less than 12 weeks prior to course start. Course catalogues, registration materials, and reporting requirements are available in the Dean's office. Prior approval is required and must be obtained prior to registration.

Activities

1. Working with a partner and the list of WHS courses (Table 3.3), create profiles and individualized course schedules for two students. Select two different students from the following:
   - a student who is twice-exceptional,
   - a student with interest and high achievement in STEM-related disciplines,
   - a student with interest and average achievement in STEM-related disciplines,
   - a student who has been radically accelerated,
   - a student who has health issues and is often unable to attend school,
   - a student who is artistically talented with average to below-average scholastic achievement,

Table 3.7
WHS Course Planning Worksheet

Grade 9

Class	Semester 1	Course Number	Semester 2	Course Number
1	English			
2	Math			
3	Economics			
4	Science			
5	Social Studies			
6	Elective			
Zero Hour				

Grade 10

Class	Semester 1	Course Number	Semester 2	Course Number
1	Pre-AP English			
2	Math			
3	History			
4	Science			
5	Elective			
6	Elective			
Zero Hour				

Grade 11

Class	Semester 1	Course Number	Semester 2	Course Number
1	U.S. History			
2	U.S. Literature			
3	Biology			
4	Math			
5	Elective			
6	Elective			
Zero Hour				

Table 3.7, continued

Grade 12

Class	Semester 1	Course Number	Semester 2	Course Number
1	English			
2				
3				
4				
5				
6				
Zero Hour				

Note. The requirements that must be taken in specific years are indicated; consult the course catalogue for class descriptions and course numbers. Students must register for courses when indicated and may choose when to fulfill other requirements.

- ⊙ a student who is musically talented and interested in attending a conservatory,
- ⊙ a student for whom English is a second language, AND
- ⊙ a student who lives in extreme poverty.

2. In a small group, role-play a conversation with a student who has average to below-average achievement but high test scores. You may choose to discuss underachievement, future goals, social and emotional needs, or other factors that may influence student achievement.

3. Create course plans for Neehar and Nayan that will prepare them to receive diplomas from WHS and prepare them for postsecondary success if the family chooses to remain in the U.S.

4. Research talent development opportunities for gifted learners available in your region. Using the medium of your choice, create a presentation in which you share information about a center for talent development's potential to augment educational experiences and prepare the students for admittance to selective universities.

5. What specific challenges do gifted learners in high school face? Develop a prioritized list. Determine if your school district is able to meet these challenges. Develop a presentation for your local school board recommending the need for changes in services.

Extensions

1. Plan a differentiated lesson for the AP class of your choice. Articulate your process for preassessment and how you will meet the learn-

ing needs of a twice-exceptional and highly gifted learner in your classroom.

2. Create a profile and high school educational plan for a gifted student living in a geographically isolated area. Indicate which courses will be taken at the high school and other curricular options that may be used to provide access to challenging and appropriate coursework. Your plan should include both school year and summer opportunities.

3. Create an outline of a guided discussion series for students who are gifted and talented or high achievers. Identify six topics for the series and four discussion items for each topic. Your plan should indicate the frequency and length of the discussions, as well as how and to whom the series will be promoted.

4. Using three or more sources, research the effectiveness of online and blended learning classes. Share key findings via a letter to the editor, a blog post, or an online video.

5. Review the data from the high school survey results (available at http://www.nagc.org/resources-publications/resources-university-professionals). What implications can you draw from these results for your state and/or high school programs across the country? Create a bumper sticker, advertisement, or product of your choice reflecting these implications and indicating the need for support of gifted programs at the high school level.

Additional Readings

Berger, S. L. (2014). *College planning for gifted students: Choosing and getting into the right college* (Updated ed.). Waco, TX: Prufrock Press.

College Entrance Examination Board. (2004). *Pre-AP: Interdisciplinary strategies for English and social studies* [Sample activity: Dialectical notebooks]. Retrieved from http://apcentral.collegeboard.com/apc/public/repository/ap04_preap_1_inter_st_35891.pdf

Dixon, F. A., & Moon, S. M. (Eds.). (2015). *The handbook of secondary gifted education* (2nd ed.). Waco, TX: Prufrock Press

Ferdig, R. E., Cavanaugh, C., & Freidhoff, J. R. (Eds.). (2012). *Lessons learned from blended programs: Experiences and recommendations from the field.* Vienna, VA: International Association for K-12 Online Learning (iNACOL).

Galbraith, J., & Delisle J. (2011). *The gifted teen survival guide: Smart, sharp, and ready for (almost) anything* (4th ed.). Minneapolis, MN: Free Spirit Publishing.

Lee, S.-Y., & Olszewski-Kubilius, P. (2006). A study of instructional methods used in fast-paced classes. *Gifted Child Quarterly, 50,* 216–237. doi:10.1177/001698620605000303

Neuhauser, C. (2002). Learning style and effectiveness of online and face-to-face instruction. *American Journal of Distance Education, 16,* 99–113. doi:10.1207/S15389286AJDE1602_4

Northey, S. S. (2005). *Handbook on differentiated instruction for middle and high schools.* Larchmont, NY: Eye on Education.

Olszewski-Kubilius, P., & Clarenbach, J. (2014). Closing the opportunity gap: Program factors contributing to academic success in culturally different youth. *Gifted Child Today, 37,* 103–110. doi:10.1177/1076217514520630

Olszewski-Kubilius, P., & Corwith, S. (2010). Distance education: Where it started and where it stands for gifted children and their educators [Special issue on distance learning]. *Gifted Child Today, 34*(3), 16–24, 64–65.

Peterson, J. S. (2011). *Talk with teens about what matters to them: Ready-to-use discussions on stress, identity, feelings, relationships, family, and the future.* Minneapolis, MN: Free Spirit Publishing.

Shelton, C. F., & James E. L. (2005). *Best practices for effective secondary school counselors.* Thousand Oaks, CA: Corwin Press.

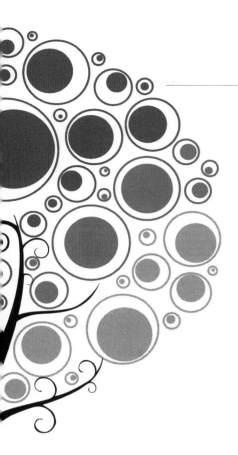

Chapter 4

Case Studies

Differentiated Instruction
in a Cluster Classroom

These case studies explore issues related to differentiated instruction for gifted learners including special populations of gifted learners (e.g., twice-exceptional, ELL, children from poverty) in the cluster classroom in early childhood, elementary, middle, and high school settings.

Dr. Ochoa's Cluster Classroom

Introduction

Dr. Ochoa's third-grade classroom accommodates learners of all types. Although she has a cluster of gifted and bright students, they do not all have the same learning strengths or interests. She modifies instruction to meet their needs through differentiated content and processes. Knowing when to push and when to pull students' learning creates dilemmas for both Dr. Ochoa and her students.

This case illustrates how differing needs and interests of third graders may be met. This case study introduces two of Dr. Ochoa's students who exhibit diverse learning strengths and interests that are influenced by age, home environment, and school environment. The case is told from the point of view of Dr. Ochoa, the students, and the parents/guardians of the students.

Mountain Crest Elementary School

The Mountain Crest Elementary School is one of 20 in the district, with 450 students in prekindergarten through fifth grade. The school has long been recognized as high achieving. It is supported by a local university through internships of student teachers, who will receive a combination teaching certificate in gifted and talented and elementary education. Until this year, the Mountain Crest campus was a neighborhood school. Due to issues at a high-poverty neighboring school, approximately 20 students per grade level are being bused to the school this year. The 20 students per grade level have been divided among three teachers per grade level.

Dr. Ochoa

Dr. Ochoa has been teaching for 20 years, the last 10 years at Mountain Crest Elementary School. Many parents moved to this school zone because of Mountain Crest's reputation of achievement, especially that of Dr. Ochoa's students.

Dr. Ochoa recently completed a Ph.D. in gifted education. Her dissertation is based on her own teaching to illustrate how she addresses differentiation within her classroom. She preassesses all students in the four core subjects so that she knows in which academic level to place them. She differentiates throughout the day with centers that address the four core subjects, mathematics, social studies, science, and English/language arts. Each content area center addresses the varying needs of the students. Dr. Ochoa always has one center in which she works directly with small groups. For the most part, differentiation is based on content and, to some extent, process. Product and affect are often the same for all students unless an independent study center is used for students who are beyond their peers in an area of study.

Natalie

Natalie is bilingual. She speaks Spanish at home, but also is proficient in English. She did not speak any English when she came to kindergarten at Mountain Crest, but quickly mastered English and enjoys manipulating language. Based on her love of language, Dr. Ochoa created a center for Natalie to learn to read and write in Spanish and to learn the history of Guatemala, her parent's homeland. When Natalie's preassessment shows that she understands the current learning concept or when she completes her work, she works at the center Dr. Ochoa created for her.

Natalie's Parents

We are excited for Natalie to learn to read and write in Spanish and to learn about Guatemala. We know how to read and write in Spanish, so we help her at home. We hope that she is able to complete a project about our homeland.

We are also happy that Natalie is able to learn at her own speed. Once she learned English, some of her classes moved too slowly for her. We try to help by taking her to the library and letting her have time to check out books and use their computer. We are saving money to buy a computer for our home.

Things to Consider

» When parents' perspectives are the same as the teacher's, the student's growth is optimal.
» Dr. Ochoa must carefully consider the diverse instructional needs of all students within her classroom.
» Teachers who meet individual student needs must have time and support for planning.

Charley

Charley's parents are both doctors. His father is a medical doctor and his mother has a Ph.D. and teaches at a local university. They are both involved in research and even though they are very busy with their own research, they include Charley when they can. Charley has a nanny who takes care of him most of the time during the school week. When his parents are busy, she comes to teacher meetings and attends all of Charley's activities at the school.

Charley is academically beyond many of his peers. His tested IQ is 148 and his Torrance Test of Creative Thinking-Figural is 130. Charley is an amazing student, but must be occupied on his thinking level or he becomes a behavior problem. Because he is generally beyond third-grade work, Dr. Ochoa offers him activities that are above fourth grade. Charley's parents prefer that he not be grade skipped because he is small for his age and other students are older.

Charley's Nanny

Charley is such an amazing young man. He understands research, he reads technical manuals that other children have no interest in reading, and he enjoys drawing and writing. As long as he is busy with an interest, he is delightful. When he seems to be at loose ends or he is missing his parents, he can be a problem. I can understand what Dr. Ochoa says about his behavior sometimes, but she agrees with me that he is an amazing child.

Dr. Ochoa

With the opinions and statements of both Natalie and Charley's parents/guardians, Dr. Ochoa is now developing individual learning plans for both students.

Discussion Questions

1. In what other ways is Dr. Ochoa currently differentiating instruction? In what other ways could she do so?
2. What types of preassessment could Dr. Ochoa use to assign students to centers?
3. What specific guidance can Dr. Ochoa give to Natalie and Charley about developing their academic and social skills?
4. Should Dr. Ochoa insist that Charley be grade skipped? Why or why not?
5. How can Dr. Ochoa help Natalie and Charley' parents guide them at home?
6. What can Dr. Ochoa do to differentiate product and affect for her students?

Activities

1. Research Dabrowski's overexcitabilities. Do any of them apply to Charley? If so, which one(s) and how? Create a T-chart showing characteristics defined by Dabrowski and those exhibited by Charley.

2. Design a unit that builds on student strengths and interests for either Charley or Natalie to study over the summer. Include options for a culminating activity in which the student shares his or her products.

3. Create lesson plans for Dr. Ochoa to help her students explore the concept of *giftedness*.

4. Research competitions available for Dr. Ochoa's students. Create a guide or brochure with bullet points that identify the skills required for one of the competitions.

5. Develop a math and science center or an English/language arts/reading center for a fictitious student in Dr. Ochoa's class.

Extensions

1. Describe a gifted student you know and define his or her learning needs. Post your description and definition on your school Facebook page and ask for comments.

2. Create a set of preassessments for one content area unit related to students in your class or on your campus.

3. Create a math and science center to accommodate three different student learning needs. Include at least three activities.

4. Develop a schematic of an English/language arts/reading center with areas for activities that will meet both social and emotional needs of gifted learners.

Additional Readings

Adams, C. M., & Boswell, C. (2012). *Effective program practices for underserved gifted students: A CEC-TAG educational resource.* Waco, TX: Prufrock Press.

Adams, C. M., & Pierce, R. L. (2010). *Differentiation that really works: Strategies from real teachers for real classrooms, grades 3–5.* Waco, TX: Prufrock Press.

Colangelo, N., Assouline, S. G., & Gross, M. U. (2004). *A nation deceived: How schools hold back America's brightest students* (Vol. 1). Iowa City: University of Iowa, The Connie Belin & Jacqueline N. Blank International Center for Gifted Education and Talent Development. Retrieved from http://www.education.uiowa.edu/belinblank/pdfs/ND_v1.pdf

Fonseca, C. (2015). *Emotional intensity in gifted students: Helping kids cope with explosive feelings* (2nd ed.). Waco, TX: Prufrock Press.

Roberts, J. L., & Boggess, J. R. (2012). *Differentiating instruction with centers in the gifted classroom.* Waco, TX: Prufrock Press.

Smutny, J. F., Walker, S. Y., & Meckstroth, E. A. (1997). *Teaching young gifted children in the regular classroom: Identifying, nurturing, and challenging ages 4–9.* Minneapolis, MN: Free Spirit Publishing.

Tillier, B. (1995, October 26). *The Theory of Positive Disintegration by Kazimierz Dabrowski* [Synopsis bibliography]. Retrieved from http://positivedisintegration.com/#synopsisbibliography

Westphal, L. E. (2011). *Ready-to-use differentiation strategies, grades 3–5.* Waco, TX: Prufrock Press.

Miss Sharma's Classroom

Introduction

Acceleration is a strategy for advancing student learning in the classroom where students receive instruction at a faster rate or earlier than age-mates. Acceleration may occur within the regular classroom, by subject, or by grade level. In the following case study, cluster classroom teacher Miss Sharma prepares for the new school year and makes a surprising discovery.

Jefferson South Elementary School (JSES) is a high-performing school located in the suburb of a large metropolitan city. Nearly 650 students in grades Pre-K through grade 5 attend. The racial demographics of the school are: 73% White, 10.6% Black, 2.3% Asian, 7.3% Hispanic, and 2.3% American Indian. Twenty-one percent of all students qualify for free and reduced lunch and 18% of all students receive special education services. Three percent of all students are considered to be limited English language proficient.

Approximately 12% of the student population has been identified as intellectually gifted and talented. These students receive accelerated instruction in mathematics and/or ELA. A top 2% score in both reading and mathematics earns a cluster classroom placement in grade 3 through grade 5. Cluster program students are assigned to an otherwise heterogeneous classroom with four to eight intellectual peers and a teacher trained to understand their unique instructional and social-emotional needs. The remaining gifted students receive differentiated instruction within the regular classroom and are eligible for enrichment activity participation.

Miss Sharma is a well-respected, veteran teacher assigned to a fourth-grade cluster classroom. She earned her master's degree in gifted and talented education from the University of St. Thomas 8 years ago and has continued on a professional development path. She has completed additional coursework in advanced differentiated instruction and recently started working on a supplementary endorsement as a reading specialist.

Over the summer, in preparation for the coming school year, Miss Sharma reads the cumulative file for each of the 26 students who will enter her classroom in the fall. She reviews their scholastic records, special education, disciplinary, medical, and special services notations. She closely examines state and local assessments, including the Northwest Evaluation Association (NWEA) Measure of Academic Progress (MAP) scores. The MAP tests in core reading and mathematics are administered to students in the fall, winter, and spring at JSES. These adaptive computerized tests align to the CCSS and are given with this frequency to monitor the progress of individual students. The tests provide specific information on student needs that can be used to inform instruction. Measuring student academic growth is a key component of the district's continuous improvement plan, and JSES teachers receive annual training, which enables them to interpret their student RIT (Rasch UnIT) scale scores.

As she reviews the files, Miss Sharma discovers two students, Kyle and Danny, who scored significantly higher than all other third graders on the MAP mathematics tests. She also determines neither was identified for cluster placement because each student's reading score was in the high average range—too low for program qualification. Miss Sharma notes that in the fall of first grade, Kyle received scores consistent with spring scores by fourth-grade students. Upon further investigation, she ascertains his mathematics scores were essentially flat during the remainder of first grade and showed little growth in second grade. By the end of third grade, Kyle's RIT score decreased by 18 points from his initial first grade test.

Danny's family moved to town one year ago. Danny was homeschooled prior to third grade, so his records are scant. A letter from his mother indicates Danny has a strong interest in mathematics and science and wants to follow his father's example and someday become a cardiologist. Danny's family hopes entry into the school system will help him make friends and enable access to competitions in mathematics, science, and robotics. The school administers the Wechsler Intelligence Scale for Children–Fourth Edition (WISC-IV) to determine placement. Although a year younger than his third-grade classmates, Danny's first school experience was successful. He was initially puzzled by the formality of school and all the testing, but he quickly adapted. His MAP test scores place him in the high average range for reading. His mathematics score was identical to Kyle's score in the fall and consistent with a fourth-grade spring score. He has shown consistent growth in mathematics and reading throughout his first school year.

Things to Consider

» A mathematics curriculum must be accelerated before it can be enriched.
» Treating mathematics as conceptual, rather than topical, raises the level of thinking for high-ability students.
» Emphasis on problems that are nonalgorithmic enhances mathematical challenge. (Johnson, 2011)

In preparation for the start of school, Miss Sharma arranges her classroom desks into four U-shaped pods. She positions six desks together in each of three pods and the remaining eight desks into a fourth pod. She assigns Kyle and Danny to adjacent seats in the eight-desk pod.

On the first day of school, Miss Sharma announces to the class she will provide opportunities for all students to prove mastery in the mathematics content matter and to move at their own pace. She observes that while most students react with excitement, Kyle appears quite indifferent about the announcement. That evening, in preparation for the initial preassessment, she prepares several worksheets to address the number and operations strand for the state standards in mathematics. She makes 35 copies of student worksheets for each of the grades two through six. Before the students arrive the next morning, she arranges the worksheets into grade-level piles on a table at the back of the room. She intentionally places the piles in a nonconsecutive grade order. During free reading time, she invites students to visit the back table one-by-one for them to select an interesting worksheet that can be completed accurately. Students are instructed to write their names on their worksheet and place it face down in a basket at the end of the back table. According to Johnson (2000), gifted learners differ from their classmates in relation to mathematical thinking (see Figure 4.1).

Discussion Questions

1. What did Miss Sharma discover and why was she surprised?
2. Why did Miss Sharma invite the students one-by-one to self-select a worksheet that was interesting and could be completed accurately? Is this type of preassessment valid? Why or why not?
3. What are Miss Sharma's next steps? Should she direct the students to complete the worksheets they've chosen? Or, should she use the worksheets to plan her lesson on the number and operations strand? Explain your rationale.
4. How should students be grouped for instruction in classrooms where a variety of skill levels exist? What issues should be considered when grouping students?
5. Why did Miss Sharma intentionally place Kyle and Danny in adjacent desks?
6. Why must mathematics curriculum be accelerated before it is enriched?

Activities

1. Research several different strategies for differentiating instruction in a cluster classroom. Select one strategy to plan a mathematics lesson that addresses one of the CCSS (or your state standards) for students

How Gifted Learners Differ From Their Classmates	Relationship to Mathematical Thinking
Pace at which they learn.	The sequential nature of math content makes pacing an issue.
Depth at which they learn.	Deeper levels of understanding and abstraction are possible for most mathematical topics, so differentiation becomes important.
Interests that they hold (Maker, 1982).	If the interest is snuffed out early, the talent may not be developed.

Figure 4.1. Gifted learners and mathematical thinking.

that differ in instructional readiness. Your lesson should include tasks with similar content and different levels of difficulty or complexity.

2. Select and read two articles on student motivation and engagement. Write a 500-word essay on factors that may influence the behaviors of Kyle and Danny in the classroom. Include a recommendation that can be shared with the students and their families.

3. Working with a partner, plan a lesson through which you introduce a new concept in mathematics. For the purposes of planning, assume your classroom will include several twice-exceptional learners and several students who have limited language proficiency.

4. Plan a preassessment strategy for a lesson aligned with the CCSS (or your state standards) in mathematics at the grade level of your choice for one of the following:
   ⊙ counting and cardinality,
   ⊙ operations and algebraic thinking,
   ⊙ number and operations in base 10,
   ⊙ measurement and data, or
   ⊙ geometry.

Extensions

1. Research and create a list of organizations that support the development of talent in STEM (science, technology, engineering, and mathematics) education. Your list should include local, regional, and national resources for educators and students.

2. Write and submit a guest editorial to either your local newspaper or a professional journal about the importance of identifying and supporting STEM education.

3. Create a presentation in PowerPoint, Prezi, or a similar format regarding the benefits of subject acceleration. Your presentation should identify at least one sample protocol for determining student eligibility.

Additional Readings

Assouline, S., & Lupkowski-Shoplik, A. (2005). *Developing math talent: A guide for educating gifted and advanced learners in math.* Waco: TX: Prufrock Press.

Assouline, S. G., & Lupkowski-Shoplik, A. (2011). *Developing math talent: A comprehensive guide to math education for gifted students in elementary and middle school* (2nd ed.). Waco, TX: Prufrock Press.

Burris, C. C., Heubert, J. P., & Levin, H. M. (2006). Accelerating mathematics achievement using heterogeneous grouping. *American Educational Research Journal, 43,* 105–136.

Cash, R. M. (2011). *Advancing differentiation: Thinking and learning for the 21st century.* Minneapolis, MN: Free Spirit Publishing.

Gentry, M. (2014). *Total school cluster grouping and differentiation: A comprehensive, research-based plan for raising student achievement and improving teacher practices* (2nd ed.). Waco, TX: Prufrock Press.

Heacox, D. (2009). *Making differentiation a habit: How to ensure success in academically diverse classrooms.* Minneapolis, MN: Free Spirit Publishing.

Johnsen, S. K., & Sheffield, L. J. (Eds.). (2013). *Using the Common Core State Standards for mathematics with gifted and advanced learners.* Waco, TX: Prufrock Press.

Ma, X. (2000). Does early acceleration of advanced students in mathematics pay off? An examination of mathematics participation in the senior grades. *Focus on Learning Problems in Mathematics, 22,* 68–79.

Reed, C. F. (2004). Mathematically gifted in the heterogeneously grouped mathematics classroom: What is a teacher to do? *The Journal of Secondary Gifted Education, 15*(3), 89–95.

Roberts, J. L., & Inman, T. F. (2009). *Strategies for differentiating instruction: Best practices for the classroom.* Waco, TX: Prufrock Press.

Roberts, J. L., & Inman, T. F. (2013). *Teacher's survival guide: Differentiating instruction in the elementary classroom, grades K–5.* Waco, TX: Prufrock Press.

VanTassel-Baska, J., & Little C. A. (Eds.). (2011). *Content-based curriculum for high-ability learners* (2nd ed.). Waco, TX: Prufrock Press.

Westphal, L. E. (2007). *Differentiating instruction with menus: Math, advanced level menus, grades 3–5.* Waco, TX: Prufrock Press.

Westphal, L. E. (2009). *Differentiating instruction with menus: Math, advanced level menus, grades 6–8.* Waco, TX: Prufrock Press.

Winebrenner, S., & Brulles, D. (2008). *The cluster grouping handbook: A school-wide model: How to challenge gifted students and improve achievement for all.* Minneapolis, MN: Free Spirit Publishing.

Academic Learning, Exploration, Resource, and Technology School (ALERTS): A Ninth-Grade Gifted Academy

Introduction

This case involves a district's decision to offer a gifted academy for ninth graders in a midsize high school. Curriculum adjustments for gifted students in core subjects are considered. This case explores one strategy to meet learning needs in core content areas so that gifted ninth-grade students are able explore core content through their interests and learning strengths.

The option found in this case is menus, which offer choices in activities and products to illustrate students' learning.

Overview

Academic Learning, Exploration, Resource, and Technology School (ALERTS) offers gifted students an extension of their grades 6 through 8 experience in a gifted academy, a Montessori school, or Pre-Advanced Placement (Pre-AP) classes across the district. Any ninth-grade student identified as gifted is automatically considered for the academy. Gifted students demonstrate that they have been succesful within their academic classes at the middle school, have passed any state-required annual examinations, have not required disciplinary interventions, and have completed or participated in at least one state-required research project or research-based academic competition. Exceptions to these requirements are made as extenuating circumstances arise.

District representation is 80% low SES. Demographics include 35% African American, 30% Hispanic, 33% White, and 2% Asian. There are two high schools in the district with 1,800 students in each. They both closely reflect the district demographics. The ALERTS cadre is 35% African American, 38% White, 25% Hispanic, and 2% Asian, and is 78% low SES.

Issues

ALERTS's school district requries the ninth-grade social studies Pre-Advanced Placement class to be Advanced Placement (AP) Human Geography. All ALERTS students are clustered in this class as well as Pre-AP English I and Pre-AP Biology 1.

Even though the ninth-grade students are clustered for the three core subjects, some students accelerate beyond the ninth-grade-level courses and some are not quite ready for the rigor of an ALERTS class that is not in their area of academic strength. For example, five students completed Algebra II and are ready for geometry. Their schedule is different because they are not clustered in the ninth-grade Algebra II class.

The school is on an eight-period day so that students have four classes that are free to be filled with electives. Choices include band, orchestra, athletics/physical education, choir, theater, mock trial, academic decathlon, and a variety of Career and Technology Education (CTE) classes. For students who qualify, Advancement Via Individual Determination (AVID) is available one class period during the day. (AVID is an elective course for students who will be first in their family to attend college. The course includes study guides, individualized study times, note-taking skills, and field trips to universities.)

Scheduling for ALERTS students demands attention. Although scheduling does not directly affect differentiation, it is important to consider because of the influence of students' interest on curriculum. To meet the needs of gifted learners, especially those from poverty, differentiation in the core content areas must be built on student interests.

Curriculum

Differentiation in coursework for ALERTS students is developed according to best practice for gifted learners. Teachers differentiate the CCSS to meet the needs of the gifted learners. This includes project-based curriculum, depth of content, complexity of thinking, accelerated pace of learning, interest-based choice of activities, and sophisticated products to illustrate learning. Teachers are encouraged to integrate subject areas.

Teachers participate in professional development in gifted education, project-based learning, and Advanced Placement. During the summer, they spend time and receive stipends to develop their curriculum and to conduct a weeklong curriclum and team building boot camp with the ALERTS students.

Things to Consider

» Differentiation within Advanced Placement requirements and CCSS need to be carefully crafted.
» Teachers and administrators understand that while learning needs of gifted students remain the same throughout their school years, expectations for final products increase with their abilities.
» Offering choice in learning activities address gifted students' interests and diverse learning needs.

An Example of Integrated Curriculum for ALERTS: Dr. Hassell and Ms. Haley

Dr. Hassell teaches Pre-AP English I and Ms. Haley teaches AP Human Geography. They determine that they can integrate one area of the CCSS in their subject area to meet the needs of their ALERTS students. Table 4.1 details the unit of study they create that uses preassessment and a menu of learning activities.

Discussion Questions

1. In what ways is it important that teachers address both the content of the subject and the students' areas of interest? Discuss the connection between these two.
2. Is there enough variety of products for students to address personal interests in this integrated unit of study? Be specific.
3. Why is preassessment for this unit of study important? In what ways does the preassessment focus on the learning that is the basis for the activities in the 20-50-80 menu?
4. How would you evaluate the activities in the 20-50-80 menu?

Activities

1. Create a new menu for this unit.
2. Create a rubric for evaluating this unit.
3. Heroes/heroism is universal topic for students of all ages. Adapt the unit in this case for a study with your students.
4. Find a 20-50-80 menu online. Adapt it for one of your units of study.
5. Create an extension for a student who completes the preassessment and menu to your satisfaction before others in the class. For example, when the student completes the work in one week for a 3-week project, how can you continue his or her learning without creating busy work or "more of the same"?
6. Instead of offering the 20-50-80 menu, develop a 3x3 tic-tac-toe menu for this unit or one of your choice.

Extensions

1. Create a menu for a teacher professional development opportunity that models the 20-50-80 or a 3x3 tic-tac-toe menu on a topic of your choice.

Table 4.1.
Heroes: Time and Place

AP Human Geography	Pre-AP English I
From the five themes of human geography, students will study *place* through the context of cultural components.	Common Core Sate Standard: *Literary and Informational Texts: Challenging and engaging literacy and informational texts.* Students will explore heroes through teacher-selected and self-selected fictional and informational texts that explore *place* through a cultural context.

Preassessment
• List three events of the 1960s that occurred in the Deep South of the U.S. (The term "Deep South" is explored before the preassessment through the engagement phase of the unit.) • Define the terms "culture" and "sense of place" relative to the Deep South with at least two examples of each. Students who answer these two assessment items to the satisfaction of the teacher are given automatic credit for 20 points on the 20-50-80 Menu (see below). Partial credit of 10 points may be given at the discretion of the teacher. Students may use the 10 points on this menu or a future one. Students who exceed the required 100 points may use the points on one future 20-50-80 menu.

Assignments
• Students read information about cultural components and sense of place through their AP Human Geography text and explore the cultural components of the Deep South in the 1960s through at least two sources of their choice. • Students read *The Secret Life of Bees* by Sue Monk Kidd (2002). (All responses will include references to *The Secret Life of Bees* and the other references chosen by the student.) • Students select two other novels, short stories, and/or informational sources that offer insight into the Deep South in the 1960s.

Activities: 20-50-80 Menu
Students will choose at least two activities from the menus below. The activities must total at least 100 points.

20 points:
- Design a bulletin board that illustrates at least three events during the 1960s in the Deep South that reflect that specific cultural way of life.
- Create a brochure that a southern city's Chamber of Commerce would produce that could reflect this southern city in the 1960s.

50 points:
- Create a newspaper advertisement that asks citizens of a town or city of the Deep South in the decade of the 1960s to nominate a local hero. The advertisement will list attributes of a hero and answer the following questions:
  - What attributes make the person a hero?
  - Who is the most courageous/heroic person you know?
  - What courageous/heroic acts define this person?
  - Is the person a traditional or inspirational hero?

- Find examples of musical and visual artists from the Deep South in the 1960s who were a part of the culture. Create a flipbook that illustrates what you find or create a musical presentation of the music and art of the time that illustrates a hero of that era.

80 points:
- "Heroic acts may be positive or negative." Explore this statement as it relates to the decade of the 1960s in the southern United States. Using *The Secret Life of Bees* (Kidd, 2002) and resources you selected, express your thoughts through a poem, essay, illustration, or play.

Table 4.1., continued

80 points, continued:
 • In a product of your choice synthesize the answers to the following questions:
   ○ What are the origins of heroes?
   ○ In what ways are heroes shaped by sense of place and local cultural context?
   ○ Why do heroes behave as they do?
   ○ Are there rules for heroes or the courage they display?
   ○ What ethics are associated with heroism?

All Students: In your work, compare and contrast heroes of the 1960s to heroes of today and write a definition of heroism for the 1960s and one for today.

2. Develop the outline of an integrated unit with a colleague who teaches a different content area.

3. Research the efficacy of using menus to evaluate student learning. Make a presentation to your campus about your findings.

4. Research on giftedness in poverty (Slocumb & Payne, 2000) suggests that teaching and learning for students in poverty must be related to their real-world experiences. In what ways can your class/campus/district meet this need? Make a list of products that relate to the experiences of your students of poverty.

Additional Readings

AVID. (2014). *What is AVID secondary?* Retrieved from http://www.avid.org/what-is-avid-secondary.ashx

Blankenship, C. (2014). *AP human geography* [social publishing platform]. Retrieved from http://scoop.it/t/ap-human-geography-by-colleen-blankenship

College Entrance Examination Board. (2004). *Pre-AP: Interdisciplinary strategies for English and social studies* [Sample activity: Dialectical notebooks]. Retrieved from http://apcentral.collegeboard.com/apc/public/repository/ap04_preap_1_inter_st_35891.pdf

Heacox, D. (2002). *Differentiating instruction in the regular classroom: How to reach and teach all learners, grades 3–12.* Minneapolis, MN: Free Spirit Publishing.

Heacox, D. (2009). *Making differentiation a habit: How to ensure success in academically diverse classrooms.* Minneapolis, MN: Free Spirit Publishing.

Hughes, C. E., Kettler, T., Shaunessy-Dedrick, E., & VanTassel-Baska, J. (2014). *A teacher's guide to using the Common Core State Standards with gifted and advanced learners in the English language arts.* Waco, TX: Prufrock Press.

Lovgren, S. (2005, July 6). "Gun, germs and steel": Jared Diamond on geography as power. *National Geographic News.* Retrieved from http://news.nationalgeographic.com/news/2005/07/0706_050706_diamond.html

National Association for Gifted Children. (n.d.). *Gifted education practices.* Retrieved from http://www.nagc.org/resources-publications/gifted-education-practices

Roberts, J. L., & Boggess, J. R. (2012). *Differentiating instruction with centers in the gifted classroom.* Waco, TX: Prufrock Press.

Roberts, J. L., & Inman, T. F. (2009). *Strategies for differentiating instruction: Best practices for the classroom.* Waco, TX: Prufrock Press.

Rosenberg, M. (2015). *The five themes of geography: Location, place, human-environment interaction, movement, and region.* Retrieved from http://geography.about.com/od/teachgeography/a/5themes.htm

Rosenberg, M. (2015). *The four traditions of geography: The spatial, area studies, man-land, and earth science traditions.* Retrieved from http://geography.about.com/od/studygeography/a/4traditions.htm

Tomlinson, C. A. (Vol. Ed.). (2004). Differentiation for gifted and talented students. In S. M. Reis (Series Ed.), *Essential readings in gifted education series: Vol. 5.* Thousand Oaks, CA: Corwin Press.

VanTassel-Baska, J. (2003). *Curriculum planning and instructional design for gifted learners.* Denver, CO: Love Publishing.

Westphal, L. E. (2012). *Ready-to-use differentiation strategies, grades 6–8.* Waco, TX: Prufrock Press.

Gifted in Poverty

Introduction

This case relates two teachers' integrated studies guided by the concepts of *relation-ships* or *systems* for their gifted students. The two teachers teach in a small, rural, Title I high school. Ninety percent of the Kent High School students are of low SES.

Kent High School offers an eight-period day with a required elective period for all students in grades 9 and 10. The elective period is designed to facilitate struggling, on-level, and advanced students.

Gifted students in grades 9 and 10 are grouped for this elective. The teachers plan together and coteach the class. This case presents two unit plans that each teacher developed. The students are given their choice of unit study and a culminating project.

A small school in a rural area with a high percentage of students of poverty does not suggest there are no gifted students. Opportunities available to gifted students in urban areas, however, are limited in a rural setting. For example, proximity to university resources, cultural venues, or entrepreneurial mentors often found in urban settings may not be in close proximity to the rural area. On the other hand, there may be more opportunities for rural gifted students to work one-on-one with local leaders or affect change though service.

Kent High School, Grades 9 and 10

Kent High School has 120 students in grades 9–12. There are 10 identified gifted students in ninth and tenth grade—six in grade 9, and four in grade 10. The ninth-grade students include two Hispanic students, two African American students, and two White students. All four of the tenth-graders are White. Eighty percent of the 10 students are of low SES.

Two years ago, Kent High School recognized that although their gifted students received excellent services at the elementary and middle school levels, the only services offered in high school were Advanced Placement courses and three Career/Technology Education courses that only appealed to a few of the gifted students.

A committee of parents, students, and educators was organized to develop program services to meet the needs of gifted students within the school day. The committee's decision was to offer an elective class for gifted students in grades 9 and 10 that would not interfere with their other chosen electives. The school's administration created a class for gifted students that paralleled extra study and tutoring class time for struggling and on-level students. The students asked that one semester focus on the humanities and one semester on studying STEM.

Teachers were selected according to the following criteria: knowledge of and certification in their subject area, professional development and/or college coursework in gifted education, and a desire to teach gifted students.

The committee determined that if the elective class for grades 9 and 10 was successful, they would extend the opportunity to junior and senior gifted students.

Influences of Poverty

Kent High School teachers selected for this class were well qualified academically and understood the social and emotional needs of gifted learners. Many sessions of professional development, however, only look at social and emotional needs of gifted students from a generic point of view—one that is often related to middle class values. The committee that determined the course of action for the 9th- and 10th-grade gifted students recognized the high levels of poverty in the class. They decided all teachers and administrators would study issues of giftedness in poverty to better meet the needs of the Kent students.

In their study, they found that educators needed to recognize the following differences of giftedness in poverty:

- While middle class students easily communicate in abstract metaphors and analogies, the analogies and metaphors from students of poverty are more concrete and relate to people and entertainers.
- Middle class students define heroes and heroic acts through their sensitivity to others' actions. Students of poverty are more likely to identify with the antihero and are more concerned with fairness than the needs of others.
- Both students of middle class and poverty learn quickly. Students of middle class may come with more background experiences, but students of poverty quickly catch up when provided experiences similar to those of the middle class students.
- Middle class students' sense of humor is thought of as being witty. Again, their humor is more abstract than their peers in poverty. Mimicking and colorful stories are marks of humor in students of poverty.
- The ability to see and understand different perspectives is similar in both. While middle class may represent different points of view through writing, gifted students of poverty are more likely to express their points of view orally or through art.

- Gifted students generally are analytical. Students of poverty are more likely to look at patterns in human behavior rather than in procedures or ideas.
- Both students of middle class and of poverty are curious. They both have extensive memories, but with different features. Students of poverty ask questions related to relationships and about people and conversations. Middle class students will ask more penetrating, abstract questions and are more independent in thinking (Slocumb & Payne, 2000).

Six of the students had participated in gifted services in grades 1–8, two students of poverty had not been identified until late elementary and two had moved away in fifth grade and returned this school year. The teachers realized that there might be gaps in their content knowledge, so they planned two sessions per week to scaffold their knowledge and skills. They also knew that the students who had not been a part of gifted services the full 8 years would be able to catch up very quickly.

With this information to guide their curriculum planning and their plan to meet the needs of some of the students, the teachers began their work.

Things to Consider

» "There is nothing so unequal as the equal treatment of unequals."—Felix Frankfurter, former U.S. Supreme Court Justice (as cited in Slocumb & Olenchak, 2006, p. 8)

» "By…[selecting] the youths of genius from among the classes of the poor, we hope to avail the State of those talents which nature has sown as liberally among the poor as the rich, but which perish without use if not sought for and cultivated."—Thomas Jefferson Notes on Virginia Q.XIV, 1782. ME 2:206 (as cited in Slocumb & Olenchak, 2006, p. 11).

» Recognition of and curriculum differentiation for the differences between gifted students from middle class and those from poverty create equal opportunities for all gifted students.

Units of Study

The two humanities teachers, Mr. Carlile and Mr. Rendón, wanted to create two options for the students that were equal in depth and complexity, but offered different avenues for products. They wanted to offer studies that would appeal to both their middle class students and students of poverty.

Mr. Carlile presented an issue related to the redevelopment of a swimming pool and park for all parts of the town to enjoy. Mr. Rendón's problem-based unit presented a high school issue about reinstituting a Winter Break celebration.

All students were given both units of study with the directions for each. Students individually decided which unit they would complete, and then Mr. Carlile and Mr. Rendón created groups of two or three based on students' choices.

Mr. Carlile's Unit of Study. Mr. Carlile presented his unit (see Table 4.2) through a problem-based scenario that looked at the community as a whole and with an opportunity for students to serve their small city. While not specifically a service-learning project, he believed the experience could lead to service opportunities and experiences for the Kent High School gifted students.

Mr. Carlile asked the students to read the problem and complete seven critical thinking questions in the order listed. After completing the questions, the students would create a response and solution based on the concept of *relationships* that could be presented to the fictitious city government. After students completed the project, they were guided to select a local issue with their ideas for resolving the issue and present their solution to their city government.

Mr. Rendón's Unit. Mr. Rendón also presented his unit (see Table 4.3) through a problem-based scenario and the concept of *systems*. He thought that an issue relating to their daily school lives would provide an opportunity for students to practice problem solving with a concrete topic.

Mr. Rendón asked the students to read the problem and complete seven critical thinking questions in the order listed. After completing the questions, the students would determine what type of Winter Break celebration, if any, would be in the best interest of the high school.

If a celebration was to be reinstituted, students would make a determination to whom to make a presentation. If the celebration is to continue to be cancelled, the students would create a presentation to the students and faculty about their decision and the systems that guided their decision.

Students would need at least a 6-week study to complete their chosen problem-based scenario. If at any time students wanted to create their own problem-based scenario that stemmed from the original one, they would submit it to Mr. Carlile or Mr. Rendón. The teachers could accept or arbitrate any changes to the original units.

Discussion Questions

1. Do the units meet the needs of gifted high school students? In what ways? If not, how could they be changed or strengthened to meet the needs of the students in this case?
2. Which unit do you think the middle class students will choose? The students from poverty? Why?

Table 4.2
Mr. Carlile's Unit of Study

The Problem
Concept: Relationships. **Generalization:** Relationships may be positive or negative.
Your mentor, the mayor of your city, leaves a message for you to meet her at the city swimming pool on the south side of town during your lunch period. She has talked with your principal to see if you can stay with her for the remainder of the school day. She says that you need to bring old clothes and shoes. She wants you to study a situation and make a recommendation and presentation for the city council. Your city has two swimming pools: the oldest one in the south part of town, called Park Cities, and a new one in the north, called The Slides of Glenview. Both are connected to a park area; again, the south is old and the north is new. You remember that there have been issues with Park Cities for the past year. Issues stem from its location and age. The pool is 40 years old and next to an old fertilizer plant. The pool was shut down at the end of the swimming season last year because of fears of leakage from the fertilizer storage tanks, as well as the old and often repaired cracks in the pool. Because of the pool's problems, age, and location, the city council decided to close it permanently. The town's citizens disagreed with their decision. For the past 6 months, citizens for both sides of the issue have appeared before the council to express their opinions. Today, the mayor and city council are meeting with local citizens, engineers, representatives from the EPA, a scientist who specializes in ground water contamination, and the county representative from Parks and Wildlife who could provide funding for rehabilitation of the pool. Their purpose is to collect data in order make a decision about the future of the pool. The citizens are ready for the council to rescind or maintain its decision because the swimming season opens in 4 weeks.
Questions
1. What is the primary issue? 2. What are the facts in this scenario? 3. What viewpoints are represented? 4. What is the aim in solving the problem? 5. What opinions are expressed? 6. What suppositions have you made or are you making about this problem? 7. What are the consequences of your suppositions? What are the consequences of your solution to the issue you identified? (Paul & Elder, 1997)

3. Does either unit address experiences and characteristics of giftedness in poverty? Why or why not?

4. Is one unit is better adapted for students from a low SES background than the other? If so, in what ways?

5. In what ways does your campus or district identify differences between gifted students of middle class and of poverty?

6. What differences do you see between gifted students from low SES in elementary, in middle school, and in high school? How are the differences manifested?

Activities

1. Looking back at the list comparing middle class students' characteristics to those of students from poverty, do you agree or disagree with

Table 4.3
Mr. Rendón's Unit of Study

The Problem

Concept: Systems.
Generalization: Systems may be influenced by other systems.

A problem has come up in a small school of 120 students, grades 9 through 12. You are a part of the leadership group that makes and arbitrates decisions related to student interests. Your group consists of 12 students: two freshmen, three sophomores, four juniors, and three seniors in the group.

It has come to your attention that a large number of the students in all four grade levels would like to have an all-school celebration prior to winter break. Because of problems in the past, some 10 years ago, this occasion was cancelled and never reinstituted.

Your group is to create a solution with a plan you devise. The plan must include, but not be limited to, the following elements:

Reinstitute Winter Celebration	No Winter Celebration; Alternative Plan
• Survey of students, parents, teachers, and administrators. • Written explanation of survey. • Written response about decision. • Presentation to school administration, student body, and/or board of trustees using your choice of technology. • Plan for ensuring success of the celebration . • Plans of details of celebration site. • Other details of requirements of celebration, such as how to hire/find entertainment, how to raise money, recipes for refreshments.	• Survey of students, parents, teachers, and administrators. • Written explanation of survey. • Written response about decision. • Presentation to school administration, student body, and/or board of trustees using your choice of technology. • Alternative plan. • Details of alternative plan.

Questions

1. What is the primary issue?
2. What are the facts in this scenario?
3. What viewpoints are represented?
4. What is the aim in solving the problem?
5. What opinions are expressed?
6. What suppositions have you made or are you making about this problem?
7. What are the consequences of your suppositions? What are the consequences of your solution to the issue you identified? (Paul & Elder, 1997)

the statements? List three points of agreement and/or disagreement with a rationale for each.

2. What are some other problem-based scenarios that would appeal to your students? Make a list of problems that could be turned into scenarios.

3. Develop a unit for your students based on a problem-based scenario. Include the questions Mr. Carlile and Mr. Rendón used to guide the students' study.

4. Create a problem-based unit of study for gifted students of poverty that incorporates the creative problem solving process (Parnes, 1992).

5. Create a professional development session that addresses giftedness in poverty for your campus or district teachers.
6. Create a compare/contrast chart of characteristics of students from poverty as defined by Slocumb and Payne (2000) and Jensen (2009).

Extensions

1. Other researchers besides Slocumb and Payne (2000) and Jensen (2009) have studies related to giftedness in poverty. Find two other points of view to compare and contrast with Slocumb and Payne as well as Jensen.
2. Access http://www.gtequity.org and select one of these areas listed for further study:
   ⊙ SES Representation in G/T programs
   ⊙ Bilingual G/T Education Model
   ⊙ Twice-Exceptional Children and G/T Services

   Create a presentation for your administration or board of trustees that explains the content in each of the areas listed as it relates to your campus or district.
3. Explore "Resources" at http://www.gtequity.org and select one. Create a reference guide for your campus or district that synthesizes the information in the areas you selected.
4. Access resources related to Dweck (2007) or Duckworth (2009). Describe how Dweck or Duckworth approaches the issue of giftedness in a short essay.

Additional Readings

Adams, C. M., & Boswell, C. (2012). *Effective program practices for underserved gifted students: A CEC-TAG educational resource.* Waco, TX: Prufrock Press.

Adams, C. M., & Chandler, K. L. (2014). *Effective program models for gifted students from underserved populations: A CEC-TAG educational resource.* Waco, TX: Prufrock Press.

Baldwin, A. Y. (Vol. Ed.). (2004). Culturally diverse and underserved populations of gifted students. In S. M. Reis (Series Ed.), *Essential readings in gifted education series*: Vol. 6. Thousand Oaks, CA: Corwin Press.

Cross, T. L., & Burney, V. H. (2005). High ability, rural, and poor: Lessons from Project Aspire and implications for school counselors. *Journal of Secondary Gifted Education, 16,* 148–156.

Cross, T. L., Coleman, L. J., & Cross, J. R. (Eds.). (2013). *Critical readings on diversity and gifted students: A CEC-TAG educational resource* (Vol. 1). Waco, TX: Prufrock Press.

Elder, L., & Paul, R. (2009). *The aspiring thinker's: Guide to critical thinking.* Dillon Beach, CA: The Foundation for Critical Thinking.

Felder, M. T., Taradash, G. D., Antoine, E., Ricci, M. C., Stemple, M., & Byamugisha, M. (2015). *Increasing diversity in gifted education: Research-based strategies for identification and program services: A CEC-TAG educational resource.* Waco, TX: Prufrock Press.

Jensen, E. (2013). *Engaging students with poverty in mind: Practical strategies for raising achievement.* Alexandria, VA: ASCD.

Lewis, S. (2014). *The rise: Creativity, the gift of failure, and search for mastery.* New York, NY: Simon & Schuster.

Paul, R., & Elder, L. (2009). *The miniature guide to critical thinking: Concepts and tools.* Tomales, CA: The Foundation for Critical Thinking.

Ripley, A. (2013). *The smartest kids in the world: And how they got that way.* New York, NY: Simon & Schuster.

Slocumb, P. D., & Payne, R. K. (2010). *Removing the mask: How to identify and develop giftedness in students from poverty* (Rev. ed.). Highlands, TX: Aha! Process.

Stambaugh, T., & Chandler, K. L. (2012). *Effective curriculum for underserved gifted students: A CEC-TAG educational resource.* Waco, TX: Prufrock Press.

Stambaugh, T., & Wood, S. M. (2015). *Serving gifted students in rural settings.* Waco, TX: Prufrock Press.

VanTassel-Baska, J. L. (Ed.). (2010). *Patterns and profiles of promising learners from poverty.* Waco, TX: Prufrock Press.

Gifted and Talented Students and the Next Generation Science Standards[1]

A precise figure for the number of gifted and talented students in the United States is not available due to the variation in identification processes from state to state. For non-dominant student groups, precise figures are further complicated as states typically rely on only one measure, resulting in fewer students receiving gifted and talented education services. These services, furthermore, are uneven across states or even districts within the same state because there is no federal mandate. The lack of national data—at best, limited national data—on science achievement of gifted and talented students makes it even more difficult to address their achievement. Although the Next Generation Science Standards (NGSS) provide academic rigor for all students, teachers can employ strategies to ensure that gifted and talented students receive instruction that meets their unique needs as science learners. Effective strategies include (1) fast pacing, (2) different levels of challenge (including differentiation of content), (3) opportunities for self-direction, and (4) strategic grouping.

Introduction

Although the following case presents real classroom experiences of NGSS implementation with diverse student groups, some considerations should be kept in mind. First, for the purpose of illustration only, the case is focused on a limited number of performance expectations. It should not be viewed as an indication of all instruction necessary to prepare students to fully understand these performance expectations. Neither does it indicate that the performance expectations should be taught one at a time. Second, science instruction should take into account that student understanding builds over time and that some topics or ideas require extended revisiting through the course of a year. Performance expectations will be attained utilizing coherent connections among disciplinary core ideas, scientific and engineering practices, and crosscutting concepts within the NGSS. Finally, the case is intended to illustrate specific contexts. It is not meant to imply that students fit solely into one demographic subgroup, but rather it is intended to illustrate practical strategies to engage all students in the NGSS.

---

1   This case has been adapted from *Case Study 7: Gifted and Talented Students and the Next Generaion Science Standards* by NGSS Lead States, 2013, Washington, DC: The National Academies Press. Retrieved from http://www.nextgenscience.org/sites/ngss/files/%287%29%20Case%20Study%20TAG%206-14-13.pdf. Copyright 2013 by NGSS Lead States. Adapted with permission.

Constructing Arguments about the Interaction of Structure and Function In Plants and Animals

Park West Elementary School in a suburb of a major metropolitan city has a population of about 450 students in grades preK–4. The demographics are 66.0% White, 4.4% Black, 6.7% Hispanic, 13.5% Asian, with the remainder multiracial. Twelve percent of the students are low-income. Approximately 12% of the students are identified as academically talented and receive accelerated instruction in reading, language, and/or mathematics in a pull-out program for grades 3–4. Otherwise, the students remain with their grade level group for other subjects, including science. The school typically scores in the 90% range on the state assessments.

Mrs. J., the classroom teacher, generally has between 22 and 25 fourth grade students in a class that reflects the school's demographics. She enjoys teaching science most and is always alert to student needs, especially in science. The challenge of teaching gifted and talented students within the diverse classroom is assessing their background knowledge and then providing productive and engaging additions to the general science curriculum within the time constraints of the daily schedule. After pre-assessing her students' current understanding either with a pretest or questioning, Mrs. J. compacts the core content to give her students credit for what they have already mastered, so that the gifted and talented students can do independent or enrichment study while the class is engaged with the content that the gifted and talented students have already mastered. Mrs. J. is flexible with her students, allowing a faster pace for the required activities and offering her students extra time to extend their learning.

This case showcases the teacher presenting alternative activities that incorporate an increased level of complexity and abstraction and reflect the interests of gifted and talented students. They are academically engaged through the strategic grouping of students with similar interests, and intellectually challenged through the introduction of advanced ideas and student-generated information. In addition, they develop their own goals and evaluate their own work. They form part of the community of learners and reinforce a prevailing quest for scientific understanding that predominates in the classroom. As a result, all students, including Jerry, Allie, Kate and Bob, have access for entry at a variety of levels through disciplinary core ideas, scientific and engineering practices, and crosscutting concepts presented in the NGSS. Classroom strategies that are particularly effective for gifted and talented students according to the research literature are highlighted in parentheses.

Things to Consider

Science Framework for K through grade 12 Science Education provides the blueprint for developing the Next Generation Science Standards (NGSS). The Framework expresses a vision in science education that requires students to operate at the nexus of three dimensions of learning: Science and Engineering Practices, Crosscutting Concepts, and Disciplinary Core Ideas. The Framework identified a small number of disciplinary core ideas that all students should learn with increasing depth and sophistication, from Kindergarten through grade 12. Key to the vision expressed in the Framework is for students to learn these disciplinary core ideas in the context of science and engineering practices. The importance of combining science and engineering practices and disciplinary core ideas is stated in the Framework as follows:

> Standards and performance expectations that are aligned to the framework must take into account that students cannot fully understand scientific and engineering ideas without engaging in the practices of inquiry and the discourses by which such ideas are developed and refined. At the same time, they cannot learn or show competence in practices except in the context of specific content. (NRC, 2012, p. 218)

The Framework specifies that each performance expectation must combine a relevant practice of science or engineering, with a core disciplinary idea and crosscutting concept, appropriate for students of the designated grade level. That guideline is perhaps the most significant way in which the NGSS differs from prior standards documents. In the future, science assessments will not assess students' understanding of core ideas separately from their abilities to use the practices of science and engineering. They will be assessed together, showing students not only "know" science concepts; but also, students can use their understanding to investigate the natural world through the practices of science inquiry, or solve meaningful problems through the practices of engineering design. The Framework uses the term "practices," rather than "science processes" or "inquiry" skills for a specific reason:

> We use the term "practices" instead of a term such as "skills" to emphasize that engaging in scientific investigation requires not only skill but also knowledge that is specific to each practice. (NRC, 2012, p. 30)

The eight practices of science and engineering, the Framework identifies as essential for all students to learn, and describes in detail, are listed below:
1. Asking questions (for science) and defining problems (for engineering)
2. Developing and using models
3. Planning and carrying out investigations
4. Analyzing and interpreting data
5. Using mathematics and computational thinking

> **Things to Consider, continued**
>
> 6. Constructing explanations (for science) and designing solutions (for engineering)
> 7. Engaging in argument from evidence
> 8. Obtaining, evaluating, and communicating information (NRC, 2012, Box 3–1, p. 42)

Gifted and Talented Connections

Jerry's naturalist interests were immediately apparent in the first week of school. He chose a classroom book on insects as an independent reading choice and excitedly shared the contents with classmates and Mrs. J. As the teacher pre-assessed Jerry by questioning him, the depth of his knowledge was evident. Jerry had an extensive knowledge about butterflies in particular, knowing their structures, species, and survival needs. Whenever a "bug" arrived at school, Jerry either knew the name or looked it up to inform the class. He would find the other animals of the food web that interacted with the animal. Jerry was the identification expert. His enthusiasm was contagious. He advocated for planting milkweed and provided seeds to the class so that classmates could add milkweed to their gardens in order to help provide food for monarch larvae. Jerry seemed to possess an unusually high interest in nature, and with the pre-assessment information, Mrs. J. could enhance the curriculum with more rigorous expectations for Jerry.

The topic of study in the 4th grade science curriculum at Park West was native barn owls' internal and external structures and their functions. Models of owls and their anatomy covered the science bulletin board. Mrs. J. was guiding the class to construct explanations about the functions of the structures, and facilitating argumentation. The class was organizing the observations by structures grouped in systems. They used the concept to focus on systems rather than memorization of individual structures of the owl itself. Owls were used as the lens by which the students studied the overall concept.

During a formal pretest, Mrs. J. found that Jerry knew most of the content of the unit. She decided that praying mantis insects could form the basis of an interest center, functioning as an anchor activity to extend Jerry's learning. Two praying mantis insects arrived along with flightless fruit flies, and students named the insects *Lost* and *Found*. Jerry immediately volunteered when the teacher suggested that they needed someone to organize the maintenance of the praying mantis and its food. He found books that included the insects, and a learning center began for those students who went into a deeper study of the animals.

The learning center became a focus for classroom activity. Not only Jerry, but also several other students, including Allie and Kate, were active participants. The center was populated with books. Then the sketches arrived. Jerry and others sketched the praying mantis and fruit fly insects, observing details in the body and researching their organs. The sketched diagrams became intricate models explaining the different functions of the animals' structures. The teacher met with Jerry and other students to discuss the goal of the interest center and their learning. The teacher reinforced that the goal was not only to describe the structures of the animals, but also to construct an explanation based on evidence about the function of those structures.

Differences between the two praying mantises were noted and questions came up as to why they were not identical. Students became scientists as they observed, looked up information in books and online, and wrote reports answering questions that were posed by other students or the teacher. The reports were posted on the bulletin board, and new information was constantly added with disorganized sticky notes to suggest modifications and more details that would refine or add to the models. Questions about other insect species like bees and ants led the students to develop arguments about the functions of the structures they observed in the praying mantis, comparing them with other classroom insects.

The students, led by Jerry, took responsibility for the insects and their learning center. The small group that condensed around the center's activities conferred daily about the growth and health of the animals. Jerry was able to find the time for the center activities because of the flexibility of pacing in the regular curriculum. He was able to complete other classroom tasks quicker than his peers; the flexibility with pacing allowed Jerry and others to continue their investigations.

A problem arose as Jerry became alarmed that the food source for the praying mantises was running out. The group of students brainstormed solutions and voted for the teacher to buy mealworms. This new insect became another subject for observation and documentation. Jerry had collaborators, Allie and Kate, who were also passionate about insects.

The mealworms went through their life cycle and the small group of students informed the class about their progress. Allie described the changes almost daily. Differences between the individual mealworms were documented and discussed. Kate researched the insects and her reports were displayed in the interest center. Kate's reports on the internal structures were helpful to the group as the students created models comparing the internal and external structures of the mealworms, praying mantises, and fruit flies. Questions about reproduction were also addressed when small mealworm larva appeared. The group shared their findings with the class, and the teacher assessed the learning based on the reports the students created.

Another opportunity for independent study arose out of a science lesson about bulbs as a food source for a growing plant. Mrs. J. brought an amaryllis bulb into the classroom for the purpose of the lesson. Bob was a quiet child who worked hard. He had a strong interest in sketching. When the potted amaryllis bulb was placed on the windowsill, Bob asked the teacher if he could document the growth of the plant, using stop motion photography. Bob collaborated with Jerry and a new interest developed. They created a chart and a way to standardize the pictures and investigate the growth of the plant. They decided on the measurement tools and controlled the variable of sampling time

When Bob and Jerry had collected enough pictures on plant growth, they created and narrated a video to illustrate the rate of growth. When the flowers bloomed, the students had questions about pollination. The idea of plant reproductive structures is a middle school topic.

Things to Consider

The incorporation of standards from an advanced grade—higher-level core scientific ideas—is an effective strategy for presenting a higher level of challenge for gifted and talented students.

The students described the structures responsible for reproduction in the flower and developed arguments to support their claim about how the flower could be pollinated. After discussing pollination methods with the teacher, Jerry decided to use a paintbrush to cross-pollinate the flowers. When the flowers dried, the students were initially disappointed that no seeds were produced as they had predicted. After carefully dissecting the flower, there was a surprising discovery: the pods contained very small seeds. This challenged a conception for the students, because they had an assumption that the seeds would be large based on the size of the flower. The students presented their findings to the class, describing their conclusions from evidence about the seeds.

Independent study of topics of interest led to real-world connections. The independent study was available to all students in the classroom, but the target group was the gifted and talented students. The classroom's wiki website provided an online place to collaborate and share interests. Students chose a topic of interest, worked alone or invited collaborators, and conferenced with the teacher. Once a topic was chosen, the students narrowed or widened the scope by asking a question to clarify their ideas about the topic.

Jerry's report on pit vipers broadened his knowledge of the subject as he found information on the physical characteristics of the animals, answering his question, "What characteristics of pit vipers make them excellent predators?" The wiki provided a versatile location that students could use at school or at home as they developed their interest reports. The science topics from just one year included flying critters, pit vipers, rock classification, falcons, robot characteristics, mastodons, zebra mussels, eclipses, and the end of the Earth. These "interest projects" provided an avenue for students to develop an expertise on self-selected topics and independent research skills.

NGSS Connections

The case illustrates gifted and talented students in a science classroom with a diverse mix of students. It highlights a range of effective classroom strategies, such as learning centers and interest projects, to support and challenge these students in the regular classroom. Students' work was informally assessed based on the products of their studies and questioning. The teacher addressed the unique learning needs of gifted and talented students who developed an understanding of science according to the three dimensions of the NGSS. The teacher designed her instruction to include higher grade band standards at a deeper and more challenging level.

Performance Expectations

4-LS1-1 Structure, Function, and Information Processing
Construct an argument that plants and animals have internal and external structures that function to support survival, growth, behavior, and reproduction.

MS-LS1-4 From Molecules to Organisms: Structures and Processes
Use argument based on empirical evidence and scientific reasoning to support an explanation for how characteristic animal behaviors and specialized plant structures affect the probability of successful reproduction of animals and plants respectively.

Disciplinary Core Ideas

LS1.A Structure and Function (by the end of grade 5)
Plants and animals have both internal and external structures that serve various functions in growth, survival, behavior, and reproduction.

LS1.B Growth, Development, and Reproduction of Organisms (by the end of grade 8)
Animals engage in characteristic behaviors that increase the odds of reproduction. Plants reproduce in a variety of ways, sometimes depending on animal behavior and specialized features.

The students were engaged in the disciplinary core ideas in life science. They explained the structures of animals and their functions. They also explored the role of specialized plant structures in the reproduction of plants, including the role of specific animal behaviors that lead to successful plant reproduction.

Scientific and Engineering Practices

Asking Questions and Defining Problems (by the end of grade 5)
Ask questions that can be investigated and predict reasonable outcomes based on patterns such as cause and effect relationships.

Planning and Carrying Out Investigations (by the end of grade 8)
Conduct an investigation to produce data to serve as the basis for evidence that meet the goals of an investigation.

Analyzing and Interpreting Data (by the end of grade 5)
Analyze and interpret data to make sense of phenomena.

Engaging in Argument from Evidence (by the end of grade 5)
Construct an argument with evidence, data, and/or a model.

Obtaining, Evaluating, and Communicating Information (by the end of grade 5)
Read and comprehend grade-appropriate complex texts and/or other reliable media to summarize and obtain scientific and technical ideas and describe how they are supported by evidence.

As the unit progressed, the students gained abilities in scientific practices through their exploration of insects and plants by *asking questions and defining problems; planning and carrying out investigations; analyzing and interpreting data; engaging in argument from evidence; and obtaining, evaluating, and communicating information.* Students argued from the evidence of their observations about the functions of the structures of plants and investigated plant growth and reproduction. The NGSS practice of *asking questions and defining problems* was illustrated when students engaged in the observations at the learning center and in the independent study.

Crosscutting Concepts

Systems and System Models (by the end of grade 5)
A system can be described in terms of its components and their interactions.

Students were able to demonstrate their understanding of the crosscutting concept of *system and system models* when they observed the structures of the insects and plants and explained how they functioned within the larger system. They generated information orally and in written and digital formats. The observations over time led the students to develop their models of internal and external structures and functions based on the crosscutting concept of *system and system models*.

Common Core State Standards Connections (CCSS) to English Language Arts (ELA) and Mathematics

The NGSS are committed to the integration of the Common Core State Standards for ELA and mathematics within the content area of science. In the case the teacher inserted reading and writing objectives of the CCSS for ELA with all students as part of her science curriculum, and differentiated outcomes for her gifted and talented students.

- ⊙ **SL4.4** Report on a topic or text . . . using appropriate facts and relevant, descriptive details to support main ideas or themes; speak clearly at an understandable pace. The scientific practice of using models was seamlessly connected to this standard.
- ⊙ **W.4.2** Write informative/explanatory texts to examine a topic and convey ideas and information clearly.

The teacher was able to raise the bar with her gifted and talented students who were presenting scientific information and explanations not only in a written and oral format, but also in a digital format. As the students developed their online reports, their work connected to the NGSS practice of *asking questions* and the CCSS.

The case also highlighted the integration of the CCSS for math:

- ⊙ **4.MD.1** Know relative sizes of measurements within one system of units including km, m, cm
- ⊙ **4.MD.4** Make a line plot to display a data set of measurements in fractions of a unit (1/2, ¼, 1/8)

Measuring and graphing plant growth highlighted this standard.

Effective Strategies from Research Literature

Gifted and talented students may have characteristics such as intense interests, rapid learning, motivation and commitment, curiosity, and questioning skills. While an "integrated theory-driven program characterized by internal consistency from goal setting to service and evaluation" is recommended (Renzulli, 2012), often teachers must make curricular decisions and choose instructional strategies that reflect the academic potential of gifted and talented students and target their unique needs as learners. Based on the research literature, teachers can employ effective differentiation strategies to promote science learning of gifted and talented students in these domains: (1) fast pacing, (2) level of challenge (including differentiation of content), (3) opportunities for self-direction, and (4) strategic grouping (Tomlinson, 2005).

First, gifted and talented students benefit from fast pacing as compared to peers. One strategy that involves pacing is called "compacting curriculum," which permits students to pretest out of curriculum already mastered and condense the content partially learned. Flexible pacing with connected extension activities allows sufficient time to explore the areas of study while avoiding redundancies. Teachers can include options for gifted and talented students to impose their own deadlines. Instead of requiring gifted and talented students to do simply more work, teachers provide differentiated instruction through the use of an anchor activity (motivating task).

The second strategy is to promote the level of challenge so that it extends the current mastery level of the student through the use of advanced materials and objectives, expectations for idea generation and creativity, complexity of ideas, and open-endedness (Tomlinson, 2005). Gifted and talented students benefit from experiences that are connected to the real world. The content should avoid repetitive tasks and be differentiated to encourage expression and foster higher-level and abstract thinking.

The third strategy is to encourage autonomy by allowing the student to follow and cultivate her/his interests and to play a role in her/his own learning trajectory. The teacher helps the student develop strengths and engage in pursuits for which the student has a passion (Tomlinson, 2005). In addition, the teacher can incorporate motivating, authentic connections to science content that allow for student-directed goal setting, exploration, and self-evaluation. Choices that reflect the different learning styles of the student should be included (Renzulli, 2012).

Finally, effective teachers encourage flexible grouping to enhance academic and socio-emotional development of gifted and talented students, such as classroom grouping that allows for both individual time on projects and opportunities in groups with like-minded peers in terms of ability and/or interests.

Effective grouping can vary between teacher-selected and student-selected in order to offer a wide range of experiences.

Context

Demographics

Reporting the demographics for gifted and talented students is difficult due to wide inconsistencies in the definition, in assessments to identify them, and in funding for gifted and talented programs across the nation.

First, the definition of gifted and talented students varies from state to state and the demographics shift accordingly. Many states have no formal state definition. For this reason it is unrealistic to arrive at an exact number of students in the United States who are gifted and talented. The National Association for Gifted Children (NAGC, 2012) defines gifted as "outstanding levels of aptitude or competence in one or more domains" and estimates that this definition describes approximately three million students, roughly 6% of all K-12 students. There are two more definitions that have been widely applied by states (NAGC, 2012). Traditionally, gifted and talented status is for those students performing at the top 5% of an assessment, such as high-stakes testing in language arts or mathematics. An alternative definition is described in Response to Intervention (RTI) as it applies to gifted and talented students. RTI suggests that 5–10% percent of high performing students in a classroom benefit from strategic, targeted, short-term instruction in addition to core; and 1–6% of the students in a given environment are considered "exceptionally gifted" and need intensive, individualized instruction.

Second, although gifted children come from every demographic group, school districts often rely on only one method of identification. Relying on only one measure may not be effective in identifying the gifted and talented students who come from underserved populations by race or ethnicity, SES, and language. In addition, students who have an area of giftedness along with a learning difficulty, referred to as twice-exceptional children, are similarly difficult to identify with only one measure (NAGC, 2012).

Finally, as there is no federal funding for gifted programs, school districts must rely on their own funds to support such programs. This results in variations in programming of support for gifted and talented students from state to state. Unfortunately, current policy and funding do not match the needs of students in poverty:

One of the barriers to developing the talents of children of poverty is inadequate resources, both financial and in terms of personnel. Developing the talents of any gifted child requires resources for special programs, classes, and support services such as counseling or testing. For children of poverty, even greater amounts of support are needed to help with basic needs of families as well as additional support services such as psychological services for children and families and social workers to assist families with issues surrounding housing and basic subsistence. (VanTassel-Baska & Stambaugh, 2007, p. 44)

Science Achievement

The *National Assessment of Educational Progress (NAEP)* does not disaggregate for gifted and talented students.

Educational Policy

In 1988, Congress passed the Jacob Javits Gifted and Talented Students Education Act to fund research grants aimed at better identifying and serving gifted and talented students, especially from underserved student populations. In 2001, ESEA (Elementary and Secondary Education Act, Title V Part D Subpart 6 Dec. 5461-5466) called for a coordination of scientifically based programs to meet the needs of gifted and talented students, and grants to assist agencies and institutions to meet educational needs of these students. ESEA (Title IX, Part A, Section 9101(22)) defines gifted and talented:

The term gifted and talented, when used with respect to students, children, or youth, means students, children, or youth who give evidence of high achievement capability in areas such as intellectual, creative, artistic, or leadership capacity, or in specific academic and diversity fields, and who need services or activities not ordinarily provided by the school in order to fully develop those capabilities.

The above definition has no mandate and only serves as a guide for states that have developed state-mandated definitions. States are not required to use this definition, nor are they federally required to identify gifted and talented students or provide services to them, leaving these decisions to the state and local governments. States, and often districts within states, differ in definitions for gifted and talented students and guidelines for services and teacher accreditation, ranging from full implementation programming to little or none. Although ESEA continued the Javits Act, funds were inconsistent over the years and the Act was defunded in 2011 (NAGC, 2012).

ESEA calls for the support of state and local efforts to increase the number and diversity of students who participate in and are successful in Advanced Placement courses (Title 1 Part G Sec 1702-1702 cited as the "Access to High Standards Act"). The US Department of Education provides awards to support activities that increase the participation of low-income students in both pre-AP and AP courses and tests.

Discussion Questions

1. What role does preassessment play in differentiating the curriculum and instruction for gifted learners? What preassessment strategies did Mrs. J. use in her classroom?
2. In what ways did Mrs. J. extend the level of content by compacting areas already mastered? Was this type of differentiation an effective strategy of pacing for gifted and talented students in her classroom? Why or why not?
3. In what ways did Mrs. J. promote autonomy and promote authentic connections to the content? Were her strategies successful? Why or why not?
4. Mrs. J. planned to extend student learning by actively engaging her class and allowing students to follow their interests. Was she successful? Why or why not?
5. How did grouping students by interest and ability impact learning in Mrs. J.'s classroom? If she had grouped the students by ability alone would the results have differed? Why?
6. What postassessment strategies did Mrs. J. use to measure student learning?
7. In what ways did Mrs. J. meet the affective needs of her students?

Activities

1. Review your state standards in one of the following: ELA, mathematics, science, or social studies. Select a standard and identify several options that can be used intended to extend learning for gifted and talented learners. Share your list of extensions with your classmates or colleagues.
2. Create a lesson plan on a science topic of your choice in which your students practice one or more of the following skills:
   - asking and defining a problem or engaging and arguing,
   - obtaining, evaluating, and communicating information,
   - planning and carrying out investigations,
   - constructing explanations,

⊙ engaging in argument from evidence, or

⊙ analyzing and interpreting data.

Ask a classroom teacher teaching the same topic to provide feedback on your lesson or, if appropriate, pilot the lesson in your own classroom.

3.   Ask students to illustrate their understanding of any standards for a review or postassessment of a chapter or unit of study (see http:// envisiongifted.com/science.html for an example). How successful is this strategy? Share your results in a discussion with a colleague.

Extensions

1.   Working with a partner or small group, select a standard in science or mathematics and then create a lesson plan in which students will complete an interest project. Determine how students will be preassessed and ways in which you can differentiate content to challenge gifted and talented students. Share your lesson plan with your classmates or at a grade level meeting.

2.   Select a grade band then compare state standards for three states in one of the following areas: ELA, mathematics, science, or social studies. Look for ways in which the standards differ in content and in assessment. Create a graphic representation of your research that can be shared with your classmates or colleagues.

3.   Develop a series of questions or activities where students reflect on their progress using Kaplan's 11 components of depth and complexity (see http://www.byrdseed.com/introducing-depth-and-complexity for examples).

Additional Readings

Adams, C. M., Cotabish, A, & Dailey, D. (2015). *A teacher's guide to using the Next Generation Science Standards with gifted and advanced learners*. Waco, TX: Prufrock Press.

Enger, S. K., & Yager, R. E. (2009). *Assessing student understanding in science: A standards-based K-12 handbook* (2nd ed.). Thousand Oaks, CA: Corwin Press.

Gavin, M. K., Casa, T. M., Adelson, J. L., Carroll, S. R., & Sheffield, L. J. (2009). The impact of advanced curriculum on the achievement of mathematically promising elementary students. *Gifted Child Quarterly, 53*(3), 188–202. doi:10.1177/0016986209334964

Johnsen, S. K., Ryser G. R., & Assouline, S. G. (2014). *A teacher's guide to using the Common Core State Standards with mathematically gifted and advanced learners.* Waco, TX: Prufrock Press.

Johnsen, S. K., & Sheffield, L. J. (Eds.). (2013). *Using the Common Core State Standards for mathematics with gifted and advanced learners.* Waco, TX: Prufrock Press.

Keeley, P. (2008). *Science formative assessment: 75 practical strategies for linking assessment, instruction, and learning.* Thousand Oaks, CA: Corwin Press.

Olszewski-Kubilius, P. (2013, May 20). Setting the record straight on ability grouping. *Education Week.* Retrieved from http://www.edweek.org/tm/articles/2013/05/20/fp_olszewski.html

Pierce, R. L., Cassady, J. C., Adams, C. M., Speirs Neumeister, K. L., Dixon, F. A., & Cross, T. L. (2011). The effects of clustering and curriculum on the development of gifted learners math achievement. *Journal for the Education of the Gifted, 34*(4), 569–594. doi:10.1177/016235321103400403

Rogers, K. B. (2006). A menu of options for grouping gifted students. In F. A. Karnes & K. R. Stephens (Series Eds.), *The practical strategies series in gifted education.* Waco, TX: Prufrock Press.

Rosebery, A. S., & Warren, B. (2008). *Teaching science to English language learners: Building on students' strengths.* Arlington, VA: NSTA.

Tomlinson, C. A. (2001). *How to differentiate instruction in mixed-ability classrooms* (2nd ed.). Alexandria, VA: ASCD.

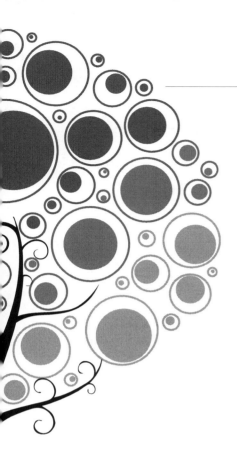

Chapter 5

Case Studies

Differentiated Instruction in
a Full-Time G/T Classroom

These case studies explore issues related to differentiated instruction for gifted learners including special populations of gifted learners (e.g., twice exceptional, ELL, children from poverty) in the full-time classroom in early childhood, elementary, middle, and high school settings. These cases focus on the differentiation of content, process, product, affective needs, and the learning environment for gifted students.

Mr. Jonathon, Lesson 1

Introduction

Mr. Jonathon is a preservice teacher who is just learning how to meet the needs of his students in a full-time gifted/blended classroom. New teachers working with learners who are gifted are faced with various challenges. Mr. Jonathon is implementing a lesson he prepared based upon geometry standards in mathematics. Follow Mr. Jonathon as he develops and teaches a lesson in geometry for his students.

Mr. Jonathon, a preservice teacher in a fourth-grade gifted/blended classroom at the Calhoun School, is assigned to a class with a very diverse population of students. The class is part of a gifted/blended program and it includes several students with special needs. One of these students has been identified with autism. Another has cerebral palsy and one student has muscular dystrophy. The Calhoun School is in a low SES area with more than 90% of the students in the school receiving free or reduced lunch. Mr. Jonathon is responsible for teaching his students every subject (social studies, language arts, science, and math). His student with autism is extremely intelligent, but has many social and emotional problems and is the only student in the class that has an IEP. All of the other students are either gifted or high-achieving students.

The gifted students catch on quickly and do not usually have to work as hard as the high achievers in the class. Mr. Jonathon is encountering many teaching responsibilities within the classroom related to attendance, grades, lesson plans, procedures, and classroom management. A behavior management program helps track different behaviors throughout the day. All of the students in the class participate in the Accelerated Reader program.

Mr. Jonathon presented the following lesson (Table 5.1) to his students.

Things to Consider

» The degree of implementation of differentiation varies in the classroom.
» Student readiness, interest, and learning profiles are key factors for classroom teachers to consider when differentiating for gifted learners.

After teaching his lesson, Mr. Jonathon made the following observations:
- The polyhedron lesson was challenging. My students had to analyze polyhedrons (number of vertices, edges, and faces). They were also required to construct different types of polyhedrons such as cubes, rectangular prisms, hexagonal prisms, and octagonal prisms.

Table 5.1
Mr. Jonathon's, Lesson 1

Lesson Topic	Three-dimensional shapes.
Subject/ Grade Level	Math/fourth grade.
Common Core State Standard	MACC.6.G.1.4. Represent three-dimensional figures using nets made up of rectangles and triangles, and use the nets to find the surface area of these figures. Apply these techniques in the context of solving real-world and mathematical problems.
Objective	By the end of the lesson, fourth-grade math students will: • describe what a net is and how to make a net of a solid figure such as a cube, pyramid, rectangular prism, pentagonal prism, or hexagonal prism; and • correctly identify faces, edges, and vertices of different polyhedrons.
Vocabulary	• **Net:** A plane figure which when folded will make a solid. • **Polyhedron:** A three-dimensional shape made of flat polygon-shaped surfaces. Prisms and pyramids are examples of polyhedrons. • **Face:** Flat polygon-shaped surfaces. Example: Squares on a cube. • **Edges:** Faces meet along segments called edges. • **Vertices:** Edges meet at points called vertices.
Materials	• 14 pages of cardstock to make the nets • 2 cube nets • 2 rectangular prism nets • 2 pentagonal prism nets • 2 hexagonal prism nets • 2 square pyramid nets • 8 octagonal prism nets • A cube box that shows where the vertex, face, and edge of polyhedral are located
Activities	• Share a PowerPoint presentation with the CCSS and essential question (How can three-dimensional shapes be represented and analyzed?). Within the PowerPoint, identify real-life examples of polyhedrons such as pyramids and boxes. • Show a nonexample (cylinder). • Show the students a real-life example box (cube), which labels the faces, edges, and vertices of a cube. • Use the prop (milk crate) to explain to the students what the faces, vertices, and edges are on a cube. • Tell class that each group will construct two 3D shapes out of a net that is on cardstock. • Students will then work in groups of two (chosen by me). The gifted students will be given more difficult 3D shapes to construct such as octahedrons and hexahedrons. They will be constructing a polyhedron from a net. • Then I will pass out a worksheet asking the students to find the number of vertices, faces, and edges. It will also ask them what the difference is between a face and an edge. • If partners finish early, they can extend the lesson by finding the number of angles in the shape. If they find the angles within the 3D shape, they can construct and analyze another figure. • Then I will return to the essential question (How can three-dimensional shapes be represented and analyzed?).
Assessments	• A worksheet, which asked the students to draw the 3D figure, the net, and find the number of vertices, faces, and edges. • A check system will be used to assess the students understanding of polyhedral (see Figure 5.1).

Note. This lesson plan has been used by permission of Van Martin, former student intern, The Webster School, St. Augustine, FL.

Check System	Yes	No
Student correctly identifies number of faces.		
Student correctly identifies number of vertices.		
Student correctly identifies number of edges.		
Student can explain the difference between a face and an edge.		

Figure 5.1. Check system.

- The students gained a deeper understanding of polyhedrons by constructing them out of cardstock and identifying the number of vertices, edges, and faces of the three-dimensional figure.
- I related the subject matter with real-world applications by asking the students to pair share and come up with a real-life example of a polyhedron. I also showed them pictures of pyramids and cubes. One of the students said that the picture I showed on the computer was an Egyptian pyramid.
- A lot of this lesson required higher order thinking because students had to actually construct a polyhedron out of cardstock. I also asked students some higher order questions during the lesson. I asked one of the students if he could tell me how a three-dimensional figure can be represented as a net.
- This lesson plan had a lot of visuals on my PowerPoint. I also incorporated group work and hands-on activities to increase student understanding of polyhedrons and nets.
- I differentiated instruction by giving the higher students more challenging polyhedrons to construct and analyze such as hexagonal and octagonal prisms. The rest of the class was given easier polyhedrons to analyze such as cubes and pyramids.
- I continuously gave my students feedback during the lesson. For example, one student drew a really good picture of a pyramid so I showed the whole class and gave praise to that student.
- If students were struggling and did not know how to identify the faces, edges, and vertices of a polyhedron I showed them a real-life example of a cube. Then I pointed to the vertices, faces, and edges that I had labeled.

Discussion Questions

1. What are the pros and cons of a gifted/blended classroom?

2. In what ways was the lesson on polyhedrons differentiated for gifted leaners in a full-time gifted/blended setting?
3. Would this lesson meet the needs of gifted learners? Why or why not?
4. What additional strategies could be used to differentiate this lesson?
5. How would you modify the lesson content, process, product, and/or affect to meet the diverse needs of learners in this full-time gifted/blended classroom?
6. What are the implications for planning for differentiation in this type of setting?
7. What are some challenges shared by teachers new to working with gifted learners?
8. How important is the postassessment? Does it align with the standard in this lesson plan? Why or why not?
9. What accommodations could be made for the students with autism, cerebral palsy, and/or muscular dystrophy?

Activities

1. Identify the pros, cons, and interesting possibilities of this lesson for this blended class of students in a PMI or graphic organizer of your choice. Share your ideas with a colleague.
2. Role-play a conversation between Mr. Jonathon and a veteran teacher reviewing this lesson plan before implementing it. Include suggestions for its revision.
3. Evaluate this lesson plan from the perspective of the school principal. Make a list of recommendations for Mr. Jonathon and his supervising teacher to consider.
4. Revise this lesson plan or devise plans to continue this unit of study. Create an assessment for the plan or plans.
5. Make a list of specific suggestions for differentiating the lesson for Mr. Jonathon's students with autism or other special needs.

Extensions

1. Compare and contrast the implications of various settings for meeting the needs of gifted learners such as inclusion classrooms, self-contained classrooms, pull-out programs, etc. Share your findings in a product of your choice.
2. Develop a plan to convince school board members to implement a specific program service for meeting the needs of gifted learners in your school or district. Include a continuum of services for the K–12 student.

3. Create a list of questions to be answered when evaluating services for gifted learners. Prioritize your list.

4. Review the latest research on differentiating curriculum and instruction for gifted learners. What does the research suggest? Do you agree or disagree? Share you results in a roundtable discussion with others.

5. What are the implications for implementing CCSS with gifted learners for teachers, programs, and students? Create a chart to help communicate your ideas with other professionals.

6. Create an annotated bibliography of resources available to teachers on best practices for teaching mathematically talented students.

Additional Readings

Assouline, S. G., & Lupkowski-Shoplik, A. (2011). *Developing math talent: A comprehensive guide to math education for gifted students in elementary and middle school* (2nd ed.). Waco, TX: Prufrock Press.

Gavin, M. K., & Adelson, J. L. (2008). Mathematics, Elementary. In J. A. Plucker & C. M. Callahan (Eds.), *Critical issues and practices in gifted education: What the research says* (pp. 367–394). Waco, TX: Prufrock Press.

Johnsen, S. K., & Kendrick, J. (Eds.). (2005). *Math education for gifted students.* Waco, TX, Prufrock Press.

Johnsen, S. K., & Sheffield, L. J. (Eds.). (2013*). Using the Common Core State Standards for* mathematics with gifted and advanced learners. Waco, TX: Prufrock Press.

Karnes, F. A., & Bean, S. M. (Eds.). (2009). *Methods and materials for teaching the gifted* (3rd ed.). Waco, TX: Prufrock Press.

National Association for Gifted Children. (n.d.). *Common Core State Standards, national science standards and gifted education.* Retrieved from http://www.nagc.org/CommonCoreStateStandards.aspx

Roberts, J. L., & Inman, T. F. (2013). *Teacher's survival guide: Differentiating instruction in the elementary classroom, grades K–5.* Waco, TX: Prufrock Press.

Rotigel, J. V., & Fello, S. (2004). Mathematically gifted students: How can we meet their needs? *Gifted Child Today, 27*(4), 46–51. doi:10.4219/gct-2004-150

Mr. Jonathon, Lesson 2

Introduction

Continue following Mr. Jonathon as he designs another lesson plan focusing on the Underground Railroad and quilts that includes a math component to build on his previous lesson in geometry. Mr. Jonathon is a preservice teacher who is just learning how to meet the needs of his students in a full-time gifted classroom.

Mr. Jonathon, a preservice teacher in a fourth-grade gifted/blended classroom at the Calhoun School, is assigned to a class with a very diverse population of students. The class is part of a gifted/blended program and it includes several students with special needs. One of these students has been identified with autism. Another has cerebral palsy and one student has muscular dystrophy. The Calhoun School is in a low SES area with more than 90% of the students in the school receiving free or reduced lunch. Mr. Jonathon is responsible for teaching his students every subject (social studies, language arts, science, and math). His student with autism is extremely intelligent, but has many social and emotional problems and is the only student in the class that has an IEP. All of the other students are either gifted or high-achieving students.

The gifted students catch on quickly and do not usually have to work as hard as the high achievers in the class. Mr. Jonathon is encountering many teaching responsibilities within the classroom related to attendance, grades, lesson plans, procedures, and classroom management. A behavior management program helps track different behaviors throughout the day. All of the students in the class participate in the Accelerated Reader program.

Mr. Jonathan presented the following lesson (Table 5.2) to his students.

Things to Consider

» The degree of implementation of differentiation varies in the classroom.
» Student readiness, interest, and learning profiles are key factors for classroom teachers to consider when differentiating for gifted learners.

Mr. Jonathon reflected about teaching his lesson and made the following observations:

⊙ When I taught my lesson about Freedom Quilts I felt like I did a good job of giving my students directions for their quilt project. I also had all of the materials for the lesson well organized the day before I taught it.

Table 5.2
Mr. Jonathon, Lesson 2

Lesson Topic	Underground Railroad and quilts.
Subject/ Grade Level	Social studies, reading, math/Grade 4.
Common Core State Standards	• LACC.4.RL.1.1. Refer to details and examples in a text when explaining what the text says explicitly and when drawing inferences from the text. • LACC.4.RL.1.2. Determine a theme of a story, drama, or poem from details in the text; summarize the text. • SS.4.G.1.4. Interpret political and physical maps using map elements (title, compass rose, cardinal directions, intermediate directions, symbols, legend, scale, longitude, latitude).
Objective	• The fourth-grade student will read a passage about quilts used on the Underground Railroad. After reading the passage, the student should know the author's purpose and main idea with supporting details. The student will also summarize the information he or she has read. • The student will create a quilt out of construction paper that has a hidden map. He or she will use symbols from a key to create a hidden map onto a quilt constructed from construction paper.
Materials	• Quilt square template • Construction paper • Scissors • Glue stick • Passage about quilts with questions on it
Hook	Show students a real-life example of a quilt. Tap prior knowledge from the book, *Sweet Clara and the Freedom Quilt*. Explain that it is believed that quilts had secret maps.
Activities	• Review the story about the Freedom Quilt. Ask a couple of students what the story was about. • Show a power point with standards, map of Underground Railroad, and pictures of where slaves hid. • Then choose partners from a list written on the board. When students pair up, give them the directions for the lesson. • First, students will work in pairs and read a passage about quilts used on the Underground Railroad. Then they will identify author's purpose, give the main idea with supporting details, and summarize the article. • After students finish the questions, they will work individually to construct a quilt out of shapes on a worksheet. Students will be given examples of patterns to use for their quilt. Then students will cut out different shapes from a worksheet. Then they will trace the shapes onto construction paper and use how ever many shapes they need for their pattern. • Students will be given a key with different symbols that they can use to create a secret map. After the students create a pattern, they can use different symbols on their key to create a map. I will show the students an example of my quilt, which has 4 orange triangles, 4 yellow triangles, 20 yellow squares, and 20 orange squares. It also has a hidden map with symbols of a boat, river, barn, and the Northern Star.
Accommodations	• If students finish early, they can identify all of the shapes, angles, reflections, and translations in the pattern. • I will cut out the shapes for one of my students who has a difficult time cutting with scissors.
Assessment	A check system will be used to assess the students' work during the lesson (see Figure 5.2).

Note. This lesson plan has been used by permission of Van Martin, former student intern, The Webster School, St. Augustine, FL.

Check System	Yes	No
Author's purpose is correct.		
Main idea is correct.		
Supporting details are correct.		
Summary is correct.		
Student correctly uses symbols to create a hidden map on the quilt made from construction paper.		

Figure 5.2. Check system.

- During this lesson I used the classroom management system (clip up is positive, clip down is negative) to keep the students focused. If a student was misbehaving, I had him or her move the clip down. If a student was behaving very well, I had him or her move the clip up.
- When I was preparing to teach my lesson about Freedom Quilts, I cut out the shapes that went into the quilt pattern for a student who would not be able to cut out the shapes independently.

Discussion Questions

1. In what ways was the lesson on Freedom Quilts differentiated for gifted learners in a full-time blended setting?
2. Would this lesson meet the needs of gifted learners? Why or why not?
3. What additional strategies could be used to differentiate this lesson?
4. How would you modify the lesson content, process, product, and/or affect to meet the diverse needs of learners in this full-time blended classroom?
5. What are the similarities and differences in the challenges shared by teachers new to working with gifted learners and veteran teachers working with gifted learners?
6. How might flexible grouping be used to meet the needs of students in this classroom?
7. Does the postassessment align with the standard in this lesson plan? Why or why not?
8. In what ways might you need to modify this lesson for Mr. Jonathon's students with autism or other special needs?
9. In the "check system," what could Mr. Jonathan do if the gifted students see something different?"

Activities

1. Research the appropriate CCSS for this lesson. Develop additional activities that align with the lesson objectives and support the mastery of the CCSS you have selected.

2. What letter grade (A, B, C, D, F) would you give this lesson plan in terms of meeting the needs of gifted learners? Identify the criteria used for this evaluation. Defend your choice to a colleague.

3. Make a list of resources available for teaching social studies to gifted learners. Select several and write a review for other teachers (see ideas at http://www.hoagiesgifted.org/social_studies.htm).

4. Review the WebQuest by Jones and Harmon (1999) "Flight to Freedom"(found at http://people.emich.edu/tjones1/flighttofreedom). How might you modify the activities to meet the needs of gifted learners? Redesign this WebQuest or create one for a topic of your own choosing (see examples at http://webquest.org/index.php).

5. Compare and contrast Mr. Jonathon's lesson plan with the lesson plan found at http://people.emich.edu/tjones1/flighttofreedom/Teachers Resources.html in a Venn or similar diagram for the WebQuest listed above. Make a list of the strengths and weaknesses for each.

6. Design tiered lessons or implement another differentiation strategy of choice (cubing, menus, learning center) for "Quilting and the Underground Railroad" or similar topic.

7. Create a differentiated PowerPoint, mini-lesson, or vocabulary lesson (see ideas at http://socialstudiesdifferentiatedinstruction.com) for social studies.

Extensions

1. Write a review for a published unit developed for social studies such as those found at the William & Mary Center for Gifted Education (CFGE; see website at http://education.wm.edu/centers/cfge/curriculum/index.php) that:
    ⊙ is interdisciplinary;
    ⊙ uses abstract concepts such as systems, cause and effect, and how things change over time;
    ⊙ places heavy emphasis on higher order reasoning;
    ⊙ provides historical analysis using primary sources;
    ⊙ includes in-depth study of content; and
    ⊙ employs the skills of discussion, writing, and research.

2. How can technology be used to support the needs of gifted learners? View the UCIrvineExtension (2013) webinar "Tech Tools to Differentiate and Engage Gifted Learners" (found at http://www.youtube.com/watch?v=7brTplFL77A). Read two articles related to this topic and write a summary about what you read. Share the summary in a venue of your choice (e.g., school newsletter, website).

3. What are the benefits of flexible grouping in meeting the needs of gifted learners? View the YouTube clip on the benefits of tiered assignments (LEARN NC, 2012; available at http://www.youtube.com/watch?v=1Rj1FA2yVlI). Research the use of flexible grouping and create a video to post on the benefits of flexible grouping.

4. View the "Revisiting 'The Differentiated Classroom': Looking Back and Ahead" webinar presented by the Association for Supervision and Curriculum Development (ASCD) and Carol Ann Tomlinson (2014; available at https://www.youtube.com/watch?v=eXfWv2EUpog). Write a reflection paper on one or more key changes that have—or should have—an impact on teaching and learning in the 15 years since the release of the first edition of Tomlinson's (1999) book *The Differentiated Classroom: Responding to the Needs of All Learners*. Be sure to include how these changes have impacted you as a teacher.

Additional Readings

Hockett, J. A. (2014). Social studies and gifted learners. In J. A. Plucker & C. M. Callahan (Eds.), *Critical issues and practices in gifted education: What the research says* (2nd ed., pp. 609–622). Waco, TX: Prufrock Press.

Jones, J. K., & Hébert, T. P. (2012, October). Engaging diverse gifted learners in U.S. history classrooms. *Gifted Child Today, 35*(4), 252–261. doi:10.1177/1076217512455476

National Association for Gifted Children. (n.d.). *Common Core State Standards, national science standards and gifted education*. Retrieved from http://www.nagc.org/CommonCoreStateStandards.aspx

Sheffield, C. C., & Duplass, J. A. (2009). Creating effective citizens: Unique opportunities for gifted education through the social studies. *Gifted Education International, 25,* 237–245. doi:10.1177/026142940902500305

Troxclair, D. A. (2000). Differentiating instruction for gifted students in regular education social studies classes. *Roeper Review, 22,* 195–198. doi:10.1080/02783190009554033

Differentiating and Assessing Products With Menus

Introduction

Differentiation for the gifted may take many forms. Content, process, and products may be differentiated. One best practice for gifted learners supports choice of learning content, ways to process learning, and/or ways to exhibit learning (products).

One choice for differentiating and assessing products is through a menu of activities. Menus may vary in focus and format. They may include choice of product to evaluate learning and to earn points for grading purposes with a rubric for evaluation.

This case explores the use of integrated core content menus to accommodate differentiation of products and their assessments in a middle school academy for gifted learners.

Wrighthouse Middle School Academy

Wrighthouse Middle School Academy is an academy for gifted students in grades 7 and 8 in a midsize public school district of 10,000 students. The academy is designed for 150 students per grade level, offers differentiation in the four core subject areas, and provides opportunities for those students who are identified as gifted in the areas of visual and performing arts, languages, creativity, and leadership. All academy students are preassessed for placement in the appropriate level of math, science, social studies, ELA, and languages (Spanish, French, German, and Mandarin Chinese). Portfolios for placement are required for those who wish to participate in advanced visual or performing arts and leadership. Creativity is enhanced through the arts, core content areas, and competitions.

District demographics are 28% African American, 28% Hispanic, 30% White, 10% Asian, and 4% Native American. Fifty-seven percent of the students are identified as coming from a low SES.

There are 166 seventh-grade students at Wrighthouse Academy and 134 in eighth grade. Academy demographics are 26% African American, 30% Hispanic, 28% White, 14% Asian, and 2% Native American. Sixty percent of the students are identified as coming from low SES.

The Wrighthouse Academy day is divided into eight periods. Students have four periods for core content, one period for languages, one period for the arts, one period for personal research and explorations, and one period of free choice for an additional language, leadership, arts, or study time. Teachers in the academy teach five sections per day, which include their core content area (four sections), one section of interest-based explorations, one period for conferences and staff meetings, one period to accommodate students' free choice period, and one period for planning.

Ms. Yokem and Mr. Hill

All core content teachers meet in the summer to refine and evaluate their curriculum from the school year that just ended and to create curriculum for the next school year based on postassessments of the students. Ms. Yokem and Mr. Hill each teach three sections of seventh-grade social studies. They have a common planning time with the seventh-grade ELA teachers.

After reflecting on the products students presented as a culmination of learning throughout the year, neither Ms. Yokem nor Mr. Hill were satisfied with the results they were seeing from the students. They decided to create a unit for their seventh-grade students that would include choices of products that illustrate students' learning, reflect their content area growth, and provide for a diversity of products to be developed. They decided they would develop the unit of study on the topic of *courage* that could be integrated with an ELA unit. They invited the ELA teachers to participate in their efforts.

Ms. Yokem and Mr. Hill determined that they would each create a 3x3 tic-tac-toe menu that included sophisticated products. By each teacher developing his or her own, each would develop one particular to their students' needs based on preassessment and would share ideas that each would want to incorporate into this menu or one they would develop in the future.

Things to Consider

» Menu choice differentiation must include deep and meaningful learning. Teachers must offer menus that include choices with depth of content, higher order thinking, and products of consequence.
» Students must have the opportunity to select product choices that meet their interests.
» Teachers must have time to create menus and develop assessments that provide meaningful feedback.

Table 5.3 details their unit.

At the beginning of the new school year, Ms. Yokem and Mr. Hill plan to meet with the ELA teachers who have the same students to discuss the activities and rubrics as they relate to the postassessment information they have for these students.

Table 5.3
Ms. Yokem and Mr. Hill's Unit

Courage	
Part 1: Courage Diary	Using novels, short stories, nonfiction, plays, print and visual diagrams, and any research material, document as many examples of courage as possible in a Courage Diary.
	Where to look for examples: Everywhere! Keep track of all examples of courage that you find in literature, at home, at school, on the street, on the news (both visual and print), in history, at church, in movies, on TV, in textbooks, in music . . . everywhere!
	How to document: Writing always works, but there many other fun ways to document: • Video-recorded interview • Audio-recorded reflections • Photographs with captions • A computer presentation • An art show • Original songs • A combination of all these The sky is the limit!
	Cite sources: As examples are collected, a running works-cited page in correct MLA format is required. If help is required in knowing how to cite a TV show or an interview with Granny and it is not found in the MLA manual, ask the teacher.
Part II: A Profile of Modern Courage	By exploring courage across the ages and by citing examples of courage you observe in the modern world, your definition of what you believe to be true courage will emerge. Complete the menu provided below to create your profile of modern courage.

Ms. Yokem's Menu

Select three activities from this menu that give you tic-tac-toe, across, down, or diagonally.

Note. Make sure that all nine are covered by students so that the sharing gives the class the information they need for the project.

Create illustrations for your Courage Diary.	List at least five characteristics of courageous people or courageous acts.	Design a T-shirt that illustrates the most courageous person or act you found for your diary.
Create a word search with characteristics of courage and courageous acts and people.	Answer a question you have about courage. For your product, select from the Product Board.	Write a short story about a person of courage or a courageous act.
Design a game to share your Courage Diary information.	Draw a comic strip about courage or courageous acts. OR Create a mural about courage or courageous acts.	Write and direct a one-act play about courage or courageous acts or people.

	Mr. Hill's Menu*		
Part II: A Profile of Modern Courage, *continued*	Select three activities from this menu that give you tic-tac-toe, across, down, or diagonally. *Note.* Make sure that all nine are covered by students so that the sharing gives the class the information they need for the project.		
	Analyze your Courage Diary to decide what society believes about courage. Based on trends and patterns in history, what are the principles on which courage is based? Illustrate your findings through an essay or with a graphic organizer of your choice.	How do the principles of courage compare to your ideas about courage? Compare and contrast these principles with a Venn diagram.	Based on society's definition and your own ideas, what criteria will you use to evaluate whether an act or person is truly courageous? Create a Creative Problem Solving (CPS) grid to evaluate your criteria. Include at least three criteria.
	Consider whether there are some people or acts that most of society would **not** consider courageous but that might be seen as courageous from a different perspective. Write an editorial expressing your perspective.	Answer a question you have about courage. For your product, select from the Product Board.	Who or what in today's world is the best example of courage? How? Create a poem or PowerPoint/Prezi to answer this question.
	Why is this study of courage important and how can it change you or your audience? Make a collage that expresses the importance of courage, how this study changed you, and how it could change others.	Create a brochure of at least three people that you define as courageous. List their characteristics, accomplishments, and anything else you want to say/ illustrate about them.	What perspective of courage do you have that has not been documented in any of your findings? Create a documentary of courage in a medium of your choice.

All answer: What is your new definition of courage?

<table>
<tr><td rowspan="1">Final Product</td><td>How to present: Presentation is up to you. Use any presentation format that will communicate all of the above with your audience. An oral presentation is not required. The Courage Diary and the profile should be able to stand alone and communicate to the audience all that you would say if you were to speak. Is a PowerPoint presentation the only other means? No. Be creative. Anything goes, as long as it communicates and meets the requirements of the rubric. Words are excellent tools for communication, but remember, the true goal is communication.</td></tr>
<tr><td>Grading</td><td>All products will be evaluated with the rubric (see Figure 5.3). For any evaluation in Novice section, work must be redone to the satisfaction of the student and teacher.
  • A: 90–100, 5 of 7 descriptors in Expert and 2 in Practitioner**
  • B: 80–89, 3 of 7 descriptors in Expert and 4 in Practitioner**
  • C: 70–79, 1 of 7 descriptors in Expert and 6 in Practitioner**

Any Novice redone by student will be evaluated as listed above.
**Determined by teacher and peers. Peer evaluations will be completed on final product.</td></tr>
</table>

Note. This menu was developed by R. Raney (personal communication, 2005). Adapted with permission.

Expert	Practitioner	Novice
Uses advanced processes to examine information; connects and evaluates information.	Uses basic processes to examine information and connect and evaluate information.	Inconsistently or inadequately analyzes information; lack of connection and evaluation of information.
Accurate information.	Mixture of accurate information and opinion.	Information inaccurate.
Well-organized, sound product.	Partially organized.	Lacks organization, clarity, and support.
Shows planning, reasoning; easy-to-follow reasoning.	Some clarity and support; lacks consistent reasoning.	Little planning.
Clear and supported with details.	Somewhat clear with minimal details.	Vague; lack of details.
Sophisticated insight and analysis.	Coherent analysis; substantive understanding.	Some analysis; inconsistent understanding.
Uses highly effective communications including supporting data, and clear, pertinent examples.	Clear communication; some supporting data with few examples.	Communication prevents audience from following ideas expressed.

Figure 5.3. Grading rubric. Adapted from *Middle School TPSP Assessment Rubric Overview* by Texas Education Agency, 2011, Austin, TX: Author, retrieved from http://www.texaspsp.org/middleschool/assessment/Middle_School_Rubric.pdf. Copyright 2011 by Texas Education Agency. Adapted with permission.

Discussion Questions

1. Which menu creates more engaged learning for seventh-grade gifted learners? Why?

2. Does one of the menus elicit deeper and more significant learning? Why or why not?

3. In what ways do the menu examples meet the criteria as a best practice for gifted learners?

4. In what ways can you teach students how to create the products required in the menus?

5. Is a rubric always necessary? Why or why not?

6. What other type(s) of evaluation could be used in conjunction with a rubric?

7. Access Laurie Westphal's (n.d.) "Menu Evaluation Checklist" on Teachers Pay Teachers (https://www.teacherspayteachers.com/Product/Menu-Evaluation-Checklist-For-Teachers-48863). Do the menus in this case study meet the criteria set by Westphal? Why or why not?

8.   Research 20-50-80 menus. Would this work be better presented and evaluated with a 20-50-80 menu?

Activities

1.   Research different types of menus. Create one of each type for your students.
2.   Find a menu online. Adapt it for one of your units of study.
3.   Create a differentiated menu for a cluster group of gifted students.
4.   Create a tic-tac-toe (3x3) menu for your students, leaving out three choices that students may develop.
5.   Ask your classroom students or students you know to select the type of menu that best fits their learning style and needs. Create a reflection for them to justify their choice.
6.   Develop a math, science, social studies, ELA/reading, or an integrated content center to use with each type of menu. Include the description of your expected learning outcomes.

Extensions

1.   Create a tic-tac-toe (3x3) menu and its evaluation rubric for a teacher professional development opportunity on a topic of your choice.
2.   Develop two novel ways to engage and evaluate teachers in a professional development session. Include visual, auditory, and kinesthetic activities.
3.   Develop a product compendium for your class or for a professional development session with teachers or administrators.

Additional Readings

Byrd, I. (n.d.). *The differentiator*. Retrieved from http://www.byrdseed.com/differentiator

Byrd, I. (2015). *Four ways to differentiate objectives: Differentiating product.* Retrieved from http://www.byrdseed.com/four-ways-to-differentiate-objectives

Chung, D. (n.d.). *Menu of products: Lit. circle products.* Retrieved from https://sites.google.com/site/davidnchung/LitCircleProductsPage.pdf?attredirects=0

Coil, C. (2000). *Teaching tools for the 21st century* (2nd ed.). Marion, IL: Pieces of Learning.

Coil, C. (2004). *Standards-based activities and assessments for the differentiated classroom.* Marion, IL: Pieces of Learning.

Coil, C., & Merritt, D. (2001). *Solving the assessment puzzle piece by piece*. Marion, IL. Pieces of Learning.

Coleman, M. R., & Gallagher, J. J. (1995). Appropriate differentiated services: Guides for best practices in the education of gifted children. *Gifted Child Today, 18*(5), 32-33.

Heacox, D. (2009). *Making differentiation a habit: How to ensure success in academically diverse classrooms*. Minneapolis, MN: Free Spirit Publishing.

Huebner, T. A. (2010). What research says about differentiated learning. *Educational Leadership, 67*(5), 79–81.

Kingore, B. (2004). *Differentiation: Simplified, realistic, and effective*. Austin, TX: Professional Associates Publishing.

Roberts, J. L., & Bogges, J. R. (2012). *Differentiating instruction with centers in the gifted classroom*. Waco, TX: Prufrock Press.

Scigiliano, D., & Hipsky, S. (2010). Three ring circus of differentiated instruction. *Kappa Delta Pi Record, 46*(2), 82–86.

Tomlinson, C. A. (2000). *What is differentiated instruction?* Retrieved from http://www.readingrockets.org/article/263

Westphal, L. E. (2012). *Ready-to-use differentiation strategies, grades 6–8*. Waco, TX: Prufrock Press.

Mr. Randall and Natalie

Introduction

Mr. Randall, a novice educator, has been teaching language arts to fifth and sixth graders. Within his double class period of gifted students, he has one highly gifted girl whose talents and abilities far exceed the rest of the class. He is finding it challenging to provide the academic rigor that she needs. In this case study, Mr. Randall considers several options on meeting the needs of this highly gifted student.

Mr. Randall has been teaching in a predominantly White suburban district in the southwest with about 5,704 students for 2 years. The community has a mix of middle and lower SES of students. His schedule is comprised of a double period of language arts for fifth-grade students identified as gifted and talented, a double period of language arts for fifth-grade students scoring in the bottom quartile in reading, and one period of English for sixth graders. Although Mr. Randall feels confident he is meeting a majority of his students' needs, he has one student, Natalie, a fifth grader whom he believes needs a more challenging and rigorous curriculum. The percent of student body by academic risk factor for Westside Independent School District (ISD) compared to the state is shown in Figure 5.6.

Things to Consider

» Learning contracts provide an opportunity for teachers to respond to the specific needs of their students.
» Learning contracts can help teachers address a wide range of cognitive and social needs students.
» Learning contracts can be used in a variety of ways (e.g., in one particular subject and grade level or across subjects and grade levels).

Mr. Randall does differentiate the curriculum and instruction for the class of students identified as gifted. Yet, he feels that he still needs to modify both for Natalie. Natalie scores in the top 99 percentile on a nationally recognized standardized test in reading and language arts. Her IQ score is 148. She excels on all tasks in his class. He notes that the one time she received less than a 95% on a class test she was truly devastated. This worried Mr. Randall and he contacted her parents to discuss his concern.

Mr. Randall is currently planning a new differentiated unit in language arts. After researching various strategies, he is considering developing a

	Economically Disadvantaged	At Risk	Limited English Proficient
Westside ISD	25.5%	31.4%	2.3%
State	59%	47.2%	16.9%

Figure 5.6. Study body by academic risk factor.

learning contract with Natalie based on her needs and interests. He found a resource, "Differentiation and Curriculum Compacting" (available at http://mediasite.dl.uconn.edu/Mediasite/Play/ba0cbe2595c84c1db6ae0b67f11b89a a1d), to help him think about the process. This is his first attempt at using this approach.

Discussion Questions

1. What do the academic risk factor data inform you about Westside ISD?
2. What is a learning contract? Under what circumstances might a learning contract be beneficial?
3. What issues should Mr. Randall consider when developing a learning contract for Natalie?
4. What role should Natalie and her parents play in the development and implementation of the learning contract?
5. Does the role of the teacher change when implementing learning contracts? If so, how?
6. What does Mr. Randall need to do next in this scenario? Why?
7. What resources and materials would be helpful in developing a learning contract?
8. What function does preassessment play in planning a learning contract?
9. Was Mr. Randall's consideration of the test data pertaining to Natalie appropriate? Why or why not?
10. Should learning styles and preferences be considered when developing a learning contract? Why or why not?
11. What other differentiation strategies might be used?

Activities

1. Research the essential or key elements of a learning contract. Specify any modifications that should be considered based on the age of the

student. Make a list of what should be included for a student with special needs such as an ELL or twice-exceptional student.

2. Create a learning contract on a specific topic or unit of study for a student(s) of your choice. Include a brief summary of the student's instructional needs and how the contract will be used. After implementing the contract, determine if it was an effective strategy to meet the needs of the gifted learner. Why or why not? What might you do differently when developing the next contract? Share your results with a colleague.

3. Develop and present a workshop for colleagues on designing learning contracts for students.

4. Make a list of all of the different ways to organize a learning contract (e.g., book title, subject area(s), etc.).

5. Research the pros and cons related to using learning contracts in the classroom. Share your results in a PMI chart.

6. Evaluate various learning contract formats (available at http://images.schoolinsites.com/SiSFiles/Schools/TN/GreenevilleCity/GreenevilleHigh/Uploads/DocumentsCategories/Documents/Learning%20Contracts.pdf). Make a list of strengths and weaknesses of the different formats.

Extensions

1. Are certain differentiation strategies more effective with certain students? What needs to be considered during the decision-making process? Create a flow chart outlining the decision-making process.

2. "Responsive teaching is flexible teaching." What does this mean to you? Invite your colleagues to share their thoughts in a brown-bag discussion.

3. What does the research tell us about the correlation between motivation and learning to achievement gains? Make a summary of your findings in a product of your choice.

4. What role do learning contracts play in Response to Intervention (RtI)? See the RtI for Gifted Students talk (available at http://www.rtinetwork.org/professional/rti-talks/transcript/talk/24; Coleman, 2010). Share something you learned from this talk with colleagues. Identify additional questions related to this topic and discuss possible answers to those questions.

Additional Readings

Association for Supervision and Curriculum Development. (2003). *Instructional strategies for the differentiated classroom 1–4*. Alexandria, VA: Author. [Video staff development set]. Retrieved from http://shop.ascd.org

Heacox, D. (2002). *Differentiating instruction in the regular classroom: How to reach and teach all learners, grades 3–12*. Minneapolis, MN: Free Spirit Publishing.

Heacox, D. (2009). *Making differentiation a habit: How to ensure success in academically diverse classrooms*. Minneapolis, MN: Free Spirit Publishing.

Kingore, B. (2004). *Differentiation: Simplified, realistic, and effective*. Austin, TX: Professional Associates Publishing.

Reis, S. M., & Renzulli, J. S. (2005). *Curriculum compacting: An easy start to differentiating for high-potential students*. Waco, TX: Prufrock Press.

Roberts, J. L., & Inman, T. F. (2015). *Strategies for differentiating instruction: Best practices for the classroom* (3rd ed.). Waco, TX: Prufrock Press.

Rogers, K. B. (2006). *A menu of options for grouping gifted students*. Waco, TX: Prufrock Press.

Smutny, J. F., & von Fremd, S. E. (2004). *Differentiating for the young child: Teaching strategies across the content areas, K–3*. Thousand Oaks, CA: Corwin Press.

Starko, A. J. (1986). *It's about time: In-service strategies for curriculum compacting*. Mansfield Center, CT: Creative Learning Press.

Tomlinson, C. A. (1999). *The differentiated classroom: Responding to the needs of all learners*. Alexandria, VA: ASCD.

Tomlinson, C. A. (2001). *How to differentiate instruction in mixed- ability classrooms*. Alexandria, VA: ASCD.

Tomlinson, C. A. (Vol. Ed.). (2004). Differentiation for gifted and talented students. In S. M. Reis (Series Ed.), *Essential readings in gifted education series: Vol. 5*. Thousand Oaks, CA: Corwin Press.

VanTassel-Baska, J. (2003). *Curriculum planning and instructional design for gifted learners*. Denver, CO: Love Publishing.

Winebrenner, S. (2001). *Teaching gifted kids in the regular classroom* (Rev. ed.). Minneapolis, MN: Free Spirit Publishing.

Winebrenner, S., & Berger, S. (1994). Providing curriculum alternatives to motivate gifted students. *Council for Exceptional Children*. Retrieved from ERIC database. (ED372553)

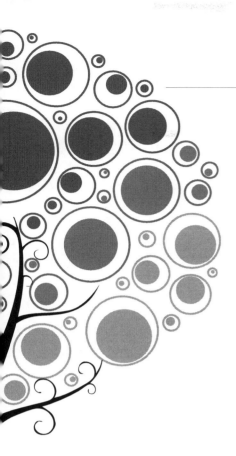

References

Association for Supervision and Curriculum Development (Producer), & Tomlinson, C. A. (Presenter). (2014, May 22). *Revisiting the differentiated classroom: Looking back and ahead* [Webinar]. Retrieved from https://www.youtube.com/watch?v=eXfWv2EUpog

Barnett, C. S., & Tyson, P. A. (1999). Case methods and teacher change: Shifting authority to build autonomy. In M. Lundberg, B. Levin, & H. Harrington (Eds.), *Who learns what from cases and how: The research base for teaching and learning with cases* (pp. 53–69). Mahwah, NJ: Lawrence Erlbaum.

Baum, S. (Vol. Ed.). (2004). Twice-exceptional and special populations of gifted students. In S. M. Reis (Series Ed.), *Essential readings in gifted education series: Vol. 7.* Thousand Oaks, CA: Corwin Press.

Baum, S. (2012, May 16). *What's in a name? Defining and reifying twice-exceptional education* [Web log post]. Retrieved from http://twiceexceptional.com/2012/05/16/whats-in-a-name-defining-and-reifying-twice-exceptional-education

Birman, B. F., Desimone, L., Porter, A. C., & Garet, M. S. (2000). Designing professional development that works. *Educational Leadership, 57*(8), 28–33.

Brame, C. J. (2013). *Flipping the classroom.* Retrieved from http://cft.vanderbilt.edu/guides-sub-pages/flipping-the-classroom

Child Welfare Information Gateway. (2011). *About CAPTA: A legislative history*. Retrieved from http://www.childwelfare.gov/pubPDFs/about.pdf

Coleman, M. R. (2010, October 9). *Re: RTI for gifted students* [Online forum]. Retrieved from http://www.rtinetwork.org/professional/rti-talks/transcript/talk/24

Dalgarno, N., & Colgan, L. (2007). Supporting novice elementary mathematics teachers' induction in professional communities and providing innovative forms of pedagogical content knowledge development through information and communication technology. *Teaching and Teacher Education, 23,* 1051–1065. doi:10.1016/j.tate.2006.04.037

Dana, N. F., Dawson, K., Wolkenhauer, R., & Krell, D. (2012). Virtual educator inquiry: Design and implementation of a year-long program to mentor virtual educators in the action research process. In K. Kennedy & L. Archambault (Eds.), *Lessons learned in teacher mentoring: Supporting educators in K-12 online learning environments* (pp. 115–129). Vienna, VA: International Association for K-12 Online Learning (iNACOL).

Dana, N. F., Dawson, K., Wolkenhauer, R., & Krell, D. (2013). Pushing the envelope on what is known about professional development: The virtual school experience. *Professional Development in Education, 39,* 240–259. doi:10.1080/19415257.2012.762417

Dana, N. F., & Yendol-Hoppey, D. (2009). *The reflective educator's guide to classroom research: Learning to teach and teaching to learn through practitioner inquiry* (2nd ed.). Thousand Oaks, CA: Corwin Press.

Danielson, C. (1996). *Enhancing professional practice: A framework for teaching*. Alexandria, VA: ASCD.

Danielson, L. M. (2009). Fostering reflection. *Educational Leadership, 66*(5). Retrieved from http://www.ascd.org/publications/educational-leadership/feb09/vol66/num05/Fostering-Reflection.aspx

Darling-Hammond, L., Wei, R. C., Andree, A., Richardson, N., & Orphanos, S. (2009). *Professional learning in the learning profession: A status report on teacher development in the United States and abroad*. Dallas, TX: National Staff Development Council.

Dawson, K., Cavanaugh, C., & Ritzhaupt, A. (2012). ARTI: An online tool to support teacher action research for technology integration. In R. Hartshorne, T. Heafner, & T. Petty (Eds.), *Teacher education programs and online learning tools: Innovations in teacher preparation* (pp. 375–391). Hershey, PA: IGI Global.

DiCamillo, K. (2000). *Because of Winn-Dixie*. Somerville, MA: Candlewick Press.

Duckworth, A. L. (2009). Backtalk: Self-discipline is empowering. *Phi Delta Kappan, 90,* 536.

Duke, N. K., & Pearson, P. D. (2002). Effective practices for developing reading comprehension. In A. E. Farstrup & S. J. Samuels (Eds.), *What research has to say about reading instruction* (3rd ed., pp. 205–242). Newark, DE: International Reading Association.

Dweck, C. S. (2007). *Mindset: The new psychology of success*. New York, NY: Random House.

Ferdig, R. E., Cavanaugh, C., & Freidhoff, J. R. (Eds.). (2012). *Lessons learned from blended programs: Experiences and recommendations from the field*. Vienna, VA: International Association for K-12 Online Learning (iNACOL).

Fisher, D., & Frey, N. (2003). Writing instruction for struggling adolescent readers: A gradual release model. *Journal of Adolescent & Adult Literacy, 46*, 396–405.

Fortune, T. W. (2015). *What research tells us about immersion*. Retrieved from http://asiasociety.org/education/chinese-language-initiatives/what-research-tells-us-about-immersion

Garrison, D. R., Anderson, T., & Archer, W. (2010). The first decade of the community of inquiry framework: A retrospective. *The Internet and Higher Education, 13*(1-2), 5–9. doi:10.1016/j.iheduc.2009.10.003

Gregory, G. H., & Chapman, C. (2013). *Differentiated instructional strategies: One size doesn't fit all* (3rd ed.). Thousand Oaks, CA: Corwin Press.

Guldberg, K., & Pilkington, R. (2006). A community of practice approach to the development of non-traditional learners through networked learning. *Journal of Computer Assisted Learning, 22*, 159–171. doi:10.1111/j.1365-2729.2006.00171.x

Idaho State Department of Education. (2010). *Twice-exceptional: Students with both gifts and challenges or disabilities* [Manual]. Retrieved from https://www.sde.idaho.gov/site/gifted_talented/twice-exceptional/docs/2E%20Manual.pdf

International Dyslexia Association. (2002). *Definition of dyslexia*. Retrieved from http://eida.org/definition-of-dyslexia

International Dyslexia Association. (2013). *Gifted and dyslexic: Identifying and instructing the twice exceptional student fact sheet*. Retrieved from http://eida.org/gifted-and-dyslexic-identifying-and-instructing-the-twice-exceptional-student-fact-sheet

International Baccalaureate Organization. (2014). *About the IB*. Retrieved from http://www.ibo.org

Jacob K. Javits Gifted and Talented Students Education Act of 2001. (2001). Pub. L. 107–110, sec. 5461.

Jensen, B. (2014). Building leader and educator capacity for transformation. In *The Microsoft in Education Transformation Framework Series*. Retrieved

from http://download.microsoft.com/download/8/E/4/8E4D5383-058A
-431E-9090-1F241AC23246/1_MS_EDU_TransformationPapers/8_
MS_EDU_BuildingLeader_EducationCapacity.pdf

Jensen, E. (2009). *Teaching with poverty in mind: What being poor does to kids'
brains and what school can do about it.* Alexandria, VA: ASCD.

Johnsen, S. K. (2012). Standards in gifted education and their effects
on professional competence. *Gifted Child Today, 35*(1), 49–57.
doi:10.1177/1076217511427430

Johnson, D. T. (2000). *Teaching mathematics to gifted students in a mixed-ability
classroom.* Retrieved from http://www.educationoasis.com/resources/
Articles/teaching_gifted_math.htm

Johnson, D. T. (2011). Adapting mathematics curricula for high-ability learners. In J. VanTassel-Baska & C. A. Little (Eds.), *Content-based curriculum
for high-ability learners* (2nd ed., pp. 187–216). Waco, TX: Prufrock Press.

Jones, T. S., & Harmon, D. A. (1999, August 15). *Flight to freedom* [WebQuest].
Retrieved from http://people.emich.edu/tjones1/flighttofreedom

Kidd, S. M. (2002). *The secret life of bees.* New York, NY: Penguin Group.

Kottmeyer, C. (2014). *Young gifted children.* Retrieved from http://www.
hoagiesgifted.org/young_children.htm

LEARN NC. (n.d.). *How does tiering benefit teachers?* Retrieved from http://
www.learnnc.org/lp/multimedia/15818

LEARN NC. (n.d.). *Rethinking the role of the teacher.* Retrieved from http://
www.learnnc.org/lp/editions/every-learner/6680

LEARN NC. (2012, March 13). *How does tiering benefit students?* [Video file]
Retrieved from http://www.youtube.com/watch?v=1Rj1FA2yVlI

Liu, F., Ritzhaupt, A., & Cavanaugh, C. (2013). Leaders of school technology innovation: A confirmatory factor analysis of the Change Facilitator
Style Questionnaire (CFSQ). *Journal of Educational Administration, 51,*
576–593. doi:10.1108/JEA-01-2012-0011

Maker, C. J. (1982). *Curriculum development for the gifted.* Rockville, MD:
Aspen Systems.

Malbin, D. (2002). *Trying differently rather than harder: Fetal Alcohol Spectrum
disorders* (2nd ed.). Portland, OR: FASCETS.

MetaMetrics. (2015). *Lexile-to-grade correspondence.* Retrieved from https://
www.lexile.com/about-lexile/grade-equivalent/grade-equivalent-chart

Mountainview Elementary School. (2014-2015). *Programme of inquiry:
Where we are in place and time.* Retrieved from http://www2.wacoisd.org/
mountainview/ib_schools.htm

Mundry, S. (2005). *What experience has taught us about professional development.*
Retrieved from http://www.sedl.org/pubs/ms90/experience_pd.pdf

National Association for Gifted Children. (n.d.). *Knowledge and skill standards in gifted education for all teachers.* Retrieved from http://www.nagc.org/resources-publications/resources/national-standards-gifted-and-talented-education/knowledge-and?id=5400#sthash.RivfRvPJ.dpuf

National Association for Gifted Children. (2010). *NAGC Pre-K–Grade 12 Gifted Programming Standards: A blueprint for quality gifted education programs.* Washington, DC: Author.

National Association for Gifted Children. (2012). *Gifted: Big picture.* Washington, DC: U.S. Department of Education.

National Association for Gifted Children, & Council for Exceptional Children. (2013a). *Advanced standards in gifted education teacher preparation.* Washington, DC: Author.

National Association for Gifted Children, & Council for Exceptional Children. (2013b). *NAGC–CEC teacher preparation standards in gifted and talented education.* Washington, DC: Author.

National Education Association. (2006). *The twice-exceptional dilemma* (pp. 7–8). Retrieved from http://www.nea.org/assets/docs/twiceexceptional.pdf

National Research Council. (2012). *A framework for K-12 science education: Practices, crosscutting concepts, and core ideas.* Committee on a Conceptual Framework for New K-12 Science Education Standards. Board on Science Education, Division of Behavioral and Social Sciences and Education. Washington, DC: The National Academies Press.

National Staff Development Council. (2001). *Standards for staff development* (Rev. ed.). Oxford, OH: Author. Retrieved from http://www.sedl.org/pubs/sedl-letter/v19n01/nsdc-standards-tools.html

Neihart, M. (2003). *Gifted children with Attention Deficit Hyperactivity Disorder (ADHD).* Retrieved from http://www.gifted.uconn.edu/siegle/tag/Digests/e649.html

NGSS Lead States. (2013). *Next Generation Science Standards: For states, by states.* Washington, DC: The National Academies Press.

Olenchak, F. R. (2001). Lessons learned from gifted children about differentiation. *The TeacherEducator, 36,* 185–198. doi:10.1080/08878730109555263

Parnes, S. J. (1992). *Source book for creative problem solving: A fifty year digest of proven innovation processes.* Scituate, MA: Creative Education Foundation.

Paul, R., & Elder, L. (1997). *The elements of reasoning and the intellectual standards.* Retrieved from http://www.criticalthinking.org/pages/the-elements-of-reasoning-and-the-intellectual-standards/480

Pearson, P. D., & Gallagher, M. C. (1983). The instruction of reading comprehension. *Contemporary Educational Psychology, 8,* 317–344.

Reid, B. D., & McGuire, M. D. (1995). *Square pegs in round holes—These kids don't fit: High ability students with behavioral problems* (RBDM 9512). Retrieved from http://www.gifted.uconn.edu/nrcgt/reidmcgu.html

Renzulli, J. S. (2012). Reexamining the role of gifted education and talent development for the 21st century: A four-part theoretical approach. *Gifted Child Quarterly, 56,* 150–159.

Sachar, L. (2000). *Holes.* New York, NY: Random House.

Sessums, C. D. (2009). *The path from insight to action: The case of an online learning community in support of collaborative teacher inquiry* (Doctoral dissertation, University of Florida). Retrieved from http://etd.fcla.edu/UF/UFE0024330/sessums_c.pdf

Sessums, C. D. (2014). Learning communities and support. In *The Microsoft in Education Transformation Framework Series.* Retrieved from http://download.microsoft.com/download/8/E/4/8E4D5383-058A-431E-9090-1F241AC23246/1_MS_EDU_TransformationPapers/7_MS_EDU_LearningCommunitiesSupport.pdf

Seuss, Dr. (1957). *The cat in the hat.* New York, NY: Random House.

Shear, L., Gallagher, L., & Patel, D. (2011). *Innovative teaching and learning research.* Retrieved from http://www.itlresearch.com/images/stories/reports/ITL%20Research%202011%20Findings%20and%20Implications%20-%20Final.pdf

Shoemaker, J. (2014, December 4). *The roles of technology and social media in the gifted classroom: An #oagctdchat topic* [Web log post]. Retrieved from https://ramblingsofagiftedteacher.wordpress.com/2014/12/04/the-roles-of-technology-and-social-media-in-the-gifted-classroom-an-oagctdchat-topic

Siegle, D. (2005). *Using media and technology with gifted learners.* Waco, TX: Prufrock Press.

Slocumb, P. D. (with Olenchak, F. R.). (2006). *Equity in gifted education: A state initiative.* Retrieved from http://www.gtequity.org/docs/equity_in_ge.pdf

Slocumb, P. D., & Payne, R. K. (2000). *Removing the mask: Giftedness in poverty.* Highlands, TX: Aha! Process.

Smutny, J. F. (2003). Differentiated instruction. *Phi Delta Kappa Fastbacks, 506,* 7–47.

Streissguth, A., & Kanter, J. (Eds.). (1997). *The challenge of Fetal Alcohol Syndrome: Overcoming secondary disabilities.* Seattle, WA: University of Washington Press.

Texas Education Agency. (2011). *Middle school TPSP assessment rubric overview.* Retrieved from http://www.texaspsp.org/middleschool/assessment/Middle_School_Rubric.pdf

Tomlinson, C. A. (1999). *The differentiated classroom: Responding to the needs of all learners.* Alexandria, VA: ASCD.

Tomlinson, C. A. (2000). Differentiated instruction: Can it work? *The Education Digest, 65*(5), 25–31. Retrieved from https://giftededucationresources.wikispaces.com/file/view/differentiated_instruct.pdf

Tomlinson, C. A. (2005). Quality curriculum and instruction for highly able students. *Theory into Practice, 44,* 160–166.

UCIrvineExtension (Producer). (2013, February 26). *Tech tools to differentiate and engage gifted learners* [Webinar]. Retrieved from http://www.youtube.com/watch?v=7brTplFL77A

U.S. Department of Education. (n.d.). *Advanced placement incentive program grants.* Retrieved from http://www2.ed.gov/programs/apincent/index.html

VanTassel-Baska, J., & Stambaugh, T. (Eds.). (2007). *Overlooked gems: A national perspective on low-income promising learners.* Conference Proceedings from the National Leadership Conference on Low-Income Promising Learners, National Association for Gifted Children and the Center for Gifted Education, College of William and Mary.

Walvoord, B. E., & Anderson, V. J. (1998). *Effective grading: A tool for learning and assessment.* San Francisco, CA: Jossey-Bass.

Warner, G. C. (1977). *The boxcar children.* Morton Grove, IL: Albert Whitman.

Weber, C. L., Boswell, C., & Behrens, W. A. (2014). *Exploring critical issues in gifted education: A case studies approach.* Waco, TX: Prufrock Press.

Westphal, L. (n.d.). *Menu evaluation checklist: For teachers.* Retrieved from https://www.teacherspayteachers.com

Wiggins, G., & McTighe, J. (2006). Examining the teaching life. *Educational Leadership, 63*(6), 26–29. Retrieved from http://www.ascd.org/publications/educational-leadership/mar06/vol63/num06/Examining-the-Teaching-Life.aspx

Woods, A. (1992). *Young Abraham Lincoln: Log-cabin president.* Mahwah, NJ: Troll Communications.

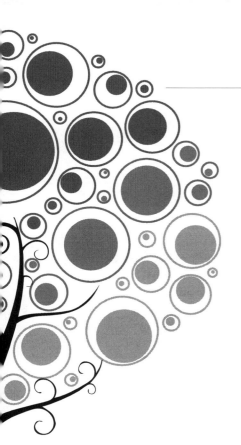

NAGC-CEC Advanced Standards in Gifted Education Teacher Preparation

Standard 1: Assessment

1.0. Gifted education specialists use valid and reliable assessment practices to minimize bias.
Key Elements
1.1. Gifted education specialists review, select, and interpret psychometrically sound, nonbiased, qualitative and quantitative instruments to identify individuals with gifts and talents and assess their abilities, strengths, and interests.
1.2. Gifted education specialists monitor the progress of individuals with gifts and talents in the general education and specialized curricula.

Assessment is critical to the advanced roles of gifted education specialists. Underlying assessment is the knowledge of systems and theories of educational assessment, along with skills in examining the technical adequacy of instruments and the implementation of evidence based practices in assessment. It is critical that assessments that minimize bias are used in the selection of instruments, methods, and procedures for both programs and individuals. With respect to assessment of individuals with gifts and talents, gifted education specialists in advanced roles apply their knowledge and skill to all stages and purposes of assessment, including identification of abilities, strengths, and interests and in monitoring and reporting learning progress in the general education curriculum as well as in the specialized curriculum in their gifted education placement.

Standard 2: Curricular Content Knowledge

2.0. Gifted education specialists use their knowledge of general[1] and specialized[2] curricula to improve programs, supports, and services at classroom, school, community, and system levels.
Key Elements
2.1. Gifted education specialists align educational standards to provide access to challenging curriculum to meet the needs individuals with exceptionalities.
2.2. Gifted educators continuously broaden and deepen professional knowledge, and expand expertise with instructional technologies, curriculum standards, effective teaching strategies, and assistive technologies to support access to and learning of challenging content.
2.3. Gifted education specialists use understanding of diversity and individual learning differences to inform the selection, development, and implementation of comprehensive curricula for individuals with exceptionalities.

1   As used, "general" or the core curricula, means the general academic content of the curricula including math, reading, English/language arts, science, social studies, and the arts.
2   As used, "specialized curricula" means the content of specialized interventions that are designed to address the unique needs of individuals with gifts and talents.

Gifted education specialists use their deep understanding of educational standards within and across domains to provide access to challenging curriculum to meet the needs of individuals with exceptionalities. Gifted education specialists continuously broaden and deepen their professional knowledge, and expand their expertise with technologies, curriculum standards, effective teaching strategies, and assistive technologies to support learning. Gifted education specialists how individual learning differences and diversity inform the selection, development and implementation of comprehensive and cohesive curricula for individuals with exceptionalities.

Standard 3: Programs, Services, and Outcomes

3.0. Gifted education specialists facilitate the continuous improvement of general and gifted education programs, supports, and services at the classroom, school, and system levels for individuals with exceptionalities.
Key Elements
3.1. Gifted education specialists design and implement evaluation activities to improve programs, supports, and services for individuals with exceptionalities.
3.2. Gifted education specialists use their understanding of cultural, social, and economic diversity and individual learner differences to inform the development and improvement of programs, supports, and services for individuals with exceptionalities.

3.3. Gifted education specialists apply knowledge of theories, evidence-based practices, relevant laws, and policies to advocate for programs, supports, and a continuum of services for individuals with exceptionalities.
3.4. Gifted education specialists design and develop systematic program and curriculum models for enhancing talent development in multiple settings.
3.5. Gifted education specialists evaluate progress toward achieving the vision, mission, and goals of programs, services, and supports for individuals with exceptionalities.

Effective gifted educators in advanced roles design and implement research activities to evaluate the effectiveness of instructional practices and to assess progress toward the organizational vision, mission, and goals of their programs. They develop procedures for continuous improvement management systems. They use their understanding of the effects of cultural, social, and economic diversity and variations of individual development to inform their development of programs and services for individuals with exceptional learning needs. Gifted educators in advanced roles apply their knowledge of cognitive science, learning theory, and instructional technologies to improve instructional programs at the school-wide and system-wide levels. They provide for a continuum of services to ensure the appropriate instructional supports for individuals with exceptional learning needs. They use their deep understanding of educational standards to help all individuals with exceptional learning needs access challenging curriculum.

Standard 4: Research & Inquiry

4.0. Gifted education specialists conduct, evaluate, and use inquiry to guide professional practice.
Key Elements
4.1. Gifted education specialists evaluate theory, research and inquiry to identify effective practices.
4.2. Gifted education specialists use knowledge of the professional literature to improve practices with individuals with exceptionalities and their families.
4.3. Gifted education specialists evaluate and modify instructional practices in response to ongoing assessment data and engage in the design and implementation of research and inquiry.

Research and inquiry inform the decisions of gifted educators in advanced roles in guiding professional practice. Gifted educators in advanced roles know models, theories, philosophies, and research methods that form the basis for evidence-based practices in gifted education. This knowledge includes information sources, data collection, and data analysis strategies. Gifted educators in advanced roles evaluate the appropriateness of research methodologies in relation to practices presented in the literature. They use educational research to improve instructional techniques, intervention strategies, and curricular materials. They foster an environment supportive of continuous instructional improvement and engage in the design and implementation of action research. Gifted educators in advanced roles are able to use the literature to resolve issues of professional practice and help others understand various evidence-based practices.

Standard 5: Leadership and Policy

5.0. Gifted education specialists provide leadership to formulate goals, set and meet high professional expectations, advocate for effective policies and evidence-based practices, and create positive and productive work environments.
Key Elements
5.1. Gifted education specialists encourage high expectations, model respect for, and use ethical practices with all individuals with exceptionalities.
5.2. Gifted education specialists support and use linguistically and culturally responsive practices.
5.3. Gifted education specialists create and maintain collegial and productive work environments that respect and safeguard the rights of individuals with exceptionalities and their families.
5.4. Gifted education specialists advocate for policies and practices that improve programs, services, and outcomes for individuals with exceptionalities.
5.5. Gifted education specialists advocate for the allocation of appropriate resources for the preparation and professional development of all personnel who serve individuals with exceptionalities.

Gifted educators in advanced roles promote high professional self-expectations and help others understand the needs of individuals with exceptional learning needs within the context of an organization's mission. They advocate laws based on solid evidence-based knowledge to support high quality education for individuals with exceptional learning needs. They also advocate for appropriate resources to ensure that all personnel involved have effective preparation. Gifted educators in advanced roles use their knowledge of organizational theory and the needs of different groups in a pluralistic society to formulate organizational goals promoting evidence-based practices and challenging expectations for individuals with exceptional learning needs. They provide leadership to create procedures that respect all individuals and permit professionals to practice ethically. They create positive and productive work environments and celebrate accomplishments with colleagues.

Standard 6: Professional and Ethical Practice

6.0. Gifted education specialists use foundational knowledge of the field and professional ethical principles and Program Standards to inform gifted education practice, engage in lifelong learning, advance the profession, and perform leadership responsibilities to promote the success of professional colleagues and individuals with exceptionalities.
Key Elements
6.1. A comprehensive understanding of the history of gifted education, legal policies, ethical standards, and emerging issues informs gifted education specialist leadership.
6.2. Gifted education specialists model high professional expectations and ethical practice, and create supportive environments that increase diversity at all levels of gifted and talented education.
6.3. Gifted education specialists model and promote respect for all individuals and facilitate ethical professional practice.
6.4. Gifted education specialists actively participate in professional development and learning communities to increase professional knowledge and expertise.
6.5. Gifted education specialists plan, present, and evaluate professional development focusing on effective and ethical practice at all organizational levels.
6.6. Gifted education specialists actively facilitate and participate in the preparation and induction of prospective gifted educators.
6.7. Gifted education specialists actively promote the advancement of the profession.

Gifted education specialists in advanced roles have a comprehensive knowledge of gifted education as an evolving and changing discipline based on philosophies, evidence-based principles and theories, relevant laws and policies, diverse and historical points of view, and issues that have influenced and continue to influence gifted education and the education of and services for individuals with exceptionalities both in school and in society. They are guided by professional ethics and practice standards. In their advanced roles gifted educators have leadership responsibilities for promoting the success of individuals with exceptional learning needs, their families, and colleagues. They create supportive environments that safeguard the legal rights of students, families, and school personnel through policies and procedures that promote ethical and professional practice. Gifted educators in advanced roles continuously broaden and deepen their professional knowledge, and expand their expertise with instructional technologies, curriculum, effective teaching strategies, and assistive technologies to support access to learning. Gifted educators in advanced roles plan, present, and evaluate professional development based on models that apply adult learning theories and focus on effective practice at all organizational levels. They are actively involved in the preparation and induction of prospective gifted educators. Gifted educators in advanced roles model their own commitment to continuously improving their own professional practice by participating in professional development themselves and promote the advancement of the profession.

Standard 7: Collaboration

7.0. Gifted education specialists collaborate with stakeholders to improve programs, services, and outcomes for individuals with gifts and talents and their families.
Key Elements
7.1. Gifted education specialists use culturally responsive practices to enhance collaboration.
7.2. Gifted education specialists use collaborative skills to improve programs, services, and outcomes for individuals with exceptionalities
7.3. Gifted education specialists collaborate to promote understanding, resolve conflicts, and build consensus for improving program, services, and outcomes for individuals with exceptionalities.

Gifted educators in advanced roles have a deep understanding of the centrality and importance of consultation and collaboration to the roles within gifted education, and they use this deep understanding to improve programs, services and outcomes for individuals with exceptional learning needs. They also understand the significance of the role of collaboration and apply their skill to promote understanding, resolve conflicts, and build consensus among both internal and external stakeholders to provide services to individuals with exceptional learning needs and their families. They possess current knowledge of research on stages and models in both collaboration and consultation and ethical and legal issues related to consultation and collaboration. Moreover, gifted educators in advanced roles have a deep understanding of the possible interactions of language, diversity, culture and religion with contextual factors and how to use collaboration and consultation to enhance opportunities for individuals with exceptional learning needs.

Glossary

Individuals with Exceptionalities: Individuals with exceptionalities include individuals with sensory, physical, emotional, social, cognitive differences, developmentally delays, exceptional gifts and talents; and individuals who are or have been abused or neglected whose needs differ sufficiently so as to require personalized special education services in addition to or in tandem with regular educational services available through general education programs and other human service delivery systems.

Special Education Service: Special education services are personalized services that appropriately credentialed special educators provide directly or indirectly to individuals with exceptionalities.

From *Advanced Standards in Gifted Education Teacher Preparation* by National Association for Gifted Children-Council for Exceptional Children, 2013, Washington, DC: Author. Copyright 2013 by National Association for Gifted Children. Reprinted with permission.

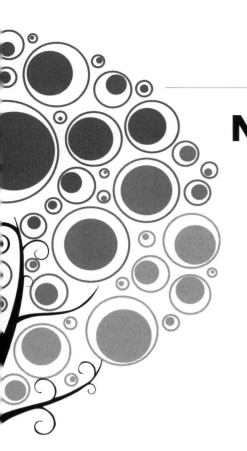

NAGC-CEC Teacher Preparation Standards in Gifted and Talented Education

Standard 1: Learner Development and Individual Learning Differences

Beginning gifted education professionals understand the variations in learning and development in cognitive and affective areas between and among individuals with gifts and talents and apply this understanding to provide meaningful and challenging learning experiences for individuals with exceptionalities.

1.1. Beginning gifted education professionals understand how language, culture, economic status, family background, and/or area of disability can influence the learning of individuals with gifts and talents.

1.2. Beginning gifted education professionals use understanding of development and individual differences to respond to the needs of individuals with gifts and talents.

Historically, gifted education professionals have placed the learning needs of the individual at the center of gifted education instruction. Gifted education professionals have altered instructional practices to optimize learning for individuals with gifts and talents. Development of expertise begins with a thorough understanding of and respect for similarities and differences in all areas of human growth and development. Like all educators, beginning gifted education professionals first respect individuals with gifts and talents within the context of human development and Individual learning differences. Not only do beginning gifted education professionals understand advanced developmental milestones of individuals with gifts and talents from early childhood through adolescence, but they also understand how exceptionalities can interact with development and learning, and create developmentally appropriate learning environments to provide relevant, meaningful, and challenging learning experiences for individuals with gifts and talents.

Beginning gifted education professionals understand the variation in characteristics between and among individuals with and without gifts and talents. They know exceptionalities can interact with multiple domains of human development to influence an individual's learning in school, community, and throughout life. Moreover, they understand that the beliefs, traditions, and values across and within cultures can influence relationships among and between students, their families, and the school community. Furthermore, these experiences of individuals with exceptionalities can influence the individual's ability to learn, interact socially, and live as fulfilled contributing members of the community. Educators of the gifted understand the phenomenon of underachievement and how it manifests itself in males and females. They understand techniques for reversing underachievement.

Beginning gifted education professionals are active and resourceful in seeking to understand how the primary language, culture, family, and areas of disability interact with the gifts and talents to influence the individual's academic and social abilities, attitudes, values, interests, and career and post- secondary options. These learning differences and their interactions provide the foundation upon which beginning gifted education professionals differentiate instruction to provide developmentally meaningful and challenging learning for individuals with exceptionalities.

Standard 2: Learning Environments

Beginning gifted education professionals create safe, inclusive, and culturally responsive learning environments so that individuals with gifts and talents become effective learners and develop social and emotional well-being.
2.1. Beginning gifted education professionals create safe, inclusive, culturally responsive learning environments that engage individuals with gifts and talents in meaningful and rigorous learning activities and social interactions.
2.2. Beginning gifted education professionals use communication and motivational and instructional strategies to facilitate understanding of subject matter and to teach individuals with gifts and talents how to adapt to different environments and develop ethical leadership skills.
2.3. Beginning gifted education professionals adjust their communication to an individual's language proficiency and cultural and linguistic differences.
2.4. Beginning gifted education professionals demonstrate understanding of the multiple environments that are part of a continuum of services for individuals with gifts and talents, including the advantages and disadvantages of various settings and teach students to adapt to these environments.

Like all educators, beginning gifted education professionals develop safe, inclusive, culturally responsive learning environments for all students. They also collaborate with colleagues in general education and other specialized environments that develop students' gifts and talents, engaging gifted students in meaningful learning activities that enhance independence, interdependence, and positive peer-relationships.

Beginning gifted education professionals modify learning environments for individual needs and risk taking. Knowledge regarding the interaction of an individual's language, family, culture, areas of disability, and other significant contextual factors with an individual's gifts and talents guides the beginning gifted educator in modifying learning environments, and provides for the maintenance and generalization of acquired skills across environments and subjects. They adjust their communication methods to an individual's language proficiency. They value and are responsive to cultural and linguistic differences avoid discrimination, stereotyping, and deficit views of differences.

Beginning gifted education professionals structure environments to encourage self-awareness, self-regulation, self-efficacy, self-direction, personal empowerment, leadership, and self-advocacy of individuals with gifts and talents, and directly teach them how to adapt to the expectations and demands of differing environments.

Standard 3: Curricular Content Knowledge

Beginning gifted education professionals use knowledge of general[1] and specialized curricula[2] to advance learning for individuals with gifts and talents.
3.1. Beginning gifted education professionals understand the role of central concepts, structures of the discipline, and tools of inquiry of the content areas they teach, and use their understanding to organize knowledge, integrate cross-disciplinary skills, and develop meaningful learning progressions within and across grade levels.
3.2. Beginning gifted education professionals design appropriate learning and performance modifications for individuals with gifts and talents that enhance creativity, acceleration, depth and complexity in academic subject matter and specialized domains.
3.3. Beginning gifted education professionals use assessments to select, adapt, and create materials to differentiate instructional strategies and general and specialized curricula to challenge individuals with gifts and talents.
3.4. Beginning gifted education professionals understand that individuals with gifts and talents demonstrate a wide range of advanced knowledge and performance levels and modify the general or specialized curriculum appropriately.

1   As used, "general" or the core curricula, means the general academic content of the curricula including math, reading, English/language arts, science, social studies, and the arts.
2   As used, "specialized curricula" means the content of specialized interventions that are designed to address the unique needs of individuals with gifts and talents.

The professional knowledge base in general education clearly indicates that educators' understanding of the central concepts and structure of the discipline and tools of inquiry related to the academic subject-matter content areas they teach makes a significant difference in student learning.

Within the general curricula, beginning gifted education professionals demonstrate in their planning and teaching, a solid foundation of understanding of the theories, central concepts and principles, structures of the discipline, and tools of inquiry of the academic subject-matter content areas they teach so they are able to organize knowledge, integrate cross-disciplinary skills, develop meaningful learning progressions and collaborate with educators in:

Using and interpreting assessments to select, adapt, and create materials to differentiate instructional strategies and general and specialized curricula to challenge individuals with gifts and talents.

Teaching the content of the general or specialized curriculum to individuals with gifts and talents across advanced performance levels.

Designing appropriate learning and performance modifications for individuals with gifts and talents in academic subject matter and specialized content domains that incorporate advanced, conceptually challenging, in-depth, distinctive, and/or complex content.

Additionally, beginning gifted education professionals use a variety of specialized curricula to individualize meaningful and challenging learning for individuals with exceptionalities.

Standard 4: Assessment

Beginning gifted education professionals use multiple methods of assessment and data sources in making educational decisions about identification of individuals with gifts and talents and student learning.
4.1. Beginning gifted education professionals understand that some groups of individuals with gifts and talents have been underrepresented in gifted education programs and select and use technically sound formal and informal assessments that minimize bias in identifying students for gifted education programs and services.
4.2. Beginning gifted education professionals use knowledge of measurement principles and practices to differentiate assessments and interpret results to guide educational decisions for individuals with gifts and talents.
4.3. Beginning gifted education professionals collaborate with colleagues and families in using multiple types of assessment information to make identification and learning progress decisions and to minimize bias in assessment and decision-making.
4.4. Beginning gifted education professionals use assessment results to develop long- and short-range goals and objectives that take into consideration an individual's abilities and needs, the learning environment, and other factors related to diversity.

> 4.5. Beginning gifted education professionals engage individuals with gifts and talents in assessing the quality of their own learning and performance and in setting future goals and objectives.

Beginning gifted education professionals understand measurement theory and practice for addressing issues of validity, reliability, norms, bias, and interpretation of assessment results.

Beginning gifted education professionals understand the policies and ethical principles of measurement and assessment related to gifted education referral/nomination, identification, program planning, differentiated instruction, learning progress, and services for individuals with gifts and talents, including individuals with culturally, linguistically, and economically diverse backgrounds.

Beginning gifted education professionals understand the appropriate use and limitations of various types of assessments and collaborate with families and other colleagues to ensure nonbiased, meaningful assessments and decision-making.

Beginning gifted education professionals select and use quantitative and qualitative assessment information to support a wide variety of decisions within gifted education. They conduct formal and informal assessments of behavior, learning, achievement, and environments to differentiate the learning experiences and document the growth of individuals with gifts and talents. Moreover, they differentiate assessments to identify above level performances and to accelerate and enrich the general curriculum.

Beginning gifted education professionals use available technologies routinely to support their assessments and employ a variety of assessments such as performance-based assessment, portfolios, and computer simulations. Using these data, beginning gifted education professionals make multiple types of assessment decisions including strategic adaptations and modifications in response to an individuals' constellation of social, linguistic, and learning factors in ways to minimize bias. They also use the results of assessments to identify above-level performance, develop long-range instructional plans anchored in both general and specialized curricula and translate these plans into carefully selected shorter-range goals and objectives to differentiate and accelerate instruction. Moreover, beginning gifted education professionals engage individuals with gifts and talents in assessing the quality of their own learning and performance and in providing feedback to guide them in setting future goals.

Like their general education colleagues, beginning gifted education professionals regularly monitor the learning progress of individuals with gifts and talents in both general and specialized content and make instructional adjustments based on these data.

Standard 5: Instructional Planning and Strategies

Beginning gifted education professionals select, adapt, and use a repertoire of evidence-based instructional strategies[3] to advance the learning of individuals with gifts and talents.
5.1. Beginning gifted education professionals know principles of evidence-based, differentiated, and accelerated practices and possess a repertoire of instructional strategies to enhance the critical and creative thinking, problem-solving, and performance skills of individuals with gifts and talents.
5.2. Beginning gifted education professionals apply appropriate technologies to support instructional assessment, planning, and delivery for individuals with gifts and talents.
5.3. Beginning gifted education professionals collaborate with families, professional colleagues, and other educators to select, adapt, and use evidence-based strategies that promote challenging learning opportunities in general and specialized curricula.
5.4. Beginning gifted education professionals emphasize the development, practice, and transfer of advanced knowledge and skills across environments throughout the lifespan leading to creative, productive careers in a multicultural society for individuals with gifts and talents.
5.5. Beginning gifted education professionals use instructional strategies that enhance the affective development of individuals with gifts and talents.

3   Instructional strategies, as used throughout this document include interventions used in general or core and specialized curricula.

In the selection, development, and adaptation of learning experiences for individuals with gifts and talents, beginning gifted education professionals consider an individual's abilities, interests, learning environments, and cultural and linguistic factors to achieve positive learning results in general and special curricula. Understanding these factors, curriculum models, and the implications of being recognized as gifted and talented guides the educator's development of scope and sequence plans; selection, adaptation, and creation of learning activities; pace of instruction; and use of differentiated evidence-based instructional strategies.

Beginning gifted education professionals possess a repertoire of evidence-based strategies to differentiate and accelerate the curriculum for individuals with gifts and talents. They select, adapt, and use these strategies to promote challenging learning opportunities in general and special curricula and to modify learning environments to enhance self-awareness, self-regulation, and self-efficacy for individuals with gifts and talents. They enhance 21st Century student outcomes such as critical and creative thinking, problem solving, collaboration, and performance skills in specific domains and allow individuals with gifts and talents opportunities to explore, develop, or research their areas of interest or talent.

Beginning gifted education professionals also emphasize the development, practice, and transfer of advanced knowledge and skills across environments throughout the lifespan leading to creative, productive careers in society for individuals with gifts and talents. Moreover, beginning gifted education professionals facilitate these actions in a collaborative context that includes individuals with gifts and talents, families, professional colleagues, and personnel from other agencies as appropriate. They are familiar with alternative and augmentative communication systems and are comfortable using technologies to support language and communication, instructional planning and differentiated instruction for individuals with exceptionalities.

Standard 6: Professional Learning and Ethical Practice

Beginning gifted education professionals use foundational knowledge of the field and professional ethical principles and programming standards[4] to inform gifted education practice, to engage in lifelong learning, and to advance the profession.
6.1. Beginning gifted education professionals use professional ethical principles and specialized program standards to guide their practice.
6.2. Beginning gifted education professionals understand how foundational knowledge, perspectives, and historical and current issues influence professional practice and the education and treatment of individuals with gifts and talents both in school and society.
6.3. Beginning gifted education professionals model respect for diversity, understanding that it is an integral part of society's institutions and impacts learning of individuals with gifts and talents in the delivery of gifted education services.
6.4. Beginning gifted education professionals are aware of their own professional learning needs, understand the significance of lifelong learning, and participate in professional activities and learning communities.
6.5. Beginning gifted education professionals advance the profession by engaging in activities such as advocacy and mentoring.

4 Pre-K–Grade 12 Gifted Education Programming Standards (2010). Washington, DC: NAGC. Retrieved from http://www.nagc.org

Beginning gifted education professionals practice in multiple roles and complex situations across wide age and developmental ranges that requires ongoing attention to legal matters and serious consideration of professional and ethical issues. Ethical principles and Program Standards guide beginning gifted education professionals. These principles and standards provide benchmarks by which gifted education professionals practice and professionally evaluate each other.

Beginning gifted education professionals understand gifted education as an evolving and changing discipline based on philosophies, evidence-based principles and theories, policies, historical points of view that continue to influence the field of gifted education and the education of and services for individuals with gifts and talents and their families in both school and society. Beginning gifted education professionals understand how these factors influence professional practice, including assessment, instructional planning, services, and program evaluation.

Beginning gifted education professionals understand the aspects of human diversity and equity as related to academic diversity. They understand aspects of human diversity and equity regarding individuals identified as gifted and talented as well as those who have potential of being identified gifted and talented.

Beginning gifted education professionals are sensitive to the aspects of diversity of individuals with gifts and talents and their families, how human diversity can influence families, cultures, and schools, and how these complex issues can each interact with the delivery of gifted education services. Of special significance is the growth in the number and prevalence of English Language Learners (ELL) and economically disadvantaged (ED) and the provision of effective gifted education services for ELL and ED learners with exceptionalities and their families. Beginning gifted education professionals also understand historical relationships of gifted education services related to diversity and equity and the organization of schools, school systems, and education-related agencies within the culture in which they practice.

Beginning gifted education professionals also understand the relationships of the organization of gifted education services to the organization of schools, school systems, and education-related agencies within cultures in which they practice. They are aware of how their own and others' attitudes, behaviors, and ways of communicating can influence their practice, and use this knowledge as a foundation to inform their own personal understandings and philosophies of special education.

Beginning gifted education professionals engage in professional activities and participate actively in professional learning communities that benefit individuals with gifts and talents, their families, colleagues, and their own professional growth. They view themselves as lifelong learners and regularly reflect on and adjust their practice, and develop and use personalized professional development plans. They plan and engage in activities that foster their professional growth and keep them current with evidence-based practices and know how to recognize their own skill limits and practice within them. They place particular emphasis on professional activities that focus on human diversity and academic diversity in all of its manifestations. Moreover, educators of the gifted embrace their special role as advocates for individuals with gifts and talents. They promote and advocate for the learning and well-being of individuals with gifts and talents across multiple and varied settings through diverse learning experiences.

Standard 7: Collaboration

> **Beginning gifted education professionals collaborate with families, other educators, related-service providers, individuals with gifts and talents, and personnel from community agencies in culturally responsive ways to address the needs of individuals with gifts and talents across a range of learning experiences.**
>
> 7.1. Beginning gifted education professionals apply elements of effective collaboration.
>
> 7.2. Beginning gifted education professionals serve as a collaborative resource to colleagues.
>
> 7.3. Beginning gifted education professionals use collaboration to promote the well-being of individuals with gifts and talents across a wide range of settings, experiences, and collaborators.

One of the significant changes in education over the past several decades is the rapid growth of collaborative educational teams to address the educational needs of students. The diversity of the students, complexity of curricular demands, growing influence of technology, and the rising targets for learner outcomes in the 21st Century has created the demand for teams of educators collaborating together to ensure all students are effectively learning challenging curricula.

Beginning gifted education professionals embrace their role as a resource to colleagues and use the theory and elements of collaboration across a wide range of contexts and collaborators. They use culturally responsive behaviors that promote effective communication and collaboration with individuals with gifts and talents, their families, school personnel, and community members. They collaborate with their general education and other special education colleagues to create learning environments that meaningfully include individuals with gifts and talents, and that foster cultural understanding, safety and emotional wellbeing, positive social interactions, and active engagement. Additionally, beginning gifted education professionals use collaboration to facilitate differentiated assessment and instructional planning to advance learning of individuals with gifts and talents across a wide range of settings and different learning experiences. They routinely collaborate with other educators in developing mentorships, internships, and vocational programming experiences to address the needs of individuals with gifts and talents. Gifted education professionals have long recognized the positive significance of the active involvement of individuals with gifts and talents and their families in the education process, and gifted education professionals involve individuals with gifts and talents and their families collaboratively in all aspects of the education of individuals with gifts and talents.

Glossary

Acceleration. Acceleration practices may include grade-based acceleration that shorten the number of years an individual is in the PK-12 system and/or subject-based acceleration that bring advanced content and skills earlier than expected for age or grade level (Rogers, 2002).

Bias. Bias may occur not only within quantitative assessments that do not have technical adequacy but also from barriers within identification procedures such as low teacher expectations, exclusive definitions, and a focus on deficits rather than strengths (Ford, 1998; Ryser, 2011).

Differentiated assessment. The practice of varying assessment in such a way that it reflects differentiation in the curriculum and/or the instruction. Differentiated assessment implies that as students experience differences in their learning, they should experience differences in their assessment. For example, students with gifts and talents may require off level/above grade level tests to accurately assess their level of ability or achievement.

Differentiated curriculum. Adaptation of content, process, and concepts to meet a higher level of expectation appropriate for advanced learners. Curriculum can be differentiated through acceleration, complexity, depth, challenge, and creativity (VanTassel-Baska & Wood, 2008).

Differentiated instruction. Multiple ways to structure a lesson so that each student is challenged at an appropriate level. Differentiated instruction may include such features as learner centeredness; planned assignments and lessons based on pre-assessment; and flexible grouping, materials, resources, and pacing (Tomlinson & Hockett, 2008).

Diversity. Differences among groups of people and individuals based on ethnicity, race, socioeconomic status, gender, exceptionalities, language, religion, sexual orientation, and geographical area (Matthews & Shaunessy, 2008; NCATE, 2010).

Technical adequacy. This term refers to the psychometric properties of an assessment instrument. Instruments with technical adequacy demonstrate validity for the identified purpose, reliability in providing consistent results, and minimize bias, and have been normed on a population matching the census data (Johnsen, 2008).

Glossary References

Ford, D. Y. (1998). The underrepresentation of minority students in gifted education: Problems and promises in recruitment and retention. *The Journal of Special Education, 32,* 4–14.

Johnsen, S. K. (2008). Identifying gifted and talented learners. In F. A. Karnes & K. R. Stephens (Eds.), *Achieving excellence: Educating the gifted and talented* (pp. 135–153). Upper Saddle River, NJ: Pearson.

Matthews, M. S., & Shaunessy, E. (2008). Culturally, linguistically, and economically diverse gifted students. In F. A. Karnes & K. R. Stephens (Eds.), *Achieving excellence: Educating the gifted and talented* (pp. 99–115). Upper Saddle River, NJ: Pearson.

National Council for Accreditation of Teacher Education (2010). Unit Standards Glossary downloaded 8/22/10 from http://www.ncate.org/public/glossary.asp?ch=155.

Rogers, K. B. (2002). Effects of acceleration on gifted learners. In M. Neihart, S. M. Reis, N. M. Robinson, & S. M. Moon (Eds.), *The social and emotional development of gifted children: What do we know?* (pp. 3–12). Waco, TX: Prufrock Press.

Ryser, G. R. (2011). Fairness in testing and nonbiased assessment. In S. K. Johnsen (Ed.), *Identifying gifted students: A practical guide* (2nd ed., pp. 63–74). Waco, TX: Prufrock Press.

Tomlinson, C. A., & Hockett, J. A. (2008). Instructional strategies and programming models for gifted learners. In F. A. Karnes & K. R. Stephens (Eds.), *Achieving excellence: Educating the gifted and talented* (pp. 154–169). Upper Saddle River, NJ: Pearson.

VanTassel-Baska, J., & Wood, S. (2008). Curriculum development in gifted education: A challenge to provide optimal learning experiences. In F. A. Karnes & K. R. Stephens (Eds.), *Achieving excellence: Educating the gifted and talented* (pp. 209–229). Upper Saddle River, NJ: Pearson.

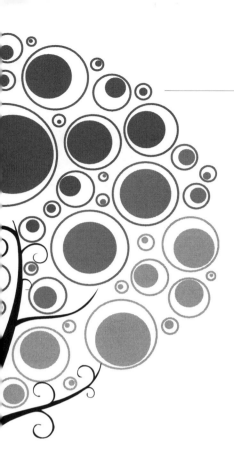

About the Authors

Christine L. Weber, Ph.D., is an associate professor of Childhood Education, Literacy, and TESOL at the University of North Florida, in Jacksonville. She instructs teachers in strategies for conceptual teaching and learning, assessment tools and meeting the needs of gifted learners. She has been a member of the Editorial Review Board for *Gifted Child Today* since 1998. Under her leadership, the *Florida's Frameworks for K–12 Gifted Learners* was developed in 2007 and disseminated to all school districts in the state. Weber has published numerous articles and presented at state, national (including the National Association of Gifted Children), and international conferences related to the education of gifted children. She currently serves as the Representative Assembly for CEC-TAG, Awards Co-Chair for the NAGC Research & Evaluation Network, and secretary for the NAGC Professional Development Network. She was awarded the Outstanding Undergraduate Teaching Award from the University of North Florida in 2007.

Wendy A. Behrens, M.A. Ed., is the Gifted and Talented Education Specialist for the Minnesota Department of Education, where she leads and advises educators, administrators, and parents. She provides technical assistance to and collaborates with institutions of higher education, educator networks, and others interested in promoting rigorous educational opportunities. Prior to her service to the state, Behrens worked as a district gifted services coordinator and a consultant for the Science Museum of Minnesota. She presents frequently on the nature and needs of gifted learners, instructional strategies, comprehensive service design, and policies that support highly able learners. She has been an invited speaker in the United States, Middle East, Far East, and Europe. Behrens is President of the Council of State Directors of Programs for the Gifted, and received the President's award from NAGC in 2013. She is an elected U.S. delegate to the World Council on Gifted, and a member of NAGC Policy Task Force and advisory councils for the Center for Talent Development, the University of St. Thomas, and Grayson School. In 2015, Behrens was named Project Director for *Project North Star*, a Javits Grant awarded to the Minnesota Department of Education. The grant is designed to elevate the identification and programming approaches provided for disadvantaged and underserved rural populations by preparing their teachers, school administrators, and communities with the knowledge and skills their gifted students need to be successful in the greater world.

Cecelia Boswell, Ed.D., has more than 40 years of experience in education. She works throughout Texas developing a variety of projects for the Texas Education Agency (TEA), and conducting research for the Texas International Baccalaureate Schools. Boswell is president of the board of the Council for Exceptional Children—Talented and Gifted Division and author of the publication on strategies for twice-exceptional gifted children, *Effective Program Practices for Underserved Gifted Students: A CEC-TAG Educational Resource* (with Cheryll Adams; 2012). She is also author of *RtI for the Gifted Student* (with Valerie Dodd Carlisle; 2010). Boswell recently served as the Executive Director of Advanced Academic Services for Waco Independent School District in Waco, TX, where she developed a new Middle School Academy for gifted and talented students, grades 6 through 8. She currently works as an independent consultant auditing gifted, advanced, and International Baccalaureate programs, creating projects for TEA, consulting for school districts, and developing products for Texas Association for Gifted and Talented as their content consultant.